SMART KIDS

William G. Durden & Arne E. Tangherlini

Center for Talented Youth, The Johns Hopkins University

SMART KIDS

How Academic Talents Are Developed and Nurtured in America

Hogrefe & Huber Publishers

Library of Congress Cataloging-in-Publication Data

Durden, William G., 1949–
Smart kids : how academic talents are developed and nurtured in
America / by William G. Durden and Arne E. Tangherlini
  p. cm.
  Includes bibliographical references and index.
  ISBN 0-88937-112-1
1. Gifted children—Education—United States. 2. Educational
acceleration. 3. Education—United States—Parent participation.
I. Tangherlini, Arne E. II. Title.
LC3993.T35   1993   371.95'6'0973—dc20   92-40190 CIP

Canadian Cataloguing in Publication Data

Durden, William G., 1949–
Smart kids : how academic talents are developed and nurtured in
America
Includes bibliographical references and index.
ISBN 0-88937-112-1
1. Gifted children—United States—Education. 2. Gifted chil-
dren—Education. I. Tangherlini, Arne E. II. Title.
LC3993.9.T35   1993   371.95'0973   C92-095771-4

P. O. Box 2487, Kirkland, WA 98083-2487
12–14 Bruce Park Ave., Toronto, Ontario M4P 2S3

Printed in USA

ISBN 0-88937-112-1
ISBN 3-8017-0685-0
Hogrefe & Huber Publishers, Seattle Toronto Bern Göttingen

Table of Contents

— Part II —

Acknowledgments

We are grateful to the many children, parents, teachers, and interested individuals who took the time to speak with us about their educational experiences. We are also thankful to the staff and faculty of the Center for Talented Youth of The Johns Hopkins University for their encouragement and enthusiastic support of this work. Unfortunately, space will not allow us to mention every individual who deserves our gratitude, but a number of individuals must be singled out. We are especially grateful to Carol Mills who read the manuscript in its various incarnations and offered continual guidance, pointing us in the direction of important issues and sharpening our arguments with her critiques. William Gustin made invaluable contributions to the formulation of the interview protocols. Christopher Weare and Daniel Tangherlini provided us guidance on the finer points of policy. Damon Krug patiently designed and revised the charts and tables. Karen Ablard, Elizabeth Albert, Gina Apostol, Linda Barnett, Charles Beckman, Linda Brody, Richard Chase, Luciano Corazza, Elke Durden, Christine Hoskins, Kristi Jacobs, Jane Kjems, Damon Krug, Heinrich Stumpf and Laura Thommen read the manuscript in draft form and offered suggestions which helped to give the book its current shape. Finally, we are deeply grateful to The Seaver Institute for having faith in our policy initiative and funding this project.

INTRODUCTION

Mapping an American Educational Landscape

A history teacher on vacation rides a greyhound from San Francisco to the Sierra Nevadas, with the excuse that he will take pictures of the Donner Pass to accompany a lesson on George and Jacob Donner's ill fated expedition but with the primary goal of skiing in the mid-April sunshine. Our teacher is the map-gazing sort, an Easterner on a rare visit to the West Coast, who hopes that by comparing the markings in his road atlas with the world he sees through the bus window he can flesh out an imagined California with highways, trees, faces, snow.

An hour into the journey, a young mother and her child, a girl about five years old, sit down next to the teacher. They are accompanied by the mother's girlfriend, who takes a seat across the aisle. The adults exchange pleasantries, then ignore each other politely. While the women tell jokes about someone called Eddie, the girl squirms in her mother's arms so she can look at the teacher's map.

The teacher shows the girl where they are and informs her that he is going to the mountains. He points out San Francisco, Sacramento, Soda Springs, and the spidery web of roads connecting them. She is reaching for the map, trying to show the teacher something, when her mother slaps her hand. "Don't disturb the man," the mother says. And for the remainder of the trip, the child sits rigidly on her mother's lap, clutching a blanket to her cheek and staring at the seat in front of her.

Starting with the first indefinite gropings, a child's business is to learn. Just as your car needs gasoline in order to get anywhere, the mental machinery of the child is constructed in such a way that it demands new challenges in order to keep running. The famous psychologist Jean Piaget called this the "drive to mastery."[1]

For the child, the drive to mastery is as keen as the need for food. Often, like the mother on the bus, instead of nourishing this desire, we stifle it — out of laziness, for the sake of propriety, or because we don't understand it. We treat curiosity as a nuisance, an unsavory beast that needs to be tamed, when in fact it is precisely this dynamic quality, this desire to interact with the environment, to observe, inquire, manipulate, adapt, and experiment which is the defining characteristic of the child's developing intellect.

By nature, all children are intellectuals, in that they are perpetually concerned with making new discoveries. They seek challenges. An education must address this fundamental drive, engaging the intellect and nourishing each child's development; otherwise, it is an encumbrance, an obstacle — oppression.

In addition to describing the drive to mastery, Piaget taught us that children develop their various abilities at different rates. What constitutes a challenge for one child does not necessarily do so for another. Some children learn to speak at six months; others wait years. Some children start reading at the age of two; others struggle into adolescence. An appropriate education is one in which an Optimal Match is created between a child's abilities and the pace and level of instruction.

Among great scientists, musicians, industrialists, writers, inventors, early intellectual development is hardly unusual. One need only skim a few biographies to find examples. Galileo Galilei was nineteen when, by watching the oscillations of a lamp in the Pisa Cathedral, he discovered the periodicity of oscillatory motion. Werner Heisenberg was twenty-six when he revolutionized physics — and philosophy — by publishing his work on the Uncertainty Principle. Kurt Godel was twenty-five when he demonstrated the impossibility of proving the consistency of arithmetic using arithmetic means — doing for mathematics what Uncertainty had done for physics. Mozart composed his first opera when he was twelve. When his first book of poems was published, Dylan Thomas was twenty, as was Jane Austen when she wrote *Pride and Prejudice*. Edwin Land invented the polaroid process as an undergraduate at Harvard and, after dropping out, organized the Polaroid Corporation at the age of twenty-six. Jean Piaget experienced particularly early success: he published his first scientific article, "Un Moineau albinos," at the age of eleven, and produced nineteen more before reaching twenty-one. He was offered a job as a curator at a museum in Geneva while still in secondary school and earned his Ph. D. at twenty-two.

When her daughter Lisa was in the second grade, Marjorie Holtz visited her class to see what the teacher was like and to get a sense of how Lisa behaved in class. For most of the time that Marjorie was there, Lisa had her head down on the desk, as if she were tired or utterly uninterested in what was going on. At one point, the teacher gave the class a spelling test. She read words aloud, carefully pronouncing each syllable, then she repeated the words and used them in sentences. Lisa wrote, but during the test she did not pick her head up from the desk once.

When Lisa came home from school, Marjorie chewed her out for being disrespectful and unmotivated. "Mom," Lisa said, "I have not missed a word all year, and yet I have to do these tests every day and the teacher repeats the words and repeats the words till I feel like screaming."

Lisa had been reading for four years when she entered the second grade. Her teacher was certainly not trying to harm her; she was merely doing her job, teaching to the middle of the class. Visiting Lisa's class was a revelation for Marjorie. "I had not known that she was so bored, that it was so painful," Marjorie observed. "You know, you don't really think of boredom as being that uncomfortable."

For talented students, proceeding from kindergarten to the twelfth grade in the nationally prescribed lock-step is often a tortuous procedure. Rather than being challenged with rigorous, high-level programs of study, children are forced to review the same material year after year, or they are given busy work in the form of extra problems — "the penalty for being bright," as one student called it. Such deprivation is most painful in the area of greatest competence — the one in which the drive to mastery is strongest.

A talent will rarely come to fruition if the environment is not geared to its unfolding. In chapter nine, we discuss the factors, personal and environmental, which appear to have the greatest impact on the development of an individual's talents. Beyond a certain proclivity for the skills of a particular field, it appears that the attainment of success (the creation of original and significant products or ideas and/or recognition in one's field of endeavor), depends largely on the interaction of the following factors: parents, peer groups, mentors, opportunities for early engagement and continual pursuit of a field, educational flexibility and rigor, out-of-school learning opportunities, stress, and motivation.

The importance of parental involvement with emergent talents is fairly consistent throughout the literature.[2] After examining the educational experiences of outstanding young mathematicians, research neurologists and artists, Benjamin Bloom and a team of investigators from the University of Chicago found that parental support was immensely important; in most cases, Bloom's subjects felt that their parents had taught them to value hard work and passionate involvement in one's undertakings. All of the subjects' parents took an interest in their talents, providing moral support and encouraging them to pursue their interests.

Bloom described three stages of talent development, each marked by an increase in autonomy and intensity. As their intellectual sophistication increased, his subjects sought opportunities to work on more difficult problems with peers who shared their interests and teachers who understood the material and were impassioned about it. For most, the opportunity to work with a mentor — an acknowledged master in the field of interest — played an invaluable role. In each case, however, intellectual development was characterized by increasing self-confidence and independence, culminating in the individual's emergence as a leader in his field.

On the whole, Bloom's subjects were dissatisfied with school. Their comments were fairly representative of talented students' attitudes towards school. "With some exceptions, in retrospect, what was intellectually exciting was what you did on your own. ... School was a drag," observed a neurologist.[3] In general, the young mathematicians and scientists in-the-making were most impressed with teachers who provided books and materials and encouraged them to work on their own. Both formally and informally, Bloom's subjects took advantage of opportunities for flexible pacing in their education.

In order to provide children with the opportunity to develop their talents, schools must be willing to adopt flexible policies which allow students to forge ahead at their own pace, especially in the areas where their capabilities and interests are greatest. Until the early part of this century, flexibility was one of the strengths of the American educational system. In one-room schools, where teachers had to balance the needs of students with large variations in age and ability, advancement was based on mastery of material rather than rigid grade-level requirements. Thus, in a single classroom, one sometimes found an eight-year-old reading the same books or performing the same math problems as some of his fifteen-year-old classmates. What has come to be called cooperative learning was a must, as teachers used their most advanced students to tutor those in need of help. While such arrangements had their shortcomings, they demonstrated an admirable intent to orchestrate the environment to encourage the emergence of talent.

In America, talent development — education — has never been limited to what goes on in the classroom. Bloom found that many of the parents of his subjects actively sought out-of-school learning experiences for their children. For many talented youngsters, Lawrence Cremin's description of the 19th century's educational landscape holds true to this day: "Individuals made their own way, irregularly, intermittently, and indeterminately through the configurations of the 19th century frontiers, going back and forth between the permeable boundaries of household, church, school, and apprenticeship, largely self-motivated and largely self-directed"[4]

More than ever before, our society is composed of individuals shaped by different cultures, experiences, political outlooks, goals, needs and abilities. In order to prepare children to take part in a pluralistic society of increasing complexity, families must have the opportunity to explore a variety of educational options. At the same time, schools must make a commitment to flexible policies which allow students to take advantage of all of the opportunities which exist in and out of the classroom, to work with knowledgeable mentors and to begin to specialize in the domains where their talents are manifest. These unique features of the American educational landscape — the permeability of the boundaries between various places of learning, flexibility, and opportunities for early specialization — are well worth rediscovering, for they can only help youngsters seeking to develop their talents.

"An Useful (and Visionary) American Education"

In the history of American education, there has always been a tension between the practical and the visionary, between serving the needs of the individual and serving those of the community. This tension was nowhere more in evidence than in Thomas Jefferson's original attempts to shape a system for public education. First and foremost, Jefferson was an advocate of "an useful American education"[5] serving distinctly practical ends: "to give every citizen the information he needs for the transaction of his own business ... to enable him to calculate for himself, and to express and preserve his ideas, his contracts and accounts, in writing ... to understand his duties to his neighbors and country ... to know his rights ... "[6]. On the other hand, Jefferson shared with his contemporaries a less modest vision of education as a means to improve not only society but ultimately the human condition: "Education," Jefferson wrote, "engrafts a new man on the native stock and improves what in his nature was vicious and perverse into qualities of virtue and social worth. And it cannot be but that each generation succeeding to the knowledge acquired by all those who preceded it, adding to it their own acquisitions and discoveries and handing the mass down for successive and constant accumulation, must advance the knowledge and well-being of mankind ... "[7]

In order for an educational system to serve the needs of the democracy, Jefferson recognized that it would have to balance various interests. On the one hand, it would have to provide all individuals with the means to earn their livelihood and participate responsibly in society. However, what is often overlooked in

Jefferson's vision of American education is his equally firm commitment to identifying the most promising students at each level and providing them with opportunities to develop their talents. "By that part of our plan which prescribes the selection of the youths of genius from among the poor," Jefferson wrote, "we hope to avail the State of those talents which nature has sown as liberally among the poor as the rich, but which perish without use, if not sought for and cultivated."[8]

The question of whether the schools exist to serve the needs of society or those of the individual has recurred throughout the history of education in America. The famous debate between Booker T. Washington and W. E. B. Du Bois was, in its essentials, an attempt to address the same tensions (between the practical and the visionary, between earning a living and cultivating "genius") for a group of people whose interests had previously been ignored in most public forums: African-Americans. While Washington favored industrial education as a means "to achieve self-respect and economic independence," Du Bois argued for "academic and professional training of the highest quality" for "the talented tenth", those individuals who showed the greatest promise of becoming leaders for the African-American community and the nation.[9]

In recent years, critics have argued that our nation's schools are neither preparing the majority of our citizenry for any but the most menial forms of employment nor nurturing "the talented tenth" to realize their full potential.[10] If any meaningful consensus has been reached in the national debate, however, it is that these goals are not antagonistic in any fundamental sense. As the economy has moved away from heavy industry, the elements of "An Useful American Education" (sic) have become increasingly technical and complex. It is one of the strange paradoxes of contemporary American society that while unemployment figures continue to rise, the business community continues to complain that it cannot find qualified employees. Recent studies have shown that over the next few decades the demand for college graduates will increase while the demand for unskilled and semi-skilled labor will continue to decrease.[11] At the same time, the vast array of problems — social, economic, political — currently facing the nation is ample testimony to the continued need to find and nurture highly talented individuals.

Du Bois's plans for the education of the "Talented Tenth" were never implemented, and during the first half of this century "youths of genius" received scant attention in the political life of the nation, as interest in the development of exceptional talent remained largely the domain of a few psychologists. Foremost among these individuals was Lewis Terman, who, in 1916, introduced the Stanford-Binet Scale of Intelligence and nine years later began his monumental work, *The Genetic Study of Genius*, which would eventually spawn the gifted child movement. While intelligence tests were used by the schools to group students according to ability from the 1920's onward, interest in exceptionally talented individuals remained largely isolated from the mainstream until 1957, when the Soviet Union launched *Sputnik*. Paradoxically, it was fear of the "red threat" that brought about what neither the Jeffersonian/Du Boisian ideal nor Terman's findings could: a national commitment to developing "the mental resources and technical skills" of its young people and to funding, through "The National Defense Education Act," more rigorous and academically challenging programs to develop those skills deemed essential to the "national defense needs of the United States."

The past thirty years have witnessed an ebb and flow of interest in the special educational needs of students with exceptional talents. The 1968 creation of a White House Task Force on Gifted Education marked the beginning of a decade of renewed interest in programs for the gifted and talented. The Marland Report, issued in 1974, provided a coherent overview of issues in gifted education and resulted in the creation of the federal Office of Talented and Gifted. Unfortunately, substantial federal funding for gifted programs, promised by the Gifted and Talented Children Act of 1978, withered in the appropriations process. Furthermore, in 1981, the federal government closed the Office of Talented and Gifted, leaving local and state governments to play the leading role in the education of gifted students. The passage of the Jacob Javits Gifted and Talented Students Act of 1988 has stimulated a renewed interest in the identification and nurturance of the nation's most talented individuals, particularly those from minority groups historically under-represented in gifted and talented programs, creating at least the illusion of a national commitment to the educational vision of Jefferson and Du Bois.

Presently, 26 states mandate programs for gifted students, and, in a peculiar twist, ten states have passed laws which place gifted students under the broader category "handicapped." Under the "Education for all Handicapped Children Act of 1975," gifted students in these states have a number of unusual rights, including the right to "a free appropriate public education" in the "least restrictive environment" and an Individualized Education Program (IEP) specifying goals and objectives and "specific educational services to be provided."[12]

The term "appropriate education" is decidedly nebulous, and while state departments often make broad recommendations in their guidelines, they tend to vest local officials with significant decision-making powers. Ultimately, the educators taking part in the "multi-disciplinary committees" which design IEPs determine what is to be considered "appropriate" for the individual student. While there is a general consensus that students with outstanding abilities have distinctive educational needs, no consensus has been established with respect to the most effective means of meeting these needs.

In attempting to provide their most talented students with "appropriate" opportunities, educators often find themselves constrained by accepted practice and highly theoretical models of intellectual development, which while serving as helpful heuristics in scholarly debate often have limited practical value. There is growing concern that current practice in gifted education is neither practical nor visionary. The conventional fare of "pull-out" programs, with their emphasis on field trips or fun and games "enrichment," addresses neither the individual need for challenging opportunities in a specific field of endeavor, nor society's need for the leaders who will negotiate future peace settlements, the scientists who will explain physical phenomena or discover cures for diseases, the artists who will create new masterpieces, or the teachers who will help others to understand such endeavors.

The Center for Talented Youth of The Johns Hopkins University and the Optimal Match

During the past fifteen years, an alternate approach to serving the needs of the nation's most talented students has emerged — an approach with profound implications for all students. The Center for Talented Youth of the Johns Hopkins University (CTY) has evolved in response to the demands of parents and students for rigorous programs which challenge students at the pace and level dictated by their abilities. Since 1979, CTY has been identifying academically talented thirteen-year-olds and providing them with the opportunity to participate in demanding courses in mathematics, science, and the humanities. Currently, CTY runs the largest international Talent Search in the world, handling in excess of 40,000 applications per year.

Based on the pioneering work of the eminent psychologist Julian Stanley, the CTY Talent Search is a two-step process. In the screening process, students scoring in the top three percentiles on a standardized grade-level test are invited to participate in the Talent Search. In the second stage, the final identification process, Talent Search participants sit for the Scholastic Aptitude Test (SAT), a test originally designed for college applicants. Students scoring the level of a college-bound male senior qualify for participation in CTY's Academic Programs.[13]

In the twelve years that the Talent Search has been in existence, research has proven the SAT to be uniquely suited to identifying students with academic talents, in that its high "ceiling allows ... precise measurement of student aptitude (the ability to grasp concepts not yet encountered in formal schooling)," and its measure of both mathematical and verbal ability yields a profile of "the degree and type of talent a student may demonstrate."[14]

While global definitions of intelligence remain elusive and controversial, there is a fairly broad consensus that individuals possess talents in a variety of domains.[15] CTY does not view talents as static, in-born qualities which certain individuals possess, but rather as dynamic tendencies which develop and reach fruition only through careful nurturing. CTY programs are designed to address the talents most closely associated with academic accomplishment and professional attainment in our society: thus, CTY offers courses in mathematics, the sciences, social sciences, and humanities. It should be noted, however, that the CTY approach has also been applied successfully to programs in the arts and shares many features with methods which have proven most effective in training young musicians and athletes.[16] CTY avoids gimmicky attempts to teach "higher order thinking" and "meta-cognitive" skills in isolation, relying instead on the rigorous traditions of the academic disciplines.

It is the guiding principle of The Center for Talented Youth that every student deserves to be treated as an individual with specific educational needs and interests. Whenever possible, an Optimal Match should be attained between a student's abilities and the program of study; that is, once a student has mastered a subject on a given level, she must be allowed to proceed to the next stage. Over the past fifty years, a substantial body of research has accumulated to support the notion that students, particularly the highly able, reap profound benefits when they are allowed to progress through the curriculum at their own pace.

Julian Stanley has amply documented the successes of students participating in accelerated mathematics courses, skipping grades, and going to college early through the Study of Mathematically Precocious Youth. Nancy and Hal Robinson have argued convincingly for early college entrance based on their research at the University of Washington. In an extensive longitudinal study of students who study mathematics in The Johns Hopkins University Center for Talented Youth's summer academic programs, Linda Barnett demonstrated that acceleration in mathematics during the middle school years serves as a catalyst for achievement in college and participation in a broader range of extra-curricular activities.[17] In a recent meta-analysis of the literature on accelerated programs for highly able students, Kulik and Kulik found that: "Academic benefits are striking and large in programs of acceleration for gifted students."[18]

CTY's academic programs, which have recently expanded to include a component for students aged 7–12, are built on a few basic principles grounded in the Optimal Match principle[19] and the liberal arts tradition. Academically talented students are not thought to require a curriculum which differs in substance from that which is offered to other students; rather, it is the pace and level of instruction which are modified to meet their distinctive needs. While instructional techniques vary across the disciplines, all CTY courses are characterized by flexible pacing, academic rigor, opportunities for individual inquiry, and intensive interaction with mentors who are specialists in the subjects they teach.

In mathematics, CTY's instructional approach is an outgrowth of Dr. Julian Stanley's work with students with exceptional abilities in mathematics. Starting in the early 1970's, Dr. Stanley discovered that students with identified talents were capable of progressing through material at a much faster pace than was permitted at school. To address this situation, Dr. Stanley developed a process of diagnostic testing and prescriptive instruction, which allows a teacher to assess a student's abilities and knowledge base and to gear instruction to his or her individual needs. Instead of wasting time and becoming frustrated as they review material which has already been mastered, students are allowed to progress at their own pace through a suitably challenging curriculum.

In CTY science courses, students are also presented with material usually reserved for older students. Fast-paced courses cover, in three weeks, what standard high school introductory courses cover in a full year. These courses provide excellent preparation for students intending to take Advanced Placement courses in high school. CTY also offers courses in archeology, astronomy, geology, paleobiology, and other sciences, which are frequently not available to middle and high school students.

In the humanities and social sciences, CTY offers a broad variety of courses, including intensive foreign language instruction, logic, American History, Russian-Soviet History, World Geopolitics, psychology, and the History of Western Music. Again, the guiding principle is that talented junior high school and high school students are capable of learning skills and studying materials usually reserved for college students. Of particular note is CTY's sequence of writing courses, which helps students to develop fluency, flexibility, and a sensitivity to the finer points of language and style. Drawing on the traditions of the Writing Seminars of The Johns Hopkins University, CTY's writing workshops help students to develop writing skills through peer criticism, discussion and analysis of literature and other media, and intensive coaching sessions with knowledgeable mentors.[20]

Building on Dr. Stanley's work, CTY's own research, and many years of experience with high ability students, CTY has developed a distinctive stance on educational policy. In sharp contrast with the adherents of "pull-out" programs for the gifted, CTY advocates tailoring educational programs to students' individual needs and abilities, involving parents in the educational process, creating a positive peer environment, utilizing out-of-school educational resources, and recapturing the flexibility which has traditionally been a strength of the American educational system.

At the heart of CTY's stance on educational policy is the notion that all students must have acccss to an intellectually engaging curriculum which is both flexible and rigorous. CTY holds that the time has come to move beyond the traditional "pull-out" enrichment programs for the gifted, which are both insular and ineffectual, and to adopt a new system of thought which will provide all students with optimal educational experiences based on regular assessments of abilities, learning styles and achievement. CTY holds that not only the "talented tenth" but all students benefit when educational programs are designed to meet individual needs, and when students are given the opportunity to engage in what Einstein termed "the holy curiosity of enquiry."[21]

Unlike many of the popular schemes to revitalize American education that rely on gimmicks and "teacher-proof" curricula, the CTY approach depends on the presence of top-notch professionals in the classroom: individuals with expertise not only in child development and instructional strategies, but most importantly, in the particular subject which they teach. CTY believes that students need mentors — teachers who serve as role models and inspire a passion for the subjects they teach. Gradually, the CTY approach is winning advocates in schools and school districts across the country and throughout the world.

The Case Studies:
Scope and Methods of the Enquiry

In this book, we present the findings of a three-year enquiry into the status of education for academically talented students in the

United States of America. The book is divided into two sections. The first eight chapters are individual case studies — a chronicle of the frustrations and triumphs of nine students and their families. Out of the dozens of interviews we initially conducted, we chose to focus on these individuals because we felt that their stories, while retaining the character of the larger sample, were, in one way or another, the most instructive.[22] In Chapter Nine, we review the individual case studies in light of current research on creative and highly successful adults, focusing on outstanding aspects of the American Education Landscape — eight features of individual intellectual development which should be of concern to every parent and educator. While every child is a unique case with specific, personal needs, many of the findings summarized in this section should serve as helpful guideposts for parents and educators working with young people.

In the second section of the book, we examine a number of programs, schools, and school systems that have implemented strategies which reflect CTY's educational philosophy. In chapters ten and eleven, we examine a school (the Hawthorne Junior High School in Yonkers, N.Y.) and a school system (Appalachia Unit 08, Pennsylvania), which have implemented programs based on the CTY model, and report on the impact that these programs are having on the youngsters they serve.

Identifying students' individual needs and tailoring educational opportunities to those needs is a logical extension of the CTY approach. Chapter Twelve is an analysis of the implementation of laws and policies on gifted education in the state of West Virginia, where officials have taken an extremely progressive stance on the implementation of flexible pacing strategies by requiring Individualized Education Programs (IEPs) for all gifted students and educational plans for all high school students. In Chapter Thirteen — the conclusion — we set forth a program for recovering our children from the system: a distinctive vision for families and educators who share a vision of an American education distinguished by its flexibility and responsiveness to the individual needs and abilities of all students.

According to Robert Yin, the strength of a case study approach rests in the ability "to retain the holistic and meaningful characteristics of real-life events — such as individual life cycles, ... neighborhood change, ... international relations. ... " As such, case studies permit the investigator "to expand and generalize theories," while addressing a wide range of questions.[23]

In the following chapters, using a case study approach, we address two sorts of question. First of all, there are matters of description: How are academically talented students educated in America? What are their distinctive needs? How are these needs being met and by whom? What are the obstacles that these young people encounter in trying to learn? How do (and don't) they overcome them? What is the role of the family in the educational process? How do families make educational decisions? What types of social adjustments do academically talented students have to make?

By portraying a broad range of students, families, and institutions from across the country, we hope to enhance the reader's sense of the educational landscape — to add depth and detail to the surface of the map. In addition to describing the present realities, we address educational policy issues. Thus, a second set of questions: How should academically talented students be educated? How can one best meet their distinctive needs? What institutional characteristics provide optimal educational conditions? Which aspects of the American educational system can best be used to serve these individuals? How can parents serve as effective advocates and promoters of their children's education? What are the best social conditions for highly able learners? Finally, and most importantly: What are the implications of these findings for all students?

After an extensive review of the literature on the education of academically talented students, a family was chosen as a test case. Following the preliminary interviews, questionnaires were developed for students, parents, and other informants. Material for each case was collected from a variety of sources. At least one interview spanning several hours was conducted with each student included in the book. Most students were interviewed two or three times. In each case, parents were also interviewed at length. Teachers, psychologists, school administrators, and other individuals familiar with the student's educational history were also interviewed.

Throughout the interview process, even when the standard protocol was used, questions were kept open-ended to allow subjects the freedom to discuss what they felt were their most significant experiences and insights.[24]

Whenever possible, various documents were examined, including teacher evaluations, psychological reports, students' work, and letters sent by parents and students. Time was also spent with students in informal settings. Often, aspects of an individual's character and insight into his or her experiences came to light only when the tape recorder had been stowed away.

The methodology for Part Two was essentially the same. A variety of knowledgeable individuals were interviewed in-depth and repeatedly. Participant-observer techniques were applied, with extensive field notes being recorded. In some instances, educational records, personal correspondence, and other internal documents were examined. Additionally, a variety of documents in the public domain were also scrutinized, including newspaper and journal articles, published research reports, data and statistics from a variety of sources, legal codes and statutes, state and local educational guidelines and policies. Again, the principles of triangulation were applied in an attempt to ensure an accurate portrayal of the events and institutions being discussed.[25]

The Appendix Section complements the narrative by providing a list of practical strategies for the parents of acedemically talented students who suspect their children have abilities requiring specific educational interventions as well as suggestions for secondary schools working with talented Attention Deficit Disorder (ADD) students.

* * * *

While conducting this study, we were consistently impressed by the creative methods employed by students and parents struggling to alter the educational status quo. In many cases, families found able and equally committed allies in teachers, principals, guidance counselors, gifted program supervisors, and school superintendents. Every student interviewed was able to tell of at least one inspiring educational experience — an independent study with a teacher who recognized her talent, a course at a local college, a project for a science fair, a class with a dynamic teacher, an experience at a summer program for the academically talented. This book is as much a testimony to the vision and hard work of the many individuals who are changing the way the educational mainstream looks at academic talent as it is a critique of mainstream misunderstandings.

The American educational landscape is as varied as the geography of the fifty states. In places it is rugged and unpredictable, continually testing the mettle of those who would cross it. In other places, it is relentlessly barren, like badlands stretching to the horizon. Everywhere, it presents challenges to individuals seeking to change it. Often it resists stubbornly — maintaining its inertial cycle like the weather, the seasons, a stream. Occasionally, when the will is present and the soil fertile, it bears the sweetest fruit — children learning.

Notes

1. Flavell, *The Developmental Psychology of Jean Piaget,* p. 16.
2. Mansfield and Busse, *The Psychology of Creativity and Discovery: Scientists and Their Work; Bloom, B., Developing Talent in Young People*; Cox, Daniel, and Boston, *Educating Able Learners*; Ochse, *Before the Gates of Excellence.*
3. Bloom, p. 377.
4. Cremin, *American Education: The National Experience 1783–1876,* p. 471.
5. Cremin, Lawrence A., *American Education: The National Experience 1783–1876,* p. 249.
6. Ibid. p. 110.
7. Ibid. 111–112.
8. Conant, James B., *Thomas Jefferson and the Development of American Education,* p. 17.
9. Cremin, Lawrence A., *American Education: The Metropolitan Experience 1876–1980,* p. 122. Du Bois, W.E.B., *"The Talented Tenth."*
10. The current debate about the quality of American education was spurred by the National Commission on Excellence in Education's report *A Nation at Risk.* In an article entitled "The Other Education Crisis," Daniel J. Singal points out failings in the education of the nation's most talented students.
11. See "What Work Requires of School," a report produced by the Secretary's Commission on Achieving Necessary Skills, U.S. Department of Labor.
12. For a fine overview of legal issues in gifted education see Karnes, F.A. & Marquardt, R.G., *Gifted Children and the Law.* In 1991, The Edu-

cation for all Handicapped Act was updated as the Individuals with Disabilities Education Act, with the major provisions of EHA remaining intact.

13. For the 1992 Talent Search, students qualified for mathematics and science courses by scoring at least 500 on the mathematics portion of the SAT and 930 combined (M+V). To qualify for humanities and social science courses, students were required to score at least 430 V and 35 on the Test of Standard Written English.

14. Barnett, Linda B. & Corazza, Luciano, "Identification of Mathematical Talent and Programmatic Efforts to Facilitate Development of Talent." For a more detailed description of the Talent Search process see Stanley, Keating & Fox (1974) *Mathematical Talent: Discovery, Description, and Development* or Stanley, J.C. (1976) "Use of tests to discover talent" in Keating (Ed.), *Intellectual Talent: Research and Development.* For further research on the suitability of the SAT as a tool for identification see Gustin, W.G. and Corazza, L. (in press) "Mathematical and Verbal Reasoning as Predictors of Scientific Achievement," *Roeper Review.*

15. Gardner, Howard, *Frames of Mind*; Feldman, D.H., Nature's Gambit; Csikszentmihalyi, M. & Robinson, R.E., "Culture, time, and the development of talent."

16. "Rembrandt to Rembrandt: A Case Study of a Memorable Painting Teacher," Zimmerman, Enid, *Roeper Review*, 13(2), 1991.

17. The research supporting acceleration of academically students is quite substantial. For an overview see Southern, W. Thomas & Jones, Eric D., eds., *The Academic Acceleration of Gifted Children.* For further reading see also Brody, L.E., & Benbow, C.P., "Accelerative Strategies: How effective are they for the gifted?"; Brody, L.E., Lupowski, A.E., & Stanley, J.C., "Early Entrance to college: A Study of academic and social adjustment during freshman year"; Brody, Linda E., Assouline, Susan G., & Stanley, Julian C. "Five Years of Early Entrants: Predicting Successful Achievement in College"; Brody, Linda E. & Stanley, J.C., "Young College Students: Assessing Factors that Contribute to Success"; and Stanley, J.C., "The case for extreme educational acceleration of intellectually brilliant youth". On early entrants at the University of Washington see Robinson, Nancy M. & Robinson, Halbert B. "The Optimal Match: Devising the Best Compromise for the Highly Gifted Student." On the impact of participation in The Johns Hopkins University Center for Talented Youth's individually-paced mathematics courses see Barnett, Linda, "Ten Years of Academic Talent: A Follow-Up." And for a meta-analysis of research on ability grouping and acceleration see Kulik, James A. & Kulik, Chen-Lin, C., "Effects of Accelerated Instruction on Students"; and idem, "Ability Grouping and Gifted Students."

18. Kulik, James A. & Kulik, Chen-Lin C., "Ability Grouping and Gifted Students," p. 191.

19. For a theoretical discussion of the psychology of optimal experience see Csikszentmihalyi, Mihaly "Toward a Psychology of Optimal Experience."

20. Tangherlini, "Of Triggerfish and Talented Youth;" Tangherlini and Durden, "Verbal Talent."

21. cited from Gruber, H.E., "On the Hypothesized Relationship between Giftedness and Creativity."

22. With a couple of notable exceptions, all of the students included in Part One are or were, at one time or another, participants in CTY's Talent Search and Academic Programs. While neither Tyrell Green nor Bob Dagleish were participants in CTY programs, both are exceptionally talented youths who came to our attention through CTY's counseling and diagnostic center.

23. Yin, Case Study Research: Design and Methods, Pp. 14–21.

24. Jackson, Bruce, *Fieldwork*.

25. Wolcott, Harry F., "A Case Study Using an Ethnographic Approach," in *Complementary Methods for Research in Education*.

PART I

Hairspray

2

Llewelyn Sczurko

Before he entered the seventh grade in Saguaro*, Arizona, Llewelyn Sczurko had spent only six months in the classroom. Except for a semester in the third grade in Fairbanks, Alaska, Llewelyn's first six years of education were conducted in his parents' home in the Alaskan bush, hundreds of miles from the nearest school.

Llewelyn had no trouble adjusting to the academic demands of his new environment; working at his own pace under the guidance of his mother, he had mastered material through the eighth grade level and beyond. However, because his parents wanted him to interact with kids his own age, they decided to enroll him in the seventh grade.

By Llewelyn's own admission, his seventh grade social life was a disaster. The problems started the first day, when he got on the bus. He was wearing a dress shirt, corduroy pants, and sunglasses, because his eyes still hadn't adjusted to the desert sun. The other kids were in t-shirts, jeans, and jams — those oversized, circus-tent-colored shorts so popular in the late eighties. As anyone who has ever been a teenager knows, no law is as ruthless as adolescent fashion. Llewelyn's clothes made him an outsider from the beginning.

---

* Town name is fictional.

And things only got worse. Llewelyn's interest in schoolwork, his seriousness, his polite manner (which endeared him to his teachers), his ignorance of the customs and habits of thirteen-year-olds, his inability to play sports, and what he called his "naïveté," alienated his classmates, made him the butt of their jokes, and earned him the most dreaded nick-name of all — "nerd."

There is an old saw that goes: "We pay for our parents' mistakes." Watching their son suffer the torments of his classmates, Bob and Linda Sczurko must have wondered more than once if Llewelyn was the victim of some of the unconventional decisions they'd made about how to live their lives.

In 1971, Bob was a successful businessman directing the East Coast distribution operations of a large retail food company. Ever since graduating from college, he'd been on the fast track. Like so many people who came of age in the sixties, however, he began to have doubts about whether or not the life he had chosen could ever be fulfilling. He remembered watching his father "work his buns off" so he could retire and fish, only to die a year too soon. He also admits to having been influenced somewhat by the musings of Timothy Leary. At any rate, because he believed there was more to life than "four-hundred-dollar suits and sixty-five-hour work weeks," Bob decided that he was going to move to the Alaskan bush.

Bob and Linda built their home with their own hands, using locally milled three-by-twelve timbers. The nearest city was hundreds of miles away; the only way to get there was by plane or dogsled. For Bob and Linda, the opportunities that the bush offered for reading, for reflection, and testing their ability to survive were exhilarating. Llewelyn's arrival was another wonder.

Homeschooling

Even before Llewelyn was born, Bob and Linda had decided that they would do everything in their power to help their child to develop his intellectual abilities. They read books on education and psychology: Piaget, Getzels, and "things like *How to Raise a Brighter Child*," Linda said, laughing self-consciously. Having studied sociology in college, Linda was particularly interested in "education and socialization."

Living in the bush gave them a lot of time to spend with Llewelyn and to experiment with some of the ideas they'd developed about how best to educate him. Besides reading to him early on, the Sczurkos used all sorts of everyday situations as teaching tools. Sandwiches and slices of cheese were used as math aids; according to Bob, Llewelyn learned to add and subtract fractions and whole numbers at about the same time. "He was probably three years old when he took a piece of American cheese and cut it in half and then cut that half in half ... and at that time he could understand the concept of fractions very well."

A few months earlier, Llewelyn had discovered the concept of zero. His mother had been drawing cats on a little magic slate, having him count them: "one cat, two cats, three cats." After a while, it occurred to her to start tearing them off. After lifting the cover sheet and making the cats disappear, she asked him how many cats there were. And Llewelyn answered, "zero."

Some of Piaget's most famous experiments have to do with children's understanding of the concept of conservation. In his experiments, Piaget would have children pour a fixed amount of water into containers of different shapes and ask if the amount of water had changed. Depending on the shape of the container, children before the age of seven or eight (the pre-operational stage) would consistently say that there was more or less water, mistaking height for volume.

From a very early age, Llewelyn had been fascinated with water. He loved to pour it from container to container and to watch it come out of the faucet and go down the drain. To encourage Llewelyn's interest, Bob and Linda developed a system with jars of different sizes and shapes and colored rice. By pouring the rice back and forth between the containers, Llewelyn learned, by the age of two, that the volume of rice was not affected by the shape of its container.

Llewelyn's official schooling started when he reached the age of five. Because of Alaska's flexible stance towards alternative education, the Sczurkos were able to school Llewelyn in their home under the supervision of the Yukon-Koyukuk School District. Once a month a supervisory teacher would fly out to check on Llewelyn's progress and bring some new materials for him to work on. The district used the Calvert School curriculum, a somewhat conservative but solid curriculum that has been used effectively for decades.

The first box of material arrived in September of Llewelyn's fifth year. It was fairly standard kindergarten fare, and already, Linda — who was to be Llewelyn's teacher — ran into a problem that would nag her the whole time she was teaching him. If she followed the lesson plan, she was supposed to teach Llewelyn the names of the various colors. But that would have been absurd, since he already knew how to spell those names and how to mix the colors to make new ones. The material simply wasn't appropriate.

The winter after Llewelyn turned five, something happened that made Linda decide that he should be tested. The family was in Belize, making plans to fly back to Alaska. Linda was trying to figure out what Llewelyn's fare would be, and she said to Bob — "that would be two-thirds of mine and mine is —, so what would that be?" And before Bob was able to give her the answer, Llewelyn came up with it.

Back in Fairbanks, the Sczurkos had Llewelyn tested by an educational psychologist, and the results were impressive. It was decided that Llewelyn should skip the first and second grade material entirely and move right into the box with third grade material. According to Linda, the only thing that gave him trouble in the third grade box was spelling, which surprised her because Llewelyn was such a good reader. The problem was solved finally when Linda explained to Llewelyn that he needed to look carefully at words, to notice how they were spelled, and then he would remember them. "It just hadn't occurred to him to pay a lot of attention, prior to that, to how the words were spelled," Linda said.

It's not unusual for academically talented kids to skip over things that don't seem important to them. A similar situation would develop later in Llewelyn's education when he ran into the multiplication tables: at first, he just could not be bothered with them. However, once he decided that they were important, he mastered them almost immediately.

The year Llewelyn turned eight, the family spent six months in Fairbanks while Bob recovered from back surgery. On the advice of a friend who was a teacher in a program for gifted children, the Sczurkos enrolled Llewelyn in the third grade even though he had already completed Calvert's fifth grade box. Academically,

Llewelyn accomplished nothing in the Fairbanks public schools. However, his parents felt that the social experience was a valuable one. "He had to learn a lot of things — like how to stand in line and how to wait for other people to be done with what he could do really quickly," Linda observed. Eventually, he turned his energies to studying the social life at the school. "I can remember he gave me a wonderful sociological interpretation of the different kinds of kids in the class, whether they were academically inclined or socially inclined," Linda said.

It is often difficult to strike a balance between accelerating a child's education and providing appropriate enrichment. To a certain extent, children supply the signals themselves. When they are bored because their school work isn't challenging, they usually let their parents know. When the work is too hard, they rarely keep it a secret. Parents are often concerned that excessive acceleration will cause social problems for a child by isolating him or her from age-mates. Most of the research on this subject indicates that acceleration does not have any adverse social effects.[1] However, the concern is certainly a legitimate one.

Returning to the bush and the homeschooling program, Linda was concerned that Llewelyn would run into problems later on if she allowed him to continue working through the material at the pace they'd initially established. In order to keep Llewelyn from finishing the twelfth grade by age twelve, Linda started exploring ways to enrich his education. As a supplement to the Calvert curriculum, with the approval of the school district, Linda began teaching Llewelyn Spanish. By the time he was twelve, Llewelyn had gained an excellent command of the language, with grammar skills comparable to those of an advanced high school student.

In addition to his formal schooling, which lasted about six hours a day, Llewelyn maintained an informal mentorship relation with his father. In particular, the two of them discussed science — a passion they've always shared. "My dad and I would be out fishing," Llewelyn explained, "and I would ask something like — 'why do the ripples go like that?' — and I would learn something about Newtonian dynamics."

Because of the conscientiousness of his parents, homeschooling proved extremely effective for Llewelyn. In addition to mastering the basics, he had many opportunities to explore particular fields of interest. Entering the regular school system, he was much better prepared academically than his classmates. In addition to a high capacity for achievement, he had a genuine interest in learning and in exploring ideas. There is no doubt that he benefitted greatly from the individual attention he received from his education at home.

Playing the Game

When Llewelyn was eleven, his family moved to Arizona so that Linda could work on a master's degree in social work. By then, Llewelyn had completed the Calvert curriculum through the eighth grade. Or, as his mother puts it — "he'd been in the eighth grade for two years." However, because they felt that it was important for Llewelyn to have the experience of interacting with age-mates, they enrolled him in the seventh grade.

Llewelyn described his classes at Saguaro Junior High School as follows: "Very few of my classes challenge me. I don't mean to be bragging or anything, but my classes get boring ... Well, there are ones that are interesting but very rarely parts that are challenging."

Once again, the lessons were mainly social. After the misery of his seventh grade year, Llewelyn decided that he would do everything in his power to shed the nerd label. To start with, he lost some of his "naïveté." As he explained: "I learned what hairspray was, what kind of clothes one should wear, stuff like that." He also learned the role that sports can play in gaining social acceptance. He became a basketball fanatic.

Next, he learned to temper his enthusiasm in class. Instead of raising his hand whenever he knew the answer, which was most of the time, he made a conscious effort to raise it only occasionally, to pretend that he didn't know as much as he did. He learned to set his standards lower. "Instead of panicking when I get under a 97, which is what I did last year," he explained, "this year I'll be satisfied with a 90." Llewelyn even admits that he cheated on occasion — not because he didn't know the answers, not because he wanted a higher score, but just so kids would think he was normal, a regular non-nerd.

On one level, Llewelyn is learning some important lessons about the nature of American society. He is learning that people are suspicious of individuals with a great deal of talent. He is learning that success depends not only on one's intellectual capabilities, but also on one's ability to conceal them. Teenage society tends to work like a convex mirror reflecting adult society; certain traits are exaggerated — the urge for sameness, and that distinctly American brand of anti-intellectualism, which Richard Hofstadter described as "a resentment and suspicion of the life of the mind and of those who are considered to represent it; and a disposition to constantly minimize the value of that life."[2]

It is no accident that the vast majority of the people receiving Ph. D.'s in science at American universities are students from other countries. The social lessons that our schools offer bright kids merely perpetuate a fundamental anti-intellectualism. In the absence of academic challenges, students learn to be wily and suspicious of intellectual enthusiasm. They learn to make fun of people who are different and to conceal their own differences; in sum, they learn to play the game.

A Physicist in the Making

Llewelyn dates his interest in physics to Christmas of his ninth year when he received a copy of the 1985–86 Science Almanac. There is no doubt, however, that his parents chose the gift in response to talents and interests that had long been in evidence. From the time of his early experiments with American cheese and colored rice to his voracious consumption of books on physics now, Llewelyn has demonstrated many of the characteristics of a scientist in the making.

During the summer after his seventh grade year, Llewelyn attended CTY summer academic programs as a Holland Scholar*.

---

* The Holland Scholarship program was set up in 1988 to honor the memory of Jerome "Brud" Holland. The program provides full scholarships for minority children and children from economically disadvantaged families.

He enrolled in a flexibly-paced math class and completed geometry in three weeks. His teacher at the CTY summer program observed that Llewelyn had "a phenomenal ability to understand complex mathematical concepts, especially theory." She went on to note that Llewelyn had even developed some interesting theories of his own.

Llewelyn enjoyed the challenge of working through geometry at his own pace. He also felt comfortable with the intellectual atmosphere at CTY; his classmates were serious about academics and did not make him feel like an outsider. Finishing second in his class helped to boost his self-confidence.

On the advice of his CTY teacher, he continued to advance in mathematics when he returned to Saguaro Junior High School. Working independently, consulting only occasionally with a teacher, Llewelyn completed Algebra II during the first semester of eighth grade. When he took the national test for certification, his score was in the 99.8th percentile. During the second semester, however, his efforts to complete trigonometry on his own bogged down. Llewelyn admits that this was due in part to the fact that he was concentrating more of his energy on basketball and social pursuits. However, working alone without the support and prodding of a teacher undoubtedly contributed to his flagging interest.

Llewelyn says that someday he would like to be flown to Stockholm at the expense of the Royal Swedish Academy. His major interests are in particle physics and quantum theory. In many respects, Llewelyn has an excellent start on his education as a scientist. His parents have been continually supportive of his interests and even though he has been forced to adapt to less than ideal social circumstances he has maintained his interest in learning.

Up until now, Llewelyn's parents have made all the decisions regarding the course of his education. They have served as advocates, pressing the schools to take into consideration his needs — first for homeschooling and later for the opportunity to continue working at his own pace in mathematics. However, he is beginning to take on more responsibility. As he sees it: "My parents allowed me to realize that it would be necessary, if I wanted to get just about any place in life, to learn things. I think that I was the one who made — shall we say, oh boy — the necessary evolution from that to the ideas of what I wanted to learn."

Linda finds that she is having some trouble letting go. She still has very definite ideas about what she thinks Llewelyn should and shouldn't be learning. But she's trying gradually to ease up her grip on Llewelyn's life. After Llewelyn finished the eighth grade, he chose to attend basketball camp instead of CTY. According to Linda, he just wasn't motivated to fill in the application. And she decided not to push him. "In the last couple of years," she said, "I've been sort of trying to back off and say, 'we'll know that you want to do something when we see you taking action towards doing it.' "

The family has moved back to a small city in Alaska where Llewelyn has started high school. Balancing academic interests with social needs will undoubtedly remain difficult. Having mastered the basics of appearing cool, however, Llewelyn should find plenty of time for his studies. Working in his favor are his profound love of learning and his parents' dedication to insuring that he gets a good education.

Notes

1. Kulik and Kulik, "Affects of Accelerated Instruction on Gifted Students."
2. Hofstadter, Richard, *Anti-intellectualism in America*.

3

Bury Three Generations

Laura Foucher

One month into her third year in high school, Laura Foucher announced her intention to graduate that spring — a year earlier than expected. She was in the process of completing the most advanced courses in science and history available at Woodbridge High School and was enrolled in two humanities courses at a local liberal arts college. Without consulting an oracle, she could scarcely have foreseen the difficulties that were to arise from her decision.

Woodbridge* is situated in the foothills of the Adirondack Mountains in upstate New York. The area is sparsely populated; to attend Woodbridge High School, some students ride the bus for hours. Towns in the area are small and old, many of them incorporated in the 1700s. Formerly, most of the area's residents made their living from the land; although dairy farming is still common, vast tracts now lie fallow as residents work in nearby cities. Yet, small-town attitudes and small-town customs persist.

The Fouchers moved to Dunne, a town just outside of Woodbridge, in 1986 when Mr. Foucher took a job as a construction

---

* The name of the town is fictional.

manager in a nearby city. At the time, Laura was in the eighth grade. She attended Woodbridge Junior High School for the remainder of the year before moving on to the high school in the fall. As a whole, the family had a hard time adjusting to the move; neighbors and people from town were cordial enough, but they hardly made an effort to welcome the Fouchers. Or, as Mr. Foucher put it: "You've heard the old expression from up in Maine — you have to bury three generations before you belong? Well, it's somewhat similar — except here it's six."

In high school, it became increasingly difficult for Laura to fit in. Not only was she an outsider, but her interests were different. She was not thrilled with the parties that played such an important role in her classmates' social lives; she was especially not interested in drinking. Experiencing a similar sense of isolation, her older brother Brian had also decided to graduate from high school a year early. But while his early graduation went off without a hitch, Laura's was complicated almost from the moment she announced her intentions.

The choice to graduate a year early posed no problem to the school's administration: the principal was well aware of the fact that, like her brother before her, Laura had all but exhausted the school's ability to provide appropriate educational opportunities. From the time of Laura's arrival in Woodbridge, the school system had in fact been relatively flexible and responsive to her individual needs. On occasion it had taken some finagling on the part her parents, but Laura had received credit and placement for work done outside of school, had been given the opportunity to cross-register at a local college, and had even been allowed to register for a Physics class which she could only attend two days a week. Now, for the second time in her school career, she was being given the opportunity to skip a grade.

Laura's problems arose when it became apparent that she was going to graduate at the top of the class into which she had just transferred. As it turned out, another girl, Margaret Malone, had been laboring since elementary school under the assumption that she was going to be valedictorian. To make matters worse, most of the kids in the school were committed to Margaret's assumption. According to Mr. Smith, Laura's math teacher in her final year, Laura handled the situation with much more poise than her classmates — the so-called "full-fledged seniors."

For seven months, Laura was ostracized by the other students. Some kids shouted nasty things at her in the hallways; others simply ignored her. According to Mr. Foucher, the students were egged on by their parents. When meetings were held to discuss the situation, other parents argued that the Fouchers hadn't been in the area long enough for Laura to be chosen valedictorian — as if the honor were a birthright. When Mr. Foucher pointed out that they had been in town for close to four years, that Laura had attended the high school for three, the parents switched arguments. Now they claimed that she wasn't old enough to be a senior.

Meanwhile, Laura concentrated on her schoolwork. With the backing of the superintendent of schools, arrangements were made so that she could fulfill the State Regents' English requirement by taking an English course at the local college where she was already cross-registered as a special student. The superintendent even arranged for the school system to pick up the tab for her transportation. He had met Laura at various award ceremonies and was impressed with her abilities. He felt that her individual needs were as much a priority as the needs of problem students who routinely received much more attention.

Before colliding with the wrath of the class of 1989, Laura and her family had taken advantage of many of the best features of the American educational system. From the start, Mr. and Mrs. Foucher monitored their children's education closely, weighing a variety of opportunities and gradually involving Laura and Brian in the decision-making processes. Before they moved to Woodbridge, the family lived in Binghamton, where both children attended a Christian day school in grades one through three. The Fouchers chose that particular school because they knew that it had a strong program in math and reading. After completing the third grade, the children were transferred to the public school, because the public school boasted superior facilities, especially for science. At first the children resented being moved away from their friends, but they adjusted quickly.

The fall before the family moved to Dunne, Laura skipped the seventh grade on the recommendation of a guidance counselor. The transition went smoothly. As Laura described it: "No one really seemed to care too terribly much, which was the good part. I mean, people seemed to accept it fairly easily, and were more like: 'Oh wow! that's sort of a neat idea.' As opposed to: 'Ooh, how weird.' "

Once again at Woodbridge, the school system responded to Laura's needs with a great deal of flexibility. While finishing up her eighth grade year, she took a French course at the high school. After taking the Regents' Exam and the high school's final exam, she was given credit and placement for a three-week European history course taken at CTY. Her last year in high school, she was allowed to cross-register at the local college, where she studied Anthropology, English, and German. The problem with class rank might have been avoided if someone in the school administration had had the foresight to count her as a sophomore when she entered Woodbridge High, since most of her classes were on the sophomore or junior level, but they were not accustomed to providing students with the sorts of flexible options that Laura required.

In addition to taking advantage of opportunities afforded by the schools, the Fouchers made ample use of other educational resources, enrolling both children in music lessons and a "College for Kids" program. After the eighth, ninth, and tenth grades, Laura attended summer sessions at CTY to study European History, astronomy and then geology. Laura was particularly inspired by her science teachers. "CTY teachers don't take you by the hand and lead you down the path," she said. "They make you think about how to solve a problem, and that's a much more effective approach."

At home, Mr. Foucher and Brian worked on electronics projects while Mrs. Foucher and Laura concentrated on various crafts — everything from needlepoint to ceramics, from pottery to weaving. Mr. Foucher encouraged Laura to take an interest in electronics as well; however, at that time, she was going through a phase, her father observed, where she didn't want to do anything that her brother was doing and was set on asserting her individuality and independence.

Without this sense of independence, without the ability to keep focused on her academic interests and goals, Laura might have suffered her classmates' affronts much less graciously. She might have given into bitterness; she might have lost track of what she was ultimately trying to accomplish.

A Precocious Child

According to her parents, Laura developed early not only intellectually but also physically, socially and emotionally. The family lore
has it that the first time Mr. Foucher saw Laura — in the nursery
at the hospital — she was picking up her head, looking around.
She walked at nine months, learned to ride a tricycle before she
was one and a half, and her mother claims that she can't remember
a time when Laura couldn't talk. From the beginning, Laura's precocity caused problems, as she continually challenged other people's expectations of what she was capable of doing.

Mr. and Mrs. Foucher read to their children constantly as they
were growing up. When Brian got his first library card, Laura was
less than two years old; still, she wanted one too. She became
furious when she learned that the library had a rule that you had
to be at least two years old in order to get a card. On the day that
she turned two, however, the Fouchers could do nothing before
they'd driven Laura down to the library to get her card.

Laura went through six or seven cards before the family moved
to Dunne. "She just plain wore them out," said her mother, her
voice accented with a crisp Upstate New York twang — like biting
into an Empire apple. "You know, she would go to the library
and it was always 'Pick whatever you want,' and she usually had
ten or fifteen books and she'd go home and three days later we'd
be back at the library for more books."

Laura's attention span also developed early. Already as a
toddler she was extremely adept at putting together puzzles. She
learned to play Monopoly at the age of four, and would spend
hours playing board games with her family. When the time came
for her brother to start school, Laura was furious that once again
she was being left out of the fun. But she didn't have to wait long.
At three years and ten months she was enrolled in a special pilot
program which combined children who had normal hearing with
hearing-impaired children.

Laura has vague memories of being taught different ways to
communicate with the children who often couldn't hear what was
being said to them. She remembers trying to act out the things she
wanted to say. Of that experience, her mother observed: "She was
going from nine in the morning till two-thirty in the afternoon,

and she had a great time. She absolutely loved it." The next year, Laura started at the Christian day school. Her parents enrolled her there, not only because of the strong math and reading programs, but also because the school had an all-day kindergarten, which was "necessary, because she was ready to go." For the next four years, things went wonderfully. Although it is hard to determine the extent to which she was being challenged, Laura progressed smoothly through elementary school.

Hardships

According to her mother, already as a child, Laura had a sophisticated understanding of social interactions, without necessarily being willing to make the adjustments in her manner that would ease the process of fitting in. After participating in relatively challenging, high-track classes throughout elementary school, she was placed in a class with students of mixed abilities in the seventh grade. She complained to her parents that her classes were boring, that she wasn't learning anything. One day, after school, Laura's mother informed her that the guidance department had suggested that she skip into the eighth grade. In response, Laura enumerated for her mother the problems she saw with that solution. She wondered whether her friends in the seventh grade would abandon her, whether she would be able to make friends with any of the eighth graders. Still, she insisted on making the jump. And although she was hurt by the loss of contact with many of her seventh grade friends, the transition went relatively smoothly and she made many new friends.

Before the family moved to Dunne, Laura had no serious social problems. By her own admission, she was never "normal." Her interests and concerns differed from those of her age-mates. Besides always being the youngest kid in her class and one of the smartest, she was also always one of the tallest. (At seventeen, she was close to six feet tall.) Her father, who was also always the tallest kid in his class, feels that all of these factors contributed to Laura's feeling that she was an outsider.

In the course of her schooling, Laura encountered some problems common to academically talented kids. When she finished assigned work, instead of allowing her to move on to more advanced topics, teachers often gave her busy-work and extra problems. Being a conscientious student, Laura would complete the assigned work only to find that the teacher didn't bother to correct it. And this frustrated her immensely.

Laura was particularly pained by the experience of being held up as an example to her classmates. According to her mother, she went out of her way to avoid calling attention to her accomplishments. Unfortunately, insensitive teachers often subjected Laura to various humiliating rituals. Standing at the front of the class with a stack of freshly graded tests, the teacher would pronounce some variation of: "I'm very disappointed in the results of this test. There was only one person who got an A." And all eyes would roll towards Laura.

Winning acceptance becomes increasingly difficult if a student's differences are constantly paraded before her classmates. Unfortunately, academic achievement — unlike accomplishments in sports or music — often does not win the admiration of peers. For Laura, learning was its own intrinsic motivation. Had the recognition been executed with a little finesse, she might also have enjoyed being recognized for her accomplishments.

During Laura's final year of high school, the issue of recognition became increasingly complex. Laura's grade average was a full two points higher than Margaret's, and Laura had worked hard to earn those grades. Naturally, Margaret's disappointment with Laura's sudden appearance in her class was understandable, but the harassment that Laura had to endure as a result was entirely unjustifiable. For months, the Fouchers agonized over how the problem might best be resolved.

Finally, Laura came up with a solution on her own: she decided to let Margaret be valedictorian. She felt no connection with her class at Woodbridge High School, and the honor of being its top student seemed hollow. She was anxious to get on with her life, to leave Woodbridge and go to college. On graduation day, Margaret gave the valedictory address, even though she was the number two student in her class.

Laura's voice gets an uncharacteristic, caustic edge when she talks about the experience. "That killed all my feelings about high school. All I wanted was to get out," she said. "If I never see any of my high school classmates again, I won't mind."

Early Entrance

In the fall of her final year in high school, Laura attended a weekend seminar at an Ivy League college for students interested in enrolling in their engineering program. She was fourteen at the time and had already decided that she was going to apply early decision to college and graduate from high school that spring. Since she was going to be on campus at the college, her mother thought it would be a good idea to schedule an interview to find out whether the school would be willing to accept a fifteen-year-old.

Laura enjoyed the seminar but the interview with the Assistant Dean of Admissions rapidly became confusing. When her mother explained that Brian had entered the college a year early and was doing extremely well, the dean sent her a puzzled look as if to say: "If you already have one child who entered a year early and there's no problem, why are we sitting here talking?" (The college in question usually does not grant interviews.) Finally Mrs. Foucher said: "You realize that Laura's only fourteen?" And the dean looked at Laura, and then he looked at Mrs. Foucher, and he said, "Really?"

The dean had had the opportunity to observe Laura over the entire weekend and had noticed no difference between her and the other students participating in the seminar. When Mrs. Foucher showed the dean Laura's SAT scores, which were both well over 700, his surprise turned to astonishment.

Laura is in her second year at the college. She is majoring in electrical engineering, but she is also completing the pre-medical requirements. Her eventual goal is to combine medicine and engineering to do research in the development of artificial limbs and other aspects of medical technology. She is doing well in college; she is enjoying the challenges that her courses present and maintaining a high grade point average.

For the first time in years, she is also happy with her social life. Outside of class, she works in the browsing library at the student union and plays in the marching band. Her mother claims that college has transformed her: "With the two of them gone last September, you would've thought the two of us would've been suffering extremely, and I don't think we did. And I think that the reason that we didn't was that we were so relieved because we knew that both kids were finally happy. And I mean, the difference in Laura — she just bubbles. She's so happy. She loves college. She finally feels that she's in an academic climate that's conducive to learning and to her and nobody cares ... how old she is."

Laura still hasn't told any of her college classmates how old she is. The years of ostracization at Woodbridge have made her wary of calling attention to her distinctiveness. No one has questioned her about her age either; in every sense — academically, socially, emotionally — she was ready to enter college when she did. Thinking about the very real possibility that she might still be a junior in high school, Laura winces; she can scarcely imagine anything worse.

Had she grown up in a city where the high school offered a lot of Advanced Placement courses, where there were other students with interests similar to her own, Laura might have considered staying in high school longer. However, she has no regrets about her current situation.

Conclusion

A number of factors were involved in Laura's successful acceleration. Participating in CTY programs for three summers and in the local college program during her last year in high school helped to prepare her for college. According to her mother, Laura had less trouble adjusting to college than did her brother. She had already had the experience of living with a roommate, and she was already familiar with the pace and discipline required by college-level classes. Laura also cited the CTY classes as an important factor in her decision to go on in science. They were her first exposure to rigorous, high-level science, and they left her hungry for more.

The social acceptance she found at CTY helped her to endure her outsider status at Woodbridge. She knew there were other kids like her.

Most important, however, was the support of her family. If anything, the family's isolation in Dunne tended to make its bond stronger. Both parents spent most of their spare time talking with their children, playing games with them, working on projects, and taking them to the movies or other extra-curricular activities. Laura was also fortunate to have parents who took an active role in overseeing her education — making sure that the schools were providing appropriate opportunities. As a rule, Mr. and Mrs. Foucher were responsive to Laura's cues — both in seventh grade when she said she was bored with her classes and in high school when she decided it was time to move on. She was by no means pushed ahead; the impetus for change always came from her.

4

A Hungry Student

Tyrell Green

A few weeks into his fifth grade year, Tyrell Green was transferred from a class for "gifted" students into a special education program. No one claimed that he lacked the ability to do the work in the gifted class, but his teacher and the school principal found him troublesome.

His behavioral problems stemmed primarily from the fact that he was not being challenged in class. Often, when he felt that an assignment was too easy, he would ask the teacher for some more interesting work. One would think that the teacher would have been gratified by her student's desire to learn. One would think that a teacher at a public school in New York City would welcome the challenge of teaching a child that the school psychologist described as having "brains and nerve and spirit." Instead, she punished him for being "disrespectful" and began picking on him systematically.

Tyrell is, without a doubt, the type of youngster that Theodore Sizer had in mind when he described the "hungry" student: "... the person who tries to find the new truth." He is not, like so many of his more successful peers, "docile, compliant, and without initiative."[1] Ill-prepared, insecure teachers are inevitably threatened by youngsters of Tyrell's caliber; or as Einstein put it — "great spirits will always encounter violent opposition from mediocre minds."

Tyrell's stubborn questioning of his teacher, his unwillingness to sit through a farcical class routine, his ability to fire verbal insults more quickly and more effectively than the teacher, won him a desk in a school for children with academic and emotional disabilities and a reputation as a trouble-maker which would follow him for the next four years. Through the eighth grade, he remained in special education classes often in the company of students functioning at the second or third grade level.

His mother, Naomi, fought to make the school system reconsider their decision, but she had a job, her own studies, and nine other kids to keep her busy. "They weren't interested in what his needs were or whether he was bright," said Ms. Green. "They were just interested in one thing, getting his conduct under control." Eventually, the situation got so bad at Tyrell's school that Ms. Green stopped sending him and let him study at home. While Tyrell received no formal schooling during the spring of his eighth grade year, he read voluminously — encyclopedia articles about subjects that interested him and classic works of literature, including Dickens novels and Shakespeare plays.

Over the years, Ms. Green had bought books as they were discarded by the local library. In this manner, she had filled an entire room of the family's first-floor housing project apartment with fiction, poetry, history, science. For Tyrell, this "library" was a sanctuary from the difficult, often threatening, world outside.

According to his mother, from a very early age, Tyrell had been something of an autodidact. He started reading when he was three years old and has been an ardent bibliophile ever since. Tyrell credits his mother with inspiring this interest. "My mother reads a lot," he said. "... Every time I see her, she's reading something."

At the suggestion of a teacher who had noticed Tyrell's exceptional abilities, he was tested when he was in the second grade. His Stanford-Binet I.Q. was 150, and his reading ability was equivalent to a sixth grader's. The evaluation team recommended that he be placed in a program for gifted and talented students. This involved transferring him to a new school.

In the third and fourth grades, things went smoothly. Although he was not particularly challenged by his classes, he had sympathetic teachers who believed in his abilities and encouraged him to develop them. One of the experiences he enjoyed most during this period was being chosen by his teacher to tutor sixth grade students who were having trouble with math. When the school principal learned of this arrangement, however, she put an end to it, because she felt that it was inappropriate for such a young student to be helping older ones. A year later, this same principal would be instrumental in having Tyrell transferred to the special education program.

After Ms. Green pulled Tyrell out of school in February of 1990, she was notified that he was due to be tested, as a part of a triennial evaluation process that all special education students in New York go through. Audrey Rose, the school psychologist charged with testing Tyrell, was astounded by the results. She found no sign of emotional disturbance — the justification for his placement in special education. There was some indication of "mild anxiety, over-sensitivity, and a tendency to perfectionism," none of which could be considered surprising, given the circumstances under which Tyrell had been operating during the last few years.

In all academic fields, Dr. Rose found Tyrell to be in the superior range. By now, he was reading on the twelfth grade level and hitting the ceiling on most of the tests that Dr. Rose usually administered. The only area where he showed relative weaknesses was in formal writing skills, where the results were closer to normal expectations for a child his age but still well above the average for an inner-city youngster. Dr. Rose and the evaluation team recommended that he be placed in a regular high school environment and that "an individualized program including appropriate college-level courses" be designed for him. However, school officials chose to ignore the recommendations of the evaluation team. As Dr. Rose explained it: "I hadn't figured on the political part of it, which is that they did this to him and now they have to justify it and keep the situation the way it is, in order to avoid being sued ...." Twenty years of experience in the New York City school system had taught Dr. Rose that young black men were often treated like pariahs: the system was more concerned with keeping them under control than with providing them with an education. She had fought for some kids in the past, but either the institutional barriers had been insurmountable or support had not been forthcoming from the children's homes. The prospect of watching yet another child fall victim to the machinations of the system horrified Dr. Rose. She decided that she would do everything in her power to get him placed in an appropriate educational setting. In Naomi Green she found a determined and equally outraged ally.

A Mother

Naomi Green is a tall, soft-spoken woman. Like her son, she is initially reserved, as if experience has taught her to approach strangers warily. However, once she begins to speak about her children or about an idea that interests her, she becomes impassioned. Her powerful hands cut at the air, silver bangles glinting on her wrists. Her speech is rich with African-American textures and nuances and self-effacing, gentle humor.

Ms. Green knew hardship from the beginning. She was born in 1940 in small-town Virginia, but remembers very little about her first years. After the war, like so many working-class blacks, her family moved to New York. She attended the first and second grades in Harlem until her mother was diagnosed with tuberculosis. At that point, she and her brother were sent to a "preventorium" for a year. After being released, she was placed in foster care. She attended high school through the twelfth grade but fell a semester short of graduating.

She was twenty-two when she had her first child; nine others would follow. Five different men would father her children, but none would stay with her to help her raise them. But she rose above her situation. In the spring of 1990 she graduated from a local college with a bachelor's degree in social work. It took her ten years from the time she enrolled, but she persisted.

Although Tyrell may be the one with the most academic facility, all of Ms. Green's children are bright. David, her fourth son, is a junior at the State University of New York, where he is studying drama and business administration. He wants to be an actor, and he wants to run his own business. Ms. Green's nineteen-year-old daughter, Kezia, is working on a degree in accounting. Two of

Ms. Green's sons have been less fortunate; the pressures of the neighborhood were too strong. Both became involved in drugs and both have done time in prison.

Ms. Green was devastated by her sons' involvement in drugs and their subsequent arrests. "I don't use them, so there's none in my house," Ms. Green explained. "But then the neighborhood — the kids in the neighborhood. Some of these drug dealers are all in the hallway and everything. It's very hard to keep your kids from being influenced." Tyrell was only thirteen years old when he was first contacted by a dealer who wanted to hire him. "And I was very stern with him," said Ms. Green. "I told him not to speak to that person again. It didn't go very far with him. You know, he hasn't used drugs ...."

Tyrell says he understands how a kid growing up in the ghetto could decide to sell drugs. "Starting salary," he said, "is a thousand dollars a week. How many kids in the city have enough talent that they can become doctors or lawyers? How many kids get the opportunity? How else are they ever going to see that kind of money?"

By definition the ghetto is a trap. But living in the ghetto is not only a function of geography but also of people's attitudes and behavior towards you. A person who lives in the ghetto is one whose right to make decisions has been taken away. As Ms. Green explains it, her children were largely ghettoized by the school system. In spite of their obvious intellectual capabilities, three of her sons were placed in special-education. Ironically, Ms. Green had to fight to get her dyslexic son Gabriel — the only one with a legitimate reason for being in Special Education — into the appropriate program. She was never consulted on these matters: the decisions were made independently by the schools. As Ms. Green explained: "I haven't had to make too many decisions, because the environment that I live in now, everything is more or less fixed .... If I was financially independent, then I would have been able to take care of the education of Tyrell better ... but being that the school system was the way it was, it was hard for me because I was constantly battling with them about decisions they would make prior to, you know, consulting me."

On a few occasions, opportunities to improve Tyrell's situation have slipped away. Sometimes because Ms. Green has not recognized them as such, sometimes because she has been slighted. After

Tyrell was tested in the second grade, arrangements were made for him to attend an elite private school in another part of the city. Ms. Green took time off from work to attend a series of meetings. However, it was an extremely stressful time for her, as she was pregnant with her youngest child and in the process of a break-up with her husband. When she missed a meeting, the school cruelly retracted its offer.

When Tyrell was in the fifth grade and the principal of the school for the "gifted" was making a stink about putting him into special education, someone suggested that he be moved, instead, to the eighth grade. It is likely that the academic challenges would have been more appropriate, and there is no doubt that Tyrell would have had no trouble fitting in socially: he has always been large for his age and unusually mature. Ms. Green was uncomfortable with this arrangement, however, because Tyrell's older brother Gabriel was in the sixth grade at that school, and she was afraid of the effects such an arrangement might have on his ego. It is hard to tell whether the jump from fifth to eighth grade was presented as a serious option; at any rate, neither Tyrell nor Ms. Green was counseled on the matter and the idea of sending him to another junior high school simply wasn't considered.

One of the most painful experiences for a parent is to witness her child being subjected to unfair treatment and to feel that she is incapable of doing anything about it. Ms. Green has certainly never stopped trying. The dream of making enough money to move to an area with better schools and less threats to the well-being of her children was one of the reasons that Ms. Green went back to school. With the same dream in mind, she got off welfare and took a job with the local schools. She had only been on the job for a year when Tyrell's teacher and the principal decided that he should be placed in special education. On a few occasions, she had to leave work to speak to the administrators at Tyrell's school. Eventually, she was fired. She was given no warning, no probation, no opportunity to discuss her situation.

There is no hard evidence, but it appears that the principal at the school where Ms. Green was working had heard from the principal at Tyrell's school that Ms. Green was making waves.

Losing the job devastated Ms. Green, financially and emotionally. Her welfare case had been closed, so she was no longer eligible for food stamps or medicaid. "Emotionally," Ms. Green said, "if I didn't have a strong belief in God — I wouldn't have been able to stand it. ... That was the only thing that kept me above water, the fact that I'm a survivor."

When Ms. Green was awarded her B. A. it was a matter of great pride in the family. All of her children came home to help her celebrate, and she regained much of her self-confidence. "Now that I've finished school," she said, "I'm going to do something about our situation." Among other things, she's considering going back for a master's degree, which would qualify her for a much more lucrative and interesting position.

The Autodidact

In *The Aims of Education*, Alfred North Whitehead wrote: "there is only one subject matter for education, and that is life in all its manifestations."[2] Quite independently of Whitehead's observation, Tyrell has shaped his own education around this principle. In spite of the fact that his last three years in the New York City school system were a waste of time, he continued to explore subjects that interested him: everything from astronomy to literature, from computer science to the workings of internal combustion engines. "I learned a lot from myself," Tyrell commented, "more from myself — venturing by myself in encyclopedias and stuff like that, than from the classrooms where they just teach you one curriculum instead of wide-spreading it."

Tyrell's curiosity manifests itself in his gestures, his attitude, his endless questions. Although shy in many social situations, particularly those involving adults, he is intellectually aggressive. Faced with a computer, a tape recorder, a car, he can hardly contain himself; he throws himself at new problems and new things with boundless curiosity and elan. Tyrell started speaking in whole sentences at the age of two; he was three when he learned to read. From the start, his mother was impressed with his memory. Everything he read, everything he saw, everything he heard, Tyrell remembered. Over time, his memory has by no means diminished; three months after writing a paper on the history of computers, he can still recite the salient developments without the slightest hesitation.

Tyrell loves jokes, riddles, and puzzles. While his sense of humor is not without its adolescent quirks, it is genuine, clever and inventive. He works on problems systematically and with determination; he often invents puzzles to test his friends. For example: A girl is stuck in a room with a piano, a saw, a table and a baseball bat. There are no windows; the door is locked and the key has disappeared. How does she get out? (See bottom of page for answers.)*

When he grows up, Tyrell wants to be a scientist or a writer. Even though his formal writing skills suffered while he was in the special education program, he has maintained his enthusiasm for writing. In his spare time, he likes to write fantasy stories. The setting for these stories is his neighborhood; the characters include himself, his brother, his friends — and various monsters. When asked why he includes the monsters, he said that he felt that a prospective reader was more likely to be interested in fantasy than reality. Until now, however, Tyrell has yet to share his stories with anyone.

Tyrell's love of science stems directly from his fascination with the way things work. His self-taught expertise ranges from bicycle mechanics to astronomy. After sitting in on a lecture about chaos theory, he began speculating immediately about whether the theory could be used to describe the dispersal of seeds by the wind.

His intellectual curiosity is accompanied by a deep sensitivity to social and political issues, particularly those affecting New York's African-American community. He devotes much of his spare time to reading books about race relations, African-American history, and the sociology of the inner-city. He is also a fan of Spike Lee's movies, hip-hop and rap music, and occasionally composes and performs his own raps.

"The most rewarding thing," observed his mother, "is that, through all the things Tyrell has gone through, it has not dimin-

---

* There are various possibilities. Among them are: a) she sits down at the piano and keeps playing a tune until she gets the right key, then she takes the key and opens the door; b) she swings the bat until she's out; c) she takes the saw and saws the table in half, puts the two halves together to make a whole, and then she climbs out the hole.

ished his belief in people ... and he's not a bad kid .... He has remained himself."

Help

While many of his teachers and school officials have waged what amounts to psychological warfare on Tyrell, he has had the good fortune of encountering a few teachers who understood his needs and were willing to take these into consideration. According to Ms. Green, "There was always somebody that took to him, always somebody there for him ... at least one teacher or somebody."

When he was in the fourth grade, there was the teacher who read his journal and encouraged him to continue working on his writing. The same teacher made the arrangements for him to tutor sixth graders who were having trouble with math. In fifth and sixth grades, at the special education school, he had another teacher who encouraged him to continue writing. Having recognized his talent, she helped him to get on the school newspaper. In sixth grade, he was chosen to edit the paper. Working on the newspaper made fifth and sixth grades bearable. "Editing is great," he said. "You get to see what goes in the newspaper and what goes out, what's not fit, what's fit, what you think."

More than anyone else, Dr. Rose, Tyrell's school psychologist, was instrumental in changing the circumstances of Tyrell's education. Tyrell had reached a dead-end as far as schooling was concerned when Ms. Green brought him in for testing at the end of his eighth grade year. Upon recognizing the extent of Tyrell's talent, Dr. Rose was determined to help him out. After school officials refused to accept the review committee's recommendation that Tyrell be decertified from the special education program and provided with an individualized educational program, Dr. Rose took things in her own hands.

First, Dr. Rose helped Ms. Green to file an appeal and then she began to meet with Tyrell on weekends, to tutor him in various subjects and to help him work through the insecurity that had developed during the past few years. When her supervisor got wind of this, she told Dr. Rose that she was overstepping her responsibilities and putting her career in jeopardy. Eventually, Dr. Rose was summoned to a meeting about her "professional conduct."

In the meantime, the appeal went nowhere, so Dr. Rose contacted the American Civil Liberties Union, and they in turn put her in touch with *Advocates for Children*, an organization which helps parents who feel their children have been wrongly placed in special education. Even though they knew that black students are much more likely than white students to be unfairly placed in special education,[3] they had never seen a case like Tyrell's. Negotiations between the schools and *Advocates for Children* produced a compromise: Tyrell was to be placed in a mainstream high school program, but the special education classification was to remain on his record for several months, until it was determined whether or not he was emotionally stable.

The school's reluctance to remove Tyrell's special education classification stemmed in part from an incident at his Junior High School. Tyrell had gotten in argument with a teacher; the teacher pushed him and knocked him over. Tyrell got up and ran to his locker. He grabbed his coat and was getting ready to storm out of the school when a razor blade — the type used to open boxes — flew out of his pocket and landed on the floor. The teacher, who had followed him, picked up the blade and accused Tyrell of planning to attack him.

According to Dr. Rose, most kids from Tyrell's neighborhood "are terrified of something happening to them — bad people hurting them or mugging them or taking their money (and it happens all the time), so that almost all of the kids have something on their person they imagine will be a weapon." Tyrell has never been involved in violence; in general, he seeks to avoid conflicts, preferring to talk things out or to walk away from problems. According to Dr. Rose, school officials pounced on the incident with the razor blade in order to maintain the image they were cultivating of Tyrell as a "terrible criminal-to-be."

Neither Ms. Green nor Dr. Rose were pleased with the compromise; once again, Tyrell's reputation would precede him along with the special education label, and no provisions were being made for his individual needs and abilities. On her own time and at her own expense, Dr. Rose decided to bring Tyrell to the CTY Counseling and Diagnostic Center to have him tested. Dr. Carol

Mills administered a series of tests that confirmed Dr. Rose's initial findings. According to Dr. Mills: "Tyrell is a young man with exceptional intellectual abilities and potential. In spite of educational 'misplacement' and virtual 'self-instruction' for the past three years, he has been able to continue to learn and is currently functioning above grade level in all areas except the mechanics of written language."

Conclusion

On the basis of Dr. Mills's evaluation and with the continued support of Dr. Rose, Tyrell was accepted with a full scholarship at a prep school in New England. In his first year, he was enrolled in standard freshman classes, but a mentorship was also set up with a teacher who had a great deal of experience working with students' individual needs. Finally, he had an opportunity to take challenging courses and explore some of his extra-curricular interests: he played football and basketball, sang in the choir, and took drawing lessons.

In his first two years at prep school, Tyrell had to face many new problems. He had not developed the study habits needed to succeed in academically rigorous courses. Barely fourteen years old, he had trouble adjusting to the demands of living away from home: doing his laundry, getting to class on time, getting along with roommates. The code of etiquette peculiar to prep schools seemed somewhat mysterious and indecipherable. Some of his teachers became frustrated with his behavior — his gregariousness, his playfulness, his apparent inattentiveness.

His experiences had given him little basis for coping with the expectations of his new school. He had trouble getting along with roommates and did poorly on his first set of examinations. He was thrown out of classes for disruptive behavior. He was placed on academic probation after smashing a window in the school's theater. He felt angry, frustrated, and isolated.

In his second year, Tyrell started out doing extremely well. Even though his advisor had left the school for another position, Tyrell had gained a great deal of confidence and poise. By mid-year, he made the honor roll and seemed to have found his niche in the school. Then a number of things occurred to send Tyrell into a crisis.

After the Rodney King trial and the ensuing riots, the atmosphere at the school seemed to change. A number of insensitive remarks which Tyrell might have ignored under other circumstances began to gnaw at him. Reading the newspapers and watching the news on television reminded him of the vast gulf that separated him from so many of his schoolmates.

He went home for a week-end to visit his mother and returned to school a day late because she did not have money to pay his bus fare. This resulted in a Saturday detention, doing maintenance on the school grounds. At a time when he needed someone to talk to, he felt abandoned and betrayed, punished for events that were beyond his control. With exams approaching, he missed his friends in New York and wondered whether prep school was really worth the effort.

Tyrell finished the school year ambivalent about returning. The high school he would attend in his home district has been described by one observer as "doing everything an inanimate object can do to keep a student from learning."[4] But prep school is not without its problems.

Tyrell sees the differences between himself and his classmates with penetrating clarity. Before the Rodney King trial brought issues of race back into the focus of the national psyche, Tyrell was disturbed primarily by issues of class and culture. Many of his schoolmates simply don't understand what it means not to have enough money to buy a shirt you like or to buy a pizza when you want one. At times, he is shocked by their behavior. "They yell at their parents," he said, shaking his head. "I would never yell at my mother. Never."

Naomi Green is proud of her son's abilities and thrilled that he has finally been given the opportunities which she always believed he deserved. "Through it all," she said, "he held out, which I always told him — 'no matter what they say,' I told him — 'it will be straightened out.' " While she is sensitive to the hardships that her son faces in an environment so different from his home, she believes it is for the best. "It's important that he know how to get along with different people," she observed, "because sometimes in life you're going to be outnumbered. That's just the way it is.

In our society, you have to learn to live with it." In describing the affect of adversity on her life, Ms. Green echoes a theme with deep roots in the African-American tradition: "It made us stronger and more determined," she says.

In a recent book, *Blacks in the White Establishment?: A Study of Race and Class in America,* Richard Zweigenhaft and William Domhoff examined "A Better Chance," a program which has been providing inner-city Black and Latino students with opportunities to attend some of the nation's elite preparatory schools for over twenty years.[5] Although the program has received mostly negative attention in the popular media, the fact is that "A Better Chance" has provided thousands of talented minority students with access to some of the best educational opportunities available in America. In spite of the difficulties that they faced attending traditionally white, upper-class schools, participants have gone on to become graduates of the nation's most prestigious universities, bank executives, reporters, scholars, lawyers, teachers, and, in one case, a world-famous musician. "The results of the program give reason to hope, for they demonstrate what is possible when black people are given an honest chance," the authors observed.[6] The unfortunate truth is that because of segregation and fiscal inequity[7] "an honest chance" is hard to find in our nation's inner-city schools. For example, sociologist John Ogbu has shown that "high-aptitude black students do only as well in public schools as blacks of average aptitude and that middle-class black students do not do as well as whites from the same background."[8] Tyrell is tremendously talented, but he is also extremely lucky. There are thousands of other talented youngsters in our cities who also deserve an honest chance.

Notes

1. Sizer, *Horace's Compromise,* p. 53.
2. Whitehead, *The Aims of Education,* p. 7
3. Kozol, *Savage Inequalities,* p. 119.
4. Kozol, *Savage Inequalities.*
5. Zweigenhaft, Richard L. and Domhoff, G. William, *Blacks in the White Establishment?: A Study of Race and Class in America.*

6. Ibid. p. 16.
7. In *Savage Inequalities* Jonathan Kozol argues convincingly that segregation and fiscal inequality have resulted in the creation of two separate school systems in America — one for the children of wealthy (mainly white) families and one for the poor. Particularly disturbing are his descriptions of students crowded into inadequate facilities. Had he remained in his neighborhood, Tyrell would in all likelihood have attended a high school which Kozol described as doing "everything an inanimate object can do to keep children from getting educated." (p. 99)
8. Ogbu, John, *Minority Education and Caste: The American System in a Cross Cultural Perspective.*

5

A Radical Accelerant

Michael Pastore

Contrary to Ordinary

At age twelve, having skipped four grades, Michael Pastore is in the eleventh grade. His schedule includes Latin IV, U. S. History (honors), Pre-Calculus, English 11 (honors), A. P. Physics, and German I. He does well in his classes; he is not always the top student but he is consistently in the top ten percent. His teachers worry more about his ability to adjust to social conditions than his ability to achieve academically. His Latin teacher expressed concern that he's missing out on a "normal" high school social life — going to dances, dating, driving around. "Getting your license is a big deal around here," said his Latin teacher, "and things like that, he's not going to do until after he graduates."

Over the years, Dr. and Mrs. Pastore have spent many sleepless nights discussing how best to meet Michael's needs. Early on, they realized that Michael was not going to have a "normal" social life no matter what they did. June Pastore is particularly concerned that her son is never going to fit in. "He lives in his own little world," she said, shaking her head. She worries about where he will go to college, whether he will get married, whether there will ever be any normalcy in his life.

Michael is an enthusiast of Norse mythology, Hellenistic studies, Macedonia, medieval history, the Civil War, computer games, fantasy novels, war strategy, karate, and the New York Yankees. Socializing is not one of his priorities. His studies absorb him; he is impatient, enthusiastic, and stubborn about learning. He has a tendency to obsess on a particular subject. "He's the only kid I know," Dr. Pastore observed, "who will come home and say 'Oh! We're going to study the medieval kings of Germany!' and be all charged up."

When he is excited about an idea, a book he's reading, or a television show, he paces and fidgets, struggling to contain his enthusiasm. When he describes a book that he enjoys, the words tumble from his mouth, as if he can't express his ideas fast enough. Michael's older sisters Toby and Margot hate to go to museums, monuments, exhibits with him. "We still talk about this, the infamous — when you're at some place and the guide asks, 'does anybody have any questions?' " says Dr. Pastore. "Everybody in the family cringes, because we know that somebody's hand is going to go up." In the movies, Michael laughs more and louder than anyone else, so his sisters make a point of sitting as far away from him as possible.

Michael was still a baby when his parents began to suspect that he was different from other children. "We never thought that this little kid's a genius," said Dr. Pastore "... we just knew he was different." When he was in pre-school, Michael's teacher observed that he didn't think like other three-year-olds. Sunday school teachers said the same thing. And gradually Michael's differences became more and more apparent.

One morning when he was four and a half years old, sitting at the breakfast table, he announced that he was going to learn how to tell time. Dr. Pastore's office is about a mile from his home; that morning when he arrived in his office the phone was ringing. It was June. "Guess what?" she said. "Michael knows how to tell time." That was to be typical of his learning pattern; once he set his mind on learning something, he learned it. At five, frustrated that he wasn't being taught to read in kindergarten, he begged his mother to work with him. After a week, he could read. By the time he was seven, he was no longer interested in the children's section of the library.

Math also came naturally. When Michael's sister Margot first encountered division, she had some trouble. In order to help, Tom and June would drill her with various problems. She was particularly frustrated when they asked her to divide a number by zero. One afternoon, four-year-old Michael looked up from the cartoon he'd been watching and explained the problem to her. "Margot, don't you understand?" he said. "You can't divide a number by zero." As Dr. Pastore sees it: "The concept was just there. No big deal."

According to his mother, Michael was born talking. Her parents, who are quiet, bookish people, had trouble accepting him. "... He was so loud compared to the girls," said Mrs. Pastore. "He monopolized every conversation." Like many bright children who happen to be talkative, Michael often intimidates adults. Stan Marshall, the minister at the Pastores' church, noted that many adults simply don't know how to react to Michael. "All of the visual data throw you off track," said Pastor Marshall. "Physically this kid is much smaller than other kids his age, so you don't know how to react when you see how he's thinking, speaking, and reading."

Being the father of such an exceptional child also has its downside. "I'm competitive like anybody else," Dr. Pastore said. "And you feel bad when you don't want to play games with your six-year-old because you know he's going to win."

Raising Michael has forced the Pastores to make constant adjustments in their assumptions about what a child can and cannot do. Michael also demanded more attention and time than his sisters. Before the school provided him with appropriate opportunities, June spent most of her time looking for ways to entertain and challenge him.

Flexibility

In trying to create an optimal match between Michael's needs and his school experience, the Pastores have worked under the assumption that if they took care of his intellectual needs, everything else would fall into place. This approach has its critics, but given the nature of Michael's talents and his character, it has been relatively successful.

The summer before he started school, Michael was looking forward to kindergarten, talking about it all the time. He had watched his sisters go off to school and come back with homework, and he was convinced that he was going to learn how to read, how to do math, and how to write reports. Reality was quick to disappoint him. After a week in kindergarten, he told his mother that he was bored, that school was a waste of time.

June spoke with Michael's teacher on various occasions about his desire to do something more challenging, but the class was large and the teacher felt that she simply didn't have time to devote to one student's individual needs. First grade was equally disappointing: Michael complained to his parents constantly that he wasn't being challenged. Again, June tried to intervene, first with Michael's teacher and then with the school's principal. "It got so bad," said Dr. Pastore, "that the principal would hide in his closet when he saw June coming."

"They thought I was just another parent," said June. "I argued a lot and cried a lot ... " In spite of June's activism, Michael was not recommended for the gifted program by his teacher. "They said: 'we don't think he would fit into the gifted program, because he seems restless; he's not very independent; he depends on the teacher all the time; he's constantly interrupting ...' " June said. "He was immature; he could maybe use another year of first grade. He was so immature," she added, icily.

After Michael finished the first grade, the Pastores realized that some serious problems were brewing. Michael, who'd initially been so enthusiastic about school, was thoroughly disillusioned and miserable. Although the teacher had not recommended him for the gifted program, he had hit the ceiling on all of the achievement tests administered by the school. So June and Tom decided to take him to see a child psychologist they knew and have him tested independently.

The results were impressive; according to the tester, Michael had an I. Q. of "at least 190" (Stanford-Binet). In their influential book, *Guiding the Gifted Child*, Webb, Meckstroth, and Tolan argue that a child with a 145 I. Q. is as different from the norm as a child with a fifty-five I. Q.[1] Undoubtedly, this is an exaggeration. In most respects high-I. Q. kids function quite normally. However, an extremely high I. Q. may indicate that a child has distinctive needs which merit individual attention; certainly, it is a strong indicator that a child's intellectual development is relatively advanced.

Michael has certain abilities which, combined with his unique personality, make fitting in a difficult proposition. He grasps ideas much more quickly than most of his peers. While classmates are struggling with material, he's begging for something new. He is impatient. Until quite recently, playing with children his own age was unbearably frustrating. They didn't understand the rules of the complex strategy games he wanted to play, they cheated, or they couldn't compete with him. "The games I play are pretty complex," he said. "So I play by myself. You always win; you always lose. No one wants to take the time to play with me." Often, he gets along better with his teachers than he does with his classmates.

After the Pastores got the results of Michael's I. Q. test, they began talking to people about the situation. Friends, neighbors, and even some teachers claimed that the public schools weren't really equipped to provide Michael with appropriate educational opportunities. For a while, Tom and June thought they might have to move to a town with a high-powered private school. That would have meant giving up their home and possibly the medical practice that Dr. Pastore had been building for fourteen years.

Emigsville is a small town in Western Miami County, Virginia, surrounded by graceful, rolling countryside dotted with white picket fences — a great place to raise a family. The Pastores' house is on a quiet street within walking distance from the church, Dr. Pastore's office, and the country club, where Tom and June have lots of friends and golf partners. Understandably, it was a home and community that the family was reluctant to abandon.

On a warm summer evening, Dr. Pastore walked up the street to the house of a neighbor, Mr. George, the then superintendent of schools in Miami County. Mr. George — a somewhat old-fashioned southern gentleman — invited Dr. Pastore to sit down on a lawn chair and listened quietly while Dr. Pastore explained Michael's situation. Later, Mr. George would admit that he was furious at the suggestion that private schools might be better equipped to serve Michael than the public schools. At the time, he told Dr. Pastore that the county school system should regard Michael as a challenge and a great opportunity. He also made the point that, while the school could work with Michael for six or seven hours a day, the Pastores had a full-time responsibility to see that his needs were being met — a fact which has never eluded Tom and June.

Mr. George held a meeting on Michael's situation with a number of his staff. Finally, he charged Dr. Jack Crane, the director of gifted and talented programs in Miami County, with doing whatever was necessary to ensure that Michael's needs were met. And since that time, Dr. Crane has worked closely with the Pastores, providing guidance and serving as a liaison with school administrators and teachers. As Dr. Crane sees it, someone like Michael has just as much right to individualized attention as a child with learning disabilities or emotional problems.

Virginia, however, is not one of the ten states which provides gifted students with Individualized Educational Programs under the Education for all Handicapped Children Act of 1975. The state provides broad guidelines for gifted programs, but leaves the design of programs and specific interventions up to the local authorities.

After Dr. Pastore's meeting with Mr. George, the Pastores decided to take Michael to CTY's Counseling and Diagnostic Center for further testing in order to get a sense of where his academic strengths and weaknesses lay. Based on Michael's test scores, Dr. Crane presented the Pastores with a series of options: 1) grade two placement with enrichment; 2) a compacted curriculum, involving grade two placement and completion of the third grade curriculum; 3) third grade placement, with gaps being filled at school and in the home. The Pastores chose option three, and Michael had a very successful year in the third grade.

Thus a pattern was established: at the end of each year, Dr. Crane presented the Pastores with a new set of educational options. Dr. Crane feels that it is essential that the family make the final decision. According to Tom Pastore, the first question that Dr. Crane asked whenever they went to see him was: "What does Michael want?"

In his second year of accelerated study, Michael skipped the fourth grade, and in addition to the regular fifth grade curriculum, he was tutored in math and English by high school teachers. A system was worked out with the elementary school teachers whereby Michael was allowed to do his homework for the high school teachers while the other children were working on their math or reading. By the end of the year, Michael's math teacher reported that he was ready to enroll in Algebra, and the English teacher noted similar progress.

At the ripe old age of nine, Michael entered Pine Wood Middle School with a mixture of sixth, seventh and eighth grade classes. On the recommendation of Dr. Carol Mills, CTY's Director of Research, he was also placed in Latin I at the high school.

The transition from elementary to middle school meant that a number of new people became involved in the decision-making process. Joan Robertson, the Assistant Principal at Pine Wood, said she was excited about the prospect of working with Michael but she was also somewhat skeptical.

A slight conflict arose with respect to physical education. On Dr. Mills recommendation, the Pastores had asked that Michael be excused from physical education. The reasoning was that he was so much smaller than his classmates that he wouldn't be on equal footing. "In theory, physical education isn't competitive," Dr. Mills observed, "but when he gets out there and the other kids can throw the ball 100 feet and he can only throw it fifty, it becomes obvious really quickly."

Ms. Robertson reluctantly agreed to excuse Michael from physical education, although she felt that this would merely allow him to neglect his physical development, a habit that did not need to be encouraged. (Michael certainly does not go out of his way to participate in sports or physical activities; he is small for his age and a bit chubby.) But in retrospect Ms. Robertson feels that the right decision was made. Another accelerated student, who came through the middle school a few years after Michael, was not excused from physical education, and the experience was miserable for her. "There's a bit of unsupervised time when the kids are going to their lockers and so on," Ms. Robertson observed. "In the future, we'll probably excuse accelerants from physical education."

The middle school does not offer Latin, and the high school Latin teacher initially doubted that Michael would be able to keep up with the class. In particular, the teacher was afraid that Michael would not be able to take notes fast enough. Dr. Pastore, with characteristic diplomacy, managed to convince the teacher to give Michael a chance. As it turned out, Michael was able to keep up without taking notes. His memory is such that once he has heard something, he seldom forgets it. In fact, Michael finished the year with the best grade in his Latin class and the highest score on the National Latin Exam.

During his second year at the middle school, Michael was again enrolled in classes on various levels. And Ms. Robertson arranged his schedule so that he could take Latin II and Geometry at the high school. For half a year, Michael was also enrolled in "Spectrum," a pull-out program for "gifted" students. The class involved working independently on a project. "I did it on the Punic Wars," Michael said. "I made a game. It wasn't really great."

A child like Michael, with exceptional academic ability, is not particularly well-served by the sort of pull-out programs that are the usual fare in "gifted" education. The problem with the designation "gifted" is that it focuses on intelligence as though it were a fixed quantity — a given; whereas, in education, it is much more useful to think of intelligence as a process. Similarly, designating children "gifted" and placing them in special pull-out programs for "gifted" students doesn't take them anywhere. Instead, it is important to focus on specific skills, needs, abilities and provide opportunities for the child to explore and develop these. Jack Crane provides another reason for preferring flexible pacing to pull-out enrichment programs. "Acceleration doesn't cost anything. In fact, if you want to look at it financially, we probably saved money by moving Michael through the school system faster," he observed, smiling wryly before hastening to add, "Of course, that's not why we did it."

Fortunately, Michael was able to benefit from the flexible programming provided by the Miami County school district. In effect, he ended up compacting three years of middle school work into two years while accumulating enough high school credit to skip the ninth grade. At the age of eleven, he entered the tenth grade with a full courseload, including Chemistry, Biology, Latin III (A. P.), English 9 (honors), World History (honors), and Algebra II.

Now in his second year of high school, Michael is doing extremely well, but he has run into some problems. His mother complains that his teachers are always finding fault with him; his work never seems to be good enough. "Even though he's skipped so many grades and makes great scores and great grades, they still have to find something, why he shouldn't be there," she said. The phenomenon is not unusual; teachers often impose much higher standards for high ability pupils. Anything less than perfection is seen as inadequate.[2]

On the other hand, June sometimes worries that Michael is developing bad work habits. "He only spends about half-an-hour on homework. He goes up to his room and immediately he's done with it." In a sense, his ability to process huge amounts of information extremely quickly is a disadvantage; he has never had to linger over a problem in order to solve it, so he hasn't developed the habit of lingering over problems. This shortcoming is most obvious in his writing. Concision is a virtue, but so is thoroughness. If Michael feels that he has said what he needs to say about a subject in a page, he will never go back and say more. According to his Latin teacher, his essays tend to be simplistic and immature, testaments to his impatience and reluctance to chew on ideas.

Tom and June are constantly struggling to get Michael to spend more time on his homework. June in particular worries that he is developing bad study habits. His honors world history teacher may have just the solution: he requires a paper a week for his class. Michael is still spending less time than his parents would like on his papers, but his writing skills are definitely improving.

Out-of-School Education

Stan Marshall, the Pastores' minister, sees Michael as an extremely reflective individual. When Michael was ten, Pastor Marshall invited him to join the communicants' class. The other youngsters in the group were thirteen and fourteen year olds, but Mr. Marshall found that Michael was beyond them in his ability to handle abstractions and analyze issues critically. For example, Michael saw almost immediately that there was no rational explanation for the trinity; he understood that it was a mystery of faith — "a mystery," as Mr. Marshall put it, "to keep probing." After

Michael's confirmation, Pastor Marshall invited him to join a class that he was teaching on the Bible for adults in the parish. Between the fifth and seventh grade, children begin to understand the Bible in a historical sense, according to Mr. Marshall. "Mike certainly understands the Bible on the historical level," Mr. Marshall observed. "At times, he even asks critical questions. The questions of a radically critical adult are not the ones Mike would ask. There is still an element of child-like faith in him .... But he will ask the tough abstract questions."

While he has been able to provide for Michael's intellectual faith needs, Pastor Marshall has experienced some frustration in trying to include Michael in the church's social activities. Michael simply does not enjoy the company of his age-mates. Playing with them frustrates him; he finds their concerns and interests childish. On the other hand, he is not ready for the boy/girl concerns of the middle school church group. Although he interacts best with adults, he tends to intimidate them so that they allow him to get away with behaviors which they would not accept with other children. "He tends to dominate," observed Pastor Marshall. "Sometimes, I have to tell him to cool his jets, to provide some discipline at the social level ... He does not have social skills commensurate with his intellectual level."

Dr. Pastore has noticed a pattern in Michael's participation in extra-curricular activities. After an initial period of passionate involvement in a club or organization, his interest invariably fades. This was the case with the boy scouts. As far as Michael was concerned, there was no substance to the meetings, and the other kids simply horsed around too much. For a while, Michael took archery lessons, but his interest waned after a few months. He has tried soccer, baseball and tennis, but no sport has really compelled him.

His favorite pastimes are intellectual; he is always reading at least two or three books, mainly fantasy, science fiction, and ancient history. He loves to play intricate war strategy and computer games. The only physical activity that has continued to engage him is karate, which certainly has a strong intellectual component.

Summers, Michael has enrolled in a number of academic programs. However, he has yet to be really challenged. He enjoyed the local university's summer enrichment program but decided not to go back after his first summer. His father has encouraged him to spend time playing with kids in the neighborhood, riding his bike and hanging out. "He needs to have a chance to be a kid," his father said. "If he doesn't want to go to school in the summer, we won't force him."

Ongoing Concerns

In many respects, Michael has benefitted from ideal circumstances. Over the years, the Miami County school system has demonstrated exemplary flexibility in responding to his needs. His parents have gone about planning his education with a lot of savvy, keeping themselves informed by attending meetings, reading and talking with other parents. In their negotiations with the school system, they have maintained a firm sense of what they believed was right for their child, but they have been willing to listen to other opinions and make compromises. In a sense, they are consummate diplomats. They realize the importance of recruiting teachers and administrators to support their cause, and they know how to hammer out an agreement.

Naturally, there are a number of concerns which remain. Even Dr. Mills worries that Michael may encounter serious problems further down the line. "Much as I do think Michael is fine, I still think he is a little bit at risk, because his father has pushed his acceleration to the edge," said Dr. Mills. But Dr. Pastore is philosophical about their decisions. "So far, he seems to be on an even keel. As I said, we haven't had any social/emotional problems, because we're trying to keep him challenged intellectually — keep him happy there. What's going to happen five years from now, ten years from now, we don't know. There's no way we can. We've gone on the premise, know as much as we can today and make the best decision we can today ... We don't want to end up saying, 'if we'd only spent the time doing this,' or 'if we'd only done that ....' " "What's most important," said Mrs. Pastore, "is that Michael is happy."

Pastor Marshall feels that trying to second-guess the Pastores is counter-productive. "Because of limited information or personal agendas, other people are not always in touch with what's going on," Pastor Marshall said. "They criticize without having all the data before them. Knowing Tom and June and having a sense of Tom's decision-making, ... I know they're going to try to be wise and considerate in their decisions."

The tendency is to assume that Michael's needs are the needs of the average child. In many respects, Michael's abilities make him an outsider no matter where he is placed in the educational system. And that will probably continue to be the case for children of exceptional ability until flexible pacing becomes the norm. In the meantime, it is important to understand that there is never a single, clear-cut educational strategy which will solve all of a child's problems. A balance will always have to be struck between intellectual and social/emotional issues; how it is struck depends on the individual child.

The Pastores have tried to handle Michael's situation with sensitivity. They are constantly making adjustments, consulting with the schools, and monitoring Michael's growth. Coping with Michael's problems has often been hard on the family. At times, his sisters have felt neglected. But in the long run the family has grown closer and everyone has learned from the experience.

Ultimately, the Pastores' work with the school system has benefitted not only Michael but other academically talented children in Miami County. In recent years, flexible pacing has gained greater acceptance throughout the county. In spite of continued resistance from some members of the educational community, Dr. Fielding, the new superintendent of schools, has given his endorsement to the educational options process which Dr. Crane adopted to address Michael's needs. As of January 1990, fifteen students were taking advantage of a variety of flexible pacing options. The Pastores have helped to form a parent's group to serve as advocates for the academically talented. And gradually the families of academically talented students are beginning to have more of a say about how their children are educated.

Notes

1. Webb, Meckstroth, & Tolan, *Guiding the Gifted Child*, p. 31.
2. Ibid.

Number
Three

Djuna Lee

A Competitor

When Djuna Lee was in the second grade, she noticed that one of the boys in her class was working on his own in a more advanced math book. This infuriated her, because she knew she was just as capable of doing the work. When she complained to the teacher, Djuna was given the same book and told that she could work on her own too.

After class, the boy would ask Djuna if she was going to take her workbook home with her. "Are you kidding?" she'd say. "I'm going to watch t. v." Then, when he wasn't looking, she'd slip the book into her bag. At home, she worked and worked until she caught up with him.

"When I was in first and second grade, I must have been so competitive," said Djuna, who is now a sophomore at the one of the nation's most selective universities.

According to her father, Dr. John Lee, Djuna has always been competitive. "From very early, she was an active child," Dr. Lee observed. "She liked to win." In school, she participated in painting contests, speaking contests, debates, and science competitions. While a junior in high school, she won the Indiana state piano competition.

A business major, Djuna describes her professional ambitions unabashedly. "My dad is a doctor and my sister's in med school. And my dad wants more doctors in the family ... I sort of compromised with him when I went to school and said I would try pre-med for a while ... But I'm more interested in making money," she said, laughing. "Actually, I like the challenge of being in a dynamic environment. I couldn't take a job that always stayed the same. I also like the social part of business, making connections, but not in a superficial way. Basically, I want [to do] something that will reflect me, my personality."

It is not difficult to imagine Djuna succeeding in business. She is dynamic, humorous, charming. According to her mother, Madeleine, she is always seeking out new challenges. "Djuna can do whatever she sets her mind to," said Madeleine. "She could go into medicine or business or law. But I feel the daily routine of medicine would be boring for her .... I'd like to see her in international business or corporate law."

Djuna is profoundly goal-oriented. "With the piano," her mother said, "if there wasn't a contest she wouldn't practice, she wouldn't go to lessons. We had to ask the teacher to sign her up for the contests. Then she practiced all the time." Djuna feels somewhat ambivalent about this aspect of her character. "I'm very, I need a goal ... I was telling my advisor I'm shooting for the stars, but it's something to shoot for," Djuna said, and then she added somewhat sarcastically: "I'm looking forward to competing for the Rhodes Scholarship."

While maintaining a healthy skepticism, Djuna pursues her goals aggressively. She has been accepted to an extremely competitive honors program; she participates in student government; she is working as a research assistant for an economics professor; and recently she spoke with the president of the university about enrolling in his course. "I think a lot of college students don't really think about calling these people. And I thought it would be a lot harder, but it ended up pretty easy .... He was really nice," said Djuna.

According to her father, Djuna is not only ambitious but also dedicated. "I think that is the difference between my boys and girls," said Dr. Lee. "For example, Djuna, when I called her this past Friday, she'd gone to the library to study. And my boy — he's at a party."

As a youngster, Djuna changed schools three times in part because she was never really challenged. "If she is not challenged, she gets bored very easily," said Madeleine Lee. But each time Djuna changed schools she had some trouble with the transition. After the second grade, her parents transferred her from the public schools to a private, Catholic school. During the first semester, she earned D's and F's; however, during the next few years, she gradually moved to the top of her class. After the seventh grade, she transferred back to the public schools because once again she was no longer being challenged.

In eighth grade, Djuna met up with her old math rival again and the competition was rekindled. She set her mind on rising to the top of her class and by the end of that year she had earned an A+ in every subject. Her father noted that the atmosphere at her school was extremely competitive. "Some people could not beat her," Dr. Lee observed. "Some people ... criticized her, you know, but what are you going to do?"

Throughout high school, Djuna continued to compete with the same small group of kids for top honors in her class. Although she was accepted in many respects, Djuna continued to feel that she was something of an outsider. There were very few Asians in her suburban Indiana hometown, and she felt a certain degree of animosity among students who were less successful and less diligent.

In Djuna's junior year, the competition became particularly grueling; kids were starting to think seriously about college and class rank was becoming ever more important. Djuna was number three in her class, the top female student. Towards the end of the year, things began to get ugly. Some of Djuna's classmates accused her of cheating on an English test; they claimed that she had written an essay at home instead of writing it in class as was required. They never confronted Djuna directly, but somehow word got back to the teacher.

The teacher eventually asked Djuna if she had anything to tell her. Djuna said she knew of the other students' accusations but told the teacher they were groundless. In the meantime the rumors continued to spread and Djuna was ostracized by many of her classmates. A few weeks later, the English teacher broke the class into groups to write plays. All of the work was to be completed in class. At home, the evening before the play was due, Djuna became inspired. She sat down at her typewriter and wrote down some scraps of dialogue that she thought would add spice to the play. The next morning she shared her ideas with the other students in her group, and they agreed that her modifications did indeed improve the play. The teacher enjoyed the play and gave everyone in the group an A.

However, when someone from the group told the teacher that Djuna had worked on it at home, the teacher became furious and changed the A's to zeroes. Djuna argued that this wasn't fair, that she couldn't help thinking about the play at home. The teacher responded that it was all right to think about the play but writing down her ideas was quite another matter, that it was supposed to be a group project. Although Djuna wrote her a letter, trying to explain the situation, the teacher remained unmoved.

Working on assignments of this sort, in which the outcome depends on the performance of other students and in which the desire to do the best job possible is stifled, is often frustrating for highly able students. In particular, someone who is as genuinely engaged in her work as Djuna has a hard time ignoring inspiration when it finds her. While promoting team-work and fair play may be an honorable pedagogical goal, one must question a teacher's judgement when a student's dedication to excellence is penalized. In the end, Djuna came away with the feeling that the teacher had decided to "nail" her one way or another. Since she hadn't been able to prove that Djuna had slipped an essay into her test, the teacher decided to get her for another infraction.

Djuna ended up with a B in the class and a bitter memory of being treated unfairly. "Out of the whole thing," Djuna said, "I just wanted them to understand that I did not cheat. Yes, the grade meant a lot to me, but the whole point was — people accused me of cheating, in a way they betrayed me. On the other hand, they didn't even give me a chance to prove my innocence."

Djuna was also frustrated that her parents did not intervene on her behalf. "And also, what I guess was really bad," she said, "was that my dad was so wrapped up in his work that he didn't really notice what was going on." Eventually, after Djuna's little brother Erik told him that Djuna was having a miserable time in school,

Dr. Lee did sit down and talk with his daughter. In retrospect, Djuna speculates that Dr. Lee did not become involved in the conflict with the school because he did not consider it an option. "My parents have always had that view," Djuna said. "Don't argue with the teacher; the teacher is always right." Out of respect, many people of Taiwanese descent simply do not question the decisions of teachers or other authorities. Whereas in Taiwan it is proper to defer to authority without question, to do so in America often implies that one agrees with a decision one might legitimately challenge.

Two Cultures

When Madeleine Lee became pregnant with her third child, she was in graduate school, trying to finish a master's degree in biology. When Djuna was born she dropped out of school to take care of the children. Having immigrated to the United States only three years before, the family was under a lot of pressure. Dr. Lee was extremely busy trying to get his medical career off the ground; he would leave early in the morning and come home late at night. Often he was on call twenty-four hours a day. "We did not really notice Djuna so much until the last years of elementary school when she gradually became the best in her class," said Dr. Lee.

Djuna did not learn to walk or talk early; she learned to read with her classmates in first grade. She did, however, demonstrate an early precocity in mathematics. "It was kind of funny, because in first grade when I was reading all these numbers and doing multiplication, division, subtraction, all that, the teacher was, like, almost trying to prevent me from doing that," Djuna said. "In the end, I had to argue with the teacher to go ahead."

Early on, Djuna discovered that by doing well in school she could win her parents' attention and affection. Although they did not put a lot of pressure on her, Djuna understood from the start that good grades were expected. "They always said they didn't care, but I always thought that if I got good grades, they would care for me more. That was one way I could receive their affection."

Djuna has always felt torn by the desire to please her parents and the need to remain true to herself. While her parents made a conscious effort to raise their kids as Americans, it was inevitable that Taiwanese values pervaded their family life. At times, Djuna felt like an American child transplanted in Taiwan and vice-versa. Aspects of her personality coupled with signals from the surrounding community created tensions with her parents.

Whereas being outgoing, dynamic, aggressive might be valued in contemporary America, that is not necessarily the case in traditional Taiwanese society. Children, particularly girls, are expected to be respectful and diligent; at best, social concerns are secondary to studies and family matters. To this day, Djuna feels that her parents exert an unreasonable influence on her personal life and that of her siblings. "I can't stand being at home too long, because my parents, they'll make me wake up at seven o'clock. They make my sister, who's 25 years old, still wake up at seven o'clock ... They tell her what to do and tell her how to dress .... They tell her — 'you need a boyfriend, you need to get married,' " Djuna said.

One time, when Djuna's parents found out that she had a boyfriend, a terrible conflict erupted in the family. Djuna met her friend during the summer after her sophomore year in high school while she was enrolled in a chemistry class for college students. She spent the summer living with her older sister, a student at the college and a teaching assistant for the chemistry class. Djuna's parents were pleased that Djuna received the top grade in the class but not that she found a boyfriend.

By the time she was sixteen, Djuna was probably ready for college not only academically but also socially. However, there was undoubtedly an element of rebellion in the way she handled the relationship with her boyfriend.

During the fall of that year, her parents left town for a weekend and she invited her boyfriend for a visit. "I invited him over, and he flew over, because we were in love, and we didn't think we'd ever see each other again. It was purely honest. He stayed in his room, and I stayed in my room. My parents found out from my brother. And when they came home, they beat me ... they called me devil and evil."

Once, Djuna noticed some scars on the back of her mother's legs. When she asked what they were, her mother said they were reminders of a bambooing she'd received from her mother. When Djuna asked why it had happened, her mother replied simply: "Because I was bad." Self-denial and submission to authority, especially parental authority, are central tenets of Taiwanese culture.[1] Although she still resents her parents' efforts to control her life, Djuna has struggled to gain a broader understanding of her experiences.

Talking to other Asian-Americans has been particularly helpful: "I think one of the reasons that I like talking to other people, especially Asian families, is because I realize that it happens to a lot of people. It's not just our family." In her freshman year at college, she took a course on Chinese sociology and found that many of the characteristics she'd believed were personal quirks and obsessions of her parents were actually expressions of Chinese culture. "The respect part," Djuna said. "And the fact that you don't spend money. You shouldn't be materialistic. You should be concentrating on your studies, and not like boys, guys. You should really do what your parents tell you to." Reading *The Joy Luck Club* reinforced the sense that she was not alone: in particular, Djuna was touched by Amy Tan's depictions of difficult mother/daughter relationships.

Djuna acknowledges that there have been problems on both sides of the relationship. "There's sort of a culture clash, you know. Taiwanese children are supposed to respect their parents and not talk back and do whatever they want to do. But I've always been the type of person that'll yell at my parents and scream at my parents whenever I think they're doing something wrong. So they've had a lot of problems with me as much as I've had problems with them." Now, Djuna openly admits that she would be disturbed if she were a parent with a sixteen-year-old daughter who suddenly found a twenty-year-old boyfriend.

When the time came for Djuna to choose a college, she ran into problems with her parents once again. "When I was applying to colleges," Djuna said, "they didn't think I would get in anywhere. I was applying to MIT and my dad was laughing at me, and was saying — 'you'll never get into any of the schools you're applying to.' Because I was applying to all Ivy League Schools and stuff like that ... He even offered me a Porsche if I got into MIT. Then once I got in, he was so shocked, he was like — 'well, you have to go.' "

Djuna feels that her father was disappointed when she chose not to attend MIT. "In Taiwan, everyone has heard of MIT but no one has heard of (my school) .... When they think of my school, they only think of sports ... " Dr. Lee admits that he was disappointed by Djuna's choice of schools. "I still feel she could have made it, but again, she might feel, in college she needs some leisure time to play around, or something like that. She did go to MIT for an interview and to look around. She was accepted, you know .... So, she went there, looked around, and she figured maybe the students there are working so hard and the people there are not very friendly. Finally she decided not to go."

Making the decision to attend her school instead of MIT and to study business instead of medicine was difficult for Djuna. "I kind of feel bad sometimes when I know that MIT would be his choice for me. It would have made him really really happy." But as she was looking at schools and trying to plan for the future she decided that she would make her decisions on the basis of her own interests. "I don't have a strong interest in medicine," she observed, "so why should I do all the schooling?"

Although Dr. Lee has regrets about Djuna's college and career choices, he is making an effort to understand her point of view. "I don't want to force her," Dr. Lee commented. "More or less, in the beginning, since I'm a doctor, maybe she felt that I want her to be a doctor, but then she found out — me, too — Djuna found out medical school (might be) a hardship for her."

Djuna says that her parents have always had trouble communicating their feelings. Although she believes that her family is "closer than the average American family," she wishes that her parents had communicated their affection more openly. "We don't hug; no one hugs in our family. No one says, 'I love you.' " Judged by American standards, this lack of effusiveness may seem peculiar; however, in a study on the Chinese concept of "heart," Julia Shiang sheds some light on what may be a fundamental cultural difference. Shiang argues that "Chinese culture is not a physically or verbally demonstrative one .... 'Heart' means to be thinking about the other person, to be willing to provide, and to anticipate desires rather than wait for requests." In observing 22 Chinese-American families over an 18 month period, Shiang found that in immigrant families conflicts often arise between tradition and the pressures to adapt to a new culture.[2]

Djuna believes that her parents are changing. She has been talking on the phone and exchanging letters with her parents. "I think
(my father) is definitely making more, trying to give more ... because he's been writing these letters to me," Djuna said. "And it's
kind of sad because he's telling me how he really feels, and it's the
first time he's ever really communicated to me and told me what's
bothering him."

Djuna feels that they still have a lot to sort out, but she is
gratified by the fact that her parents are beginning to accept her
on her own terms. "I'd really like her to be a doctor," Dr. Lee
said. "But I don't have that. I don't really care anymore. I told
her, you know, do whatever you want. You are pretty smart anyway. So, as long as you are happy, do something you like and I
think you will be okay."

Educating a Restless Mind

According to Madeleine Lee, until her senior year of high school,
Djuna was rarely challenged in school. "She thinks differently
from myself and my other children," observed Madeleine. "She
absorbs information much faster." Djuna studied hard and did
well in school, but she was always looking for something more.
"In my schooling," she said rather wistfully, "no one would let
me jump grades; no one would let me accelerate."

While Djuna has certainly had to struggle both with personal
and educational obstacles, she has also taken advantage of many
of the best features of American education. After eighth grade she
attended the CTD at Northwestern University, a summer academic program modeled on CTY. The following summer she studied math at CTY. After her sophomore year in high school, she
enrolled in a college chemistry course. And during her senior year
at a private preparatory school in Chicago, she really found her
academic niche, taking two courses at the local university on top
of a full senior schedule. Both at her public high school and at her
prep school, Djuna benefitted immensely by working closely with
teachers who served as mentors, spending spare time with her,
challenging and inspiring her. Extra-curricular activities — de-

bate, speaking contests, piano lessons, student government — also played an important role in her education.

She found that CTD and CTY were particularly valuable socially. "I discovered boys at CTD and CTY," said Djuna. "At school, it didn't matter if I liked a boy, because I was just considered this academic thing." She also enjoyed meeting other Asian-American students with whom she could trade experiences of growing up with two entirely different, often contradictory cultures.

Having attended challenging summer academic programs like CTD and CTY was a double-edged experience for Djuna. On the one hand, it made high school easier to endure, but, on the other, it made her long to finish sooner. "Socially (you) become more confident," Djuna said. "You have fun ... but on the other hand it makes you realize — I want to go to college, because if this is how college is going to be, where people are more academic, they don't care so much about your looks and stuff like that .... And you're sort of caught in a Catch-22 because you want to graduate from high school early; you know you're prepared .... You're more confident, you're able to enjoy what you have and you know there are good things to come, but, on the other hand, you're like — great, I'm stuck here; I can't do anything about it."

Djuna's father did not think it would be a good idea for her to skip grades, and, anyway, her public high school did not permit it. In a sense, respite came by default: after the run-in with classmates and her junior high school English teacher, life became impossible for Djuna at her hometown high school and she transferred to the prep school in Chicago. While in prep school, she enrolled in two courses at the University of Chicago — introductory physics and calculus. But more importantly she took courses in European history, the history of economics, the history of political thought and international relations with Ralph Haight, a teacher who would have a profound impact on her life. "... I admired him so much that ... I tried my hardest in his class," Djuna observed. "I wanted to gain his admiration and liking .... He was so challenging; he taught me how to write .... He really tied in world events. Like history, as I had learned it in public school, was just memorization. But in Mr. Haight's class, I was there after class to argue with him. I was there before."

In many ways, Djuna's description of Mr. Haight is a description of the ideal teacher for academically talented students. His expectations are high; he constantly challenges his students to look at material in new ways and to express their ideas. He is passionate and knowledgeable about the subject he teaches and he makes himself available to his students for discussion and guidance. Djuna once asked him why he doesn't teach college. "High school is really where the kids listen to you. You get to know the kids more. College is more distant," he told her.

Djuna's admiration for Mr. Haight may only be rivalled by his admiration of his former student. "Djuna's a hard-working kid," he said, "motivated and bright, has a very good attitude towards school and teachers .... She's a very mature girl. She really has, and had, her head on straight coming into (our) school." Mr. Haight worries, however, that Djuna may actually suffer from a surfeit of talent. "She obviously can do anything she wants to do and do it well, which may be a curse as much as a blessing."

In *Nature's Gambit*, a study of prodigies, D.H. Feldman examined the role played by coincidence in the fulfillment of the promise implied by great gifts.[3] According to Feldman, "individuals with a single talent are more likely to pursue that field; the more talents there are competing with the target one, the more likely time and resources will be split."[4] At some point, individuals like Djuna with a broad range of talents must ask themselves variants of the following questions: What sort of endeavor will allow me to make the greatest contribution? Which pursuits will provide me with a sense of fulfillment? Often, they find themselves addressing this sort of question again and again.

While in college Djuna has certainly experimented with a variety of interests. Her extra-curricular activities include tutoring prison inmates and serving as co-chair of the university's Student Health Advisory Board. She spent the summer between her sophomore and junior years in northwest Hawaii doing research on the behavior of seals. She is deeply concerned about social and environmental issues and has considered a career in environmental law.

In the twenty-seven years that Mr. Haight has been teaching, he has come into contact with thousands of extremely bright students. More than anything else, he feels that success in life is born of inner drive. "Djuna definitely has that drive," he observed. He is not confident, however, that Djuna will be fulfilled in business. "I think the hard side of business is not going to be something she'll like .... It just doesn't seem to be a good fit," he observed. "I think she'd be more natural in something academic, dealing with people in a more humanitarian way .... But I could be wrong."

After three successful years of college and a summer at a prominent New York investment bank, where she completed an internship in the mergers and acquisitions division, Djuna disagrees with Mr. Haight. She feels that it is only since she began studying business that she has "come into her own." At the start of her senior year of college, she is one of only five students in all three of the University's honors programs; she is earning a 3.6 average, taking six courses, teaching a course in statistics at the evening school, and continuing her research on marketing. Recently, she won a State Farm Exceptional Student Fellowship Award — a prestigious national fellowship awarded to business students demonstrating excellence in leadership and academic achievement — and was chosen one of the ten most exceptional women college students in America by a prominent magazine.

Djuna is not particularly worried about the "hard" side of business; she feels that overcoming childhood adversity has made her tough and adaptable. "I don't think I'm going to have difficulty with the ruthless part [of business]. What might deter me is the role that luck plays in whether or not you make it to the top," Djuna observed. "People have different aspects to their personalities. In Mr. Haight's class, I think maybe I was assertive in a quiet sort of way. But I can be very assertive when I have to."

Djuna has not abandoned the idea of applying for a Rhodes Scholarship or other fellowships that would give her time to study and reflect, but she is skeptical about academia, finding it insular, impersonal, and overly theoretical. She has been offered a position as a full-time analyst in the investment bank where she worked during the summer after her junior year, and is seriously considering the offer. "I've been given this tremendously attractive opportunity at the bank, so it's difficult to say no," she said. "Things are starting to come together for me in a way they never have before. But we'll have to see. I'm still only 21 years old."

Notes

1. On the importance of discipline and traditional values in contemporary Taiwan see Lee, Ger Bei, "Moral Education in the Republic of China." For a comparison of the values of Taiwanese children and American children see McDaniel, Ernest D. & Soong, Wayne, "Comparisons of Self-Concept Scores of Children in America and in Taiwan." For an examination of how these values may translate into academic success see Mordkowitz, Elliot R. & Ginsburg, Herbert P., "Early Academic Socialization of Successful Asian-American College Students."
2. Shiang, Julia, "'Heart' and Self in Old Age: A Chinese Model."
3. Feldman, D.H., *Nature's Gambit*.
4. Ibid. p. 65.

7

"You're Born Knowing Boolean Logic"

Stig Nielsen

Trusting what you see, you may be deceived. Well under five feet tall, Stig Nielsen, at age twelve, looked like a sandlot baseball player or Norman Rockwell kid — the kind Jimmy Stewart would pat on the head, the kind that all America gets wobble-kneed over: an Opey, a Beaver Cleaver or Richie Cunningham. Stig has been acting since he was three and a half; he did his first commercial when he was five. His presence borders on the luminous.

To dwell on appearances, however, is to do Stig a grave injustice. A five-minute conversation with him convinces the skeptic that his intellect eclipses even his presence. Stig's vocabulary and the patterns of his sentences are distinctly adult; there is a quickening in his voice when he speaks about something that interests him — Antarctica, physics, William Faulkner — but no adolescent indirection. He knows what he wants to say and knows how to say it clearly, precisely.

During the 1989–90 academic year, at the age of twelve, Stig was enrolled at a magnet high school in a city in the South, taking junior English, A. P. Computer Science, A. P. Chemistry, A. P. Calculus (B. C.), and French I/II. He was also taking a course on fractal geometry at the local university. Throughout his school career, Stig has won math competitions and spelling bees; one year, he placed second in the National French Competition and won a city-wide science fair with a project involving computer simulations of chaotic motion of subatomic particles.

According to Aloysius Stone, the principal at Stig's middle school, Stig was one of a kind. "In the thirty years I've been in education, I've run across a lot of good students, many of whom now hold leadership positions in the city, and nationally," observed Mr. Stone. "But his was a situation that was far above anything I had run into." Not only is Stig capable academically, he is well-liked and able to fit into almost any social situation. In Mr. Stone's words: "Stig has a wonderful personality. And everyone thought the world of him."

In many respects, Stig is the model "gifted" child. His talents are prodigious and impossible to overlook; he hits the ceiling on every standardized test he takes and the forms that teachers fill out to identify "gifted" children seem to have been designed with him in mind. His early development was extremely precocious: he learned to read at three and, according to his mother, "instantly" put puzzles together. Like Michael Pastore (chapter four), he wins every game he plays — chess, monopoly, scrabble. And although his ability to speak his parents' native language is rudimentary at best, he consistently beats them at Scrabble in that language. Nevertheless, his first four or five years of school were immensely frustrating as little was done to meet his individual needs. When he was finally allowed to advance, his acceleration was carried out in fits and starts without what could be considered an orderly plan. "To an extent, much more than we would have wanted, it has been a process of crisis management," said Stig's father, Dr. Leif Nielsen. "We were in situations where we had to do things, rather than sitting and making a consistent plan for what we wanted Stig to do during his years in school."

Age Appropriateness

When Stig was in the fourth grade, his teacher assigned a book report, telling her students to choose a book from a list she had prepared. None of the titles interested Stig; he asked if he might be allowed to read an Agatha Christie mystery or a Shakespearean tragedy instead. The teacher felt that these works were inappropriate. "She got very upset .... 'There's so much good children's literature,' she said, 'so it was not necessary,' " said Ingrid Nielsen, Stig's mother.

With a student like Stig the best way to ensure that he will do something is to tell him that he can't do it. "She said I wouldn't understand it until I was twenty," said Stig. "But I went ahead and read those books anyway — had no trouble with Agatha Christie or Shakespeare .... Well, not *no* trouble. I mean it wasn't as difficult as I might have anticipated."

On one level, Stig's teacher was right: he certainly couldn't read Shakespeare with the same sensitivity as he will when he is an adult, but allowing a youngster to stretch the limits of his abilities is rarely a harmful experience. At worst, Stig might have discovered that he didn't understand a word of Shakespeare. What was more likely and what did finally occur (when he read *Macbeth* on his own) was that he gained respect for Shakespeare and decided that the tragedies would be worth revisiting later in life.

Notions of "age appropriateness," with the profound influence they exert on the development of school curricula, have inhibited the natural progress of many academically talented students. Inflexible assumptions about what children should and shouldn't be able to do at a certain age or grade level are often harmful. At age four, when Stig entered kindergarten, he already knew how to read, how to do the multiplication tables, and how to interact with other children — but being taught how to do those things was considered "age appropriate." Forced to learn what he already knew, Stig became enormously frustrated with his first school experience.

For weeks on end, he stayed home from school, suffering from headaches, nausea, sinus infections. A few years later, a pediatrician told Mrs. Nielsen that Stig's physical problems stemmed largely from his frustration with his school situation. "The doctor said straight out that his immune system is so sensitive because he has so many problems with the school. That there is nothing we can do ... till something comes up," said Mrs. Nielsen. Now, whenever Stig complains of a sinus infection, his parents immediately ask how things are going at school. Unlike his older brother Jorgen, who has always felt comfortable telling his parents what is bothering him, Stig internalizes his problems. "He would become depressed if things got boring in class or if a class didn't seem to be going in a positive direction," said Louise Pisacane, one of his seventh grade teachers. "He's such a true intellectual; he lives in the mind a lot." For bright kids like Stig, the separation between mental and physical suffering is slight. Boredom is painful.

Before Stig finished kindergarten, the Nielsens had lived on the West Coast and both boys had attended public schools. When the family moved to the South, Stig and his older brother Jorgen were enrolled in a Catholic school. The nuns must have taken golden-haired Stig for one of the cherubim, for they immediately began making otherworldly demands of him. "In the first through fourth grades, I went to a Catholic school, and the way they dealt with me there and treated me has actually made a big impression that really has hurt me," said Stig. "I was expected to be a sort of perfect child, to be a good little boy. And they didn't really understand my problem. Or they didn't want to understand. They just sort of stuck me and kept me in the classes."

Ingrid felt the pressure from the school as well. "I felt that very much as a parent — the pressure from his teachers and the principal, on both of us for the whole family, not only on Stig," Ingrid said, a faint Scandinavian lilt coloring the cadence of her speech. "There was a pressure to always have the best report card, because if he didn't they could always throw that in my face if I had a complaint. So, I thought if you're going to get something, you need to be perfect. Maybe I exaggerated, because I wasn't used to this Catholic school. You know, there was a dress code, again something I wasn't used to, so I always was afraid that my kids weren't properly dressed, and I went out of my way to really do it as well as I could, but it seemed that somehow if something went wrong, it always happened with us. And other parents could allow their kids to go with patches on their pants. But if I allowed my kids to go with something [the teachers] didn't like, I always got a letter home, I found. And I really wondered why. So, I understand why

Stig could have internalized and felt the pressure from me and from us, because it was there. It was there very much indeed."

While on the one hand, the school's officials expected perfect behavior and perfect performances from Stig, they were unwilling to give him the opportunity to work on challenging material. "In first grade, I remember them teaching us the alphabet and the vowel sounds. You have the little u's to make the sound short and the little bars to make them long. And I remember this one instance — a teacher telling us about the short i and it sounds like "i" — "iiiiitch" and she was scratching her arm the whole time, repeating the word, drilling those vowel sounds into your brain and ... I was bored out of my skull," Stig said, amusement mingling with disgust in his voice. "The problem I've had most, I guess, was review — the problem of review. In that school, every year, two-thirds of the year was spent on review and then you'd get something that was barely new .... Like division instead of multiplication, or something like that."

Over the years Stig has built up a lot of anger about the various educational techniques to which he's been subjected. "A lot of people seem to think the way to treat a gifted child is to give it (sic) work. They're gifted, so they're able to do more work. So, you just give them more problems, and it's just busy work, which I can't stand. And there's also the enrichment thing: they're bored with what they're doing, give them something else. Logic puzzles, magic squares and things like that to figure out. And, I mean, they can be challenging, but they're just not what I'm looking for .... They don't go anywhere. I mean, in doing enrichment, you don't learn anything. You might be able to learn some basic logic skills, but you're born with Boolean logic."

Bright kids are often held back because of the widespread belief that there are valuable social lessons to be learned from coevals. Often, teachers use their most advanced students as instructors. But like Stig, many academically talented students have little patience for people who can't process information or perform higher order thinking skills as quickly as they can. "To be able to explain something to other people is important," Stig observed. "I mean, teaching what you're learning kind of makes your knowledge concrete .... But I've been explaining things to other students for quite a while now .... It gets to me, like say in the computer lab, if there's a person standing over the printer, complaining how it never works and it just won't print her document, and then I go over and turn the printer on — that's kind of frustrating."

Often, the only thing smart kids learn by being held back is contempt — for their teachers, for other students, and especially for the system.

Out of Chaos

The crisis struck when Stig was halfway through the fourth grade. He was spending more time home on antibiotics than he was spending in school. The pediatrician who had linked his illness with his school situation referred the Nielsens to a school counselor. On the basis of the counselor's recommendations, they started exploring other options. They applied to an assortment of private schools, but for one reason or another all of the schools turned them away — the poshest of them because they felt Stig's I. Q. was too high.

Up to this point, the Nielsens had avoided the city schools because Leif's colleagues at the university had expressed nothing but contempt for public education. In desperation, Dr. Nielsen spoke with the superintendent of schools, who arranged a "staffing" — a meeting between the Nielsens and various school officials to discuss Stig's situation. Most importantly, Dr. Nielsen discovered that under the law in the state where the family resided, "giftedness" is considered the equivalent of a handicap; thus, gifted children have the right to Individualized Educational Programs (IEP's) and other special educational provisions. This knowledge would prove invaluable as they struggled to provide optimal learning experiences to both Stig and Jorgen.

Initially, the officials from the public school system were skeptical of Stig's abilities and reluctant to make special arrangements for him. He was transferred from the fourth grade at the Catholic school into the fourth grade at the neighborhood public school. It was Stig's good fortune, however, that the principal at his new school was an open-minded and flexible individual. After a meeting with Stig and the Nielsens, she put him in fifth and sixth grade classes and let him participate in the most advanced "gifted" pull-out program. The promotion was an unofficial, de facto, arrangement.

The following year, when Stig returned to the local elementary school, there was a new principal who was less sympathetic to his situation. Three weeks into the school year, it became obvious that repeating the sixth grade simply wouldn't be challenging. Leif and Ingrid requested another "staffing." Dr. Diana Whitcomb, the city's supervisor of elementary and middle school gifted programs, made a strong case for promoting Stig to junior high school. Dr. Whitcomb recounted, "We're in the staffing and the teachers are saying, 'We can't accelerate this child. He's so young. It would be unfair to him.' And here's a child sitting here, who at nine can say: 'Do you think it's fair for me to teach myself at the back of the room? Shouldn't I be allowed to interact?' " In the end, Dr. Whitcomb prevailed. And over the years, she was one of a handful of people who continued to support and advocate for the Nielsens.

At his junior high school, Stig was once again fortunate to encounter an open minded administration. Aloysius Stone, the school's principal, a dapper southern gentleman of the old school, was an unlikely proponent of radical acceleration. At first, he was a bit uncomfortable with Stig's advancement. "As I look back," said Mr. Stone, "there are so many things about high school that I thought were a part of growing up. The junior and senior proms, dating. It bothers me that (he's) not going to experience that." However, as Mr. Stone got to know Stig, his skepticism gradually evaporated.

"Everyone thought the world of him," said Mr. Stone. "He was the star in our musical that year. He was Oliver. He just fit in. There was never any conflict, never any feelings like — well, this little smart-aleck." In part, Stig fit in so well because he was finally allowed to work on a level that corresponded to his ability rather than his age. After Stig had spent three weeks in the seventh grade and proved how well he could do, Mr. Stone suggested a promotion to the eighth grade.

Leaps and Bounds

During the summer after he completed the eighth grade, Stig attended CTY's summer academic programs. At the age of ten, he was the youngest student on campus. And even at CTY, his abilities made him stand out. "I've never seen anyone like him," said one student. "He had this trick where he would have you shuffle a deck of cards. He'd look through the cards once, and then without looking he'd recite the cards back to you, in order."

In part because he was so young and in part because he did not enjoy the self-paced structure of CTY's math course (he had already spent so many years working on his own with a book), Stig did not particularly enjoy his first three-week session at CTY. The second three weeks were quite another story. He had signed up for a course in ancient Greek. He described the exhilaration of the experience in a letter: "Greek opened me up to the new world of not only languages but classical studies. Greek culture! Archeology! The possibilities were endless! But most of all, I discovered that I worked well with languages."

While CTY provided Stig's brother Jorgen with an opportunity to accelerate his math studies and to make friends, it allowed Stig to experience what his mother called "exotic adventures." "CTY opened his eyes to a new world," said Ingrid. "Until then, it had been math, math, and science. The same stuff over and over." In his second summer at CTY, he took courses in statistics and political science. And again he loved the experience. In particular, he was pleased with his teachers. "Probably the best plus in those courses compared to other courses I've had is that the teachers were interesting people. They didn't just teach what they were teaching; they were enthusiastic and they went into discussions about it and about other things, and in a deeper way than just scratching the surface."

Stig's Greek teacher in particular had a profound influence on his attitude towards his studies. "He was starting a career in the topic. He was really into Greece, the culture and the language. One thing, it wasn't only the language. There was some discussion about the culture and the art and the architecture, which was interesting." No experience is more valuable for a child with an active intellect than the opportunity to interact with adults who are both enthusiastic and knowledgeable. As R. Ochse observed, "One of the keys to the development of creative genius is the acquisition of values relating to intellectual achievement."[1]

After the summer at CTY, Stig was fortunate to be admitted to a local magnet high school. During his first year he took a mix of freshman and sophomore courses. In his spare time, he continued to study ancient Greek with a private tutor, he acted in several commercials and plays, he wrote programs for his Macintosh, he rode his bicycle and went for long walks in the woods with his parents and brother Jorgen. After two years of high school, at the age of twelve, he had accumulated A. P. credit in Biology, Chemistry, Pascal, and Calculus B.C. and had aced his course in fractal geometry at the university. In the spring of 1991, after a year in an International Baccalaureate program, he enrolled at the university in his parents' native Scandinavia; at age thirteen, he was the youngest person ever to enter that university.

Although he remains uncertain about his future (his career options are almost limitless), he leans towards graduate work in science. His award-winning science project involved creating computer models of chaotic systems, but physics is not his first passion. More than anything else, he would like to study penguins. "I recall a documentary I saw that dealt with penguins," Stig said. "I remember a clip. It was like a seventy, eighty mile an hour gale going on, and they were just jumping off ice-floes into the water and having a ball in this wind. And it just kind of struck me as interesting."

Up to this point much of Stig's success can be attributed to his wonderful relationship with his parents, they have been continuously supportive and open. At times, Stig has felt pushed, he said, but in retrospect he is happy. "When they realized that I had a problem when I was bored, they could have held me back like a lot of parents do, but they've been supportive," Stig remarked. "Over the years, when I've had problems of any kind, they've tried to sit down and talk to me." Whether it was a matter of making phone calls, writing letters, or attending endless meetings, Dr. and Mrs. Nielsen have always been willing to do whatever was necessary to ensure that his educational needs were being met.

So far, it seems that Stig's acceleration has not hampered his social/emotional development. Louise Pisacane, one of his junior high school teachers, commented that Stig was not singled out for teasing and when kids did pick on him, his response was very good-natured. She did observe, however, that some of his classmates resented his intelligence and intensity. "The kids got tired of him always being this way, always being so intellectual, always having a serious angle on things, always being the one that has the answer. There's the little urge to want to knock somebody down who does that. I think he experienced some of that. But I never heard him say that though. So I don't know if he notices things." Stig can get impatient with his peers; he has little tolerance for wrong answers on what appear to him to be easy questions, little patience for individuals whose learning processes are slower. He is never nasty, but at times he can come across a bit haughty.

Dr. Nielsen believes that Stig has been strengthened by enduring the many hardships that have confronted him, but he sometimes worries that Stig has been forced to grow up a little too quickly. In particular, he worries that Stig's experiences as a professional actor have made him suspicious of other people's judgement. Stig worries, for example, that the judges at science fairs will be as arbitrary as producers at auditions. "And that's hard to argue with," said Dr. Nielsen. "In many ways that's a tough burden to bear for someone as young as that — to understand so much."

8

A Drop-out of Sorts

Jorgen Nielsen

Whereas Stig has tended to get cute, break-your-heart parts in ads, more often than not his brother Jorgen (who is four years older) has been cast as a nerd — a number-spouting child genius, a bit gawky, a bit oblivious. While schoolwork comes almost effortlessly to Stig, Jorgen has often had to work hard. Whereas Stig has always been athletic and popular in school, Jorgen suffers from Ehlers-Danlos syndrome, a genetic disorder of the connective tissue, which makes it difficult and sometimes dangerous for him to play sports and has contributed to his social isolation. According to his parents, Jorgen has always been reflective, cautious, soft-spoken. While he might not have the raw talent of his brother Stig, he does possess the rare quality which often distinguishes the great individual from the merely gifted: drive.

In spite of the fact that he has lived most of his life in the United States, Jorgen's manner is more European than his brother's. Like his parents, he seems never to have assimilated entirely. Nothing in his language gives him away; like his brother, he has the diction of a professional actor. His otherness comes across in less palpable things — the way he carries himself, his frankness which borders sometimes on naïveté, his vulnerability. Adults who have worked with Jorgen invariably comment on his maturity. Already in elementary school he suffered from being out of synch with his classmates. "He talked like a teenager when he was seven," said his mother. "The other kids just didn't have the patience; they didn't understand what he was talking about."

Being different is hard on children, but in adolescence, it is an unforgivable sin. At the exclusive, all-boys academy that Jorgen attended in seventh and eighth grade, boys are supposed to be jocular, rowdy, loudmouthed, ruddy. Except for children with medical excuses, after-school sports are mandatory. Because of his medical condition, Jorgen spent the after-school period practicing the piano instead of playing ball. Inevitably, he was teased, called a sissy, ostracized.

At one point, he tried to explain his disability to a classmate in the belief that knowledge would result in understanding or at least tolerance. Instead, the boy spread nasty rumors about Jorgen, and the teasing was redoubled. Being teased and ostracized is a painful experience. Jorgen, unfortunately, was tortured. Classmates began making obscene phone calls to his home. Once they hired a prostitute to call the house and ask him for a date. Ingrid Nielsen answered the phone and was so mortified she could never bring herself to tell Jorgen. Another time, a bed-wetting agency called to ask if the family had a thirteen-year-old with a bladder problem. Eventually the phone calls became so frequent and disturbing that the Nielsens had their number changed. Oddly enough, the customer service representative said she'd run into many instances where families with bright adolescents had been forced to get unlisted numbers to avoid harassment.

When Dr. and Mrs. Nielsen contacted the administrators at Jorgen's school about the other students' behavior, they were told that nothing could be done, since no one knew who was making the phone calls. Problems with the school reached a climax at the beginning of Jorgen's freshman year of high school (at the time when Stig had finally been allowed to advance to the appropriate level). One afternoon when Jorgen was sitting in the school library studying, some students snuck up on him. They rolled him in a carpet and swung him around in the air, all the while taunting and threatening him.

Because they feared for his safety, the Nielsens decided to take Jorgen out of the school. The family found some consolation in the fact that a number of teachers called from the school to express their outrage at what had happened and their regret at losing a student with Jorgen's ability and interest. But sympathy was of little use in terms of figuring out what to do next.

As opposed to Stig, who had always been frustrated by the level of the material he was being presented with, up to this point, Jorgen had often struggled academically. In the fourth, fifth and sixth grades, it had sometimes seemed to his parents that he was being overwhelmed by his schoolwork. Jorgen was in fact a bit of an underachiever; although he had the ability to do well in school, for many years he just didn't care. He was also hampered by a mild case of dyslexia.

To get Jorgen out of the slump during his sixth-grade year, Dr. and Mrs. Nielsen prepared a wall chart on which they listed Jorgen's responsibilities and assigned points to them. By keeping his room clean, practicing the piano, and devoting a certain amount of time to school work every day, Jorgen earned points. Once he had earned a number of points agreed upon in advance, he would be given a computer. According to Jorgen, the strategy was effective. "I was very excited about that computer," he said. "This friend, Peter, and I and another friend who was also into computers, in the fifth and sixth grade ... we created and planned our own computer software company — CSS, Combined Skills Software .... And I created a word-processor, that I got the backbone for out of a textbook .... I embellished it beyond recognition and I was really proud of it."

In her book *Before the Gates of Excellence*, R. Ochse argues that the distinction between intrinsic and extrinsic motivation is rather artificial. While the humanist tradition in psychology maintains that extrinsic motivators are not as valuable as intrinsic ones, it fails to account for the fact that in most individuals the two are intimately linked. "Despite what psychologists have said to the contrary, productive creative behavior apparently offers various types of extrinsic satisfaction," Ochse wrote. Trollope was even more direct: "All material progress has come from man's desire to do the best he can for himself and those about him."[2]

When Jorgen enrolled in the private academy, his parents suggested making a new wall chart. But Jorgen decided that it was no longer necessary. "He came and he said, 'I don't need this stuff anymore. I really like to get good grades,' " observed Ingrid Nielsen. "And that was a breakthrough for him." After the sixth grade, apart from his social isolation, Jorgen was tremendously successful in school, ranking among the top students in all of his classes. And when school did not always sustain his intellectual interests, he now had his computer to explore.

Jorgen and his parents have always been extremely close. While Jorgen's schooling experiences were at least as painful as Stig's, he was always able to talk with his parents about his problems. "I feel very lucky," Jorgen said. "Across the years, my parents have always been there to talk to." Dr. Nielsen agrees: "I feel that we have a relationship with him that is very similar to the one that we had when he was two or three years old, I mean, adjusting for age and maturity. It's the same kind of acceptance and openness, and tenderness. I really feel that."

In a sense, Jorgen's ostracization from the society of his classmates is emblematic of the isolation that Dr. and Mrs. Nielsen experienced in the south. From the beginning, the family felt like outsiders. In part, their situation may have been aggravated by a certain mistrust of the south, a lack of awareness of southern culture and a strong aversion to many aspects of it. Southern manners, southern values, southern customs may have clashed with their own. But the fact remains that after two years in the South, the Nielsens (who are warm, thoughtful and generous) had encountered very few people whom they could consider friends. In particular, they found the university's social scene, with all of its history and rituals, virtually impenetrable. The Nielsens' feelings not withstanding, there were more people who allied themselves with their cause than they might be able to believe. (Ingrid, in particular, was deeply hurt by the fact that people were suspicious of her attempts to change the system and create optimal educational conditions for her children.)

After the carpet incident at the academy, the Nielsens would have found it unthinkable to send Jorgen back. Since Stig was having some success in the public schools, they decided that they might try the same route with Jorgen. In comparing the problems they would encounter in the public schools to those they'd encountered in the private, Dr. Nielsen tends to emphasize process. In the public schools, there is a due process; if you are willing to expend the energy, write the letters, make the phone calls, something will eventually happen. You have specific rights and they're written in black and white. In the private system, you depend entirely on the whims of individual administrators. Experience, unfortunately, would come to temper the Nielsens' faith in due process.

The Emperor's New Clothes

We live in an image-conscious society — a society in which people like to believe that reality is a certain way simply because someone has said that it is so. After the Nielsens had taken Jorgen out of the private academy and were trying to figure out where to send him next, they went to visit one of the local public high schools. They were impressed with what the principal told them; she promised that all sorts of arrangements would be made to meet Jorgen's needs. A few weeks into the school year, however, it became evident that a broad chasm separated the principal's promises from reality.

When Jorgen's computer teacher found out that her students weren't going to receive high school credit for her PASCAL course, she decided that it wasn't worth teaching and told the students to play computer games instead. Some of Jorgen's teachers would simply neglect to show up for class; others never returned graded homework. "I always found myself nagging the teachers," said Jorgen, "as if they were the delinquent students ... " According Barbara Smith, Jorgen's Latin teacher, who worked with him independently during her preparation period because she felt that his needs could not be met in any of the school's regularly scheduled classes, the school was a "facade."

"We write up these wonderful brochures about what's going on in our school and what kinds of programs we have," said Mrs. Smith. "And we have all these wonderful math courses and dadi-dadi-da, but the reality is that we've got math teachers asleep during class. That's what I mean by facade. And there's a lot of that going on, sad to say. I don't believe in producing facades; I believe in producing students." After a while, the school's administration put pressure on Mrs. Smith to stop tutoring Jorgen independently. "They said I was working a hardship on my colleagues." But Mrs.

Smith had no intention of giving the class up. "Working with him was the bright spot of the day," she said. "He was the only really stimulating student I had." Echoing her sentiments, Jorgen said: "Mrs. Smith's class was one of the only reasons I kept going."

At first, Dr. and Mrs. Nielsen brushed Jorgen's complaints aside: the school couldn't possibly be that bad. Jorgen tried to talk to his teachers; he asked for more challenging work, but to no avail. In January or February, when it became apparent that the situation was as bad as Jorgen reported it to be, the Nielsens made an appointment to see the principal, Ms. Hodgkins.

On a day when the schools were shut down because of the ice on the roads, Jorgen and his parents visited Ms. Hodgkins. Jorgen had just begun explaining the situation to her — the inattention of some teachers, the unchallenging nature of his classes — when she flew into a rage. She swore at the Nielsens, insulted them, and threatened to take them to court if they made false claims. Overwhelmed by the tirade, Jorgen began to cry. After a while, Ms. Hodgkins calmed down and offered to leave the room for a while so that Jorgen could collect himself. The Nielsens waited in an unheated office for half an hour; when Ms. Hodgkins returned, she had regained her composure somewhat, but she still refused to acknowledge the problems that Jorgen had pointed out.

Later, a meeting was arranged with some officials from the city's schools. Among the officials present was Mr. Hodgkins — the husband of the principal at Jorgen's school. At one point, Mr. Hodgkins suggested that special arrangements might be made for Jorgen. But by this time, the Nielsens felt that there were profound problems at the school that needed to be brought into the open. "The strategy that we had chosen — well, it wasn't really a choice," said Dr. Nielsen. "What we had reacted to was that the teachers in the school didn't do their jobs in the first place. Okay, so Mr. Hodgkins was able to deflect, to make it that Jorgen had special needs. Like he had a need for teachers coming to class."

A solution — satisfactory to none of the parties concerned — was finally arrived at. Since Jorgen was so far ahead of his classmates and so determined to continue his studies, he would be allowed to work in the library. The experience was lonely and frustrating. With the exception of Ms. Smith, the teachers who were supposed to be his tutors were reluctant to work with him. He had to badger them to get their attention.

Towards the end of his freshman year, Jorgen wrote an editorial which appeared in the local newspaper. Without naming the school, he criticized some problems that he had observed. In spite of the fact that the students were required to take a health class in which the importance of a good diet was emphasized, a concession in the school basement sold all sorts of junk food. "Before class," Jorgen said, "you'd see all these kids standing around in the halls, munching Fritos and sipping Cokes." He also observed that when students drove to away games, they would pile into the back of pick-up trucks and zoom off down the highway, without the slightest attention to safety.

The next day, another student, outraged by Jorgen's observations, spent her free periods passing out enlarged photocopies of the editorial. A number of students voiced their discontent to the principal, and a meeting was called. Ms. Hodgkins told Jorgen that she was disappointed that he hadn't spoken with her first. The tone of the meeting was generally hostile. "Do you want these students to like you?" the principal asked him at one point, gesturing at the other students in the room.

Jorgen tried to explain that he didn't think that the editorial was such a big deal; he'd merely expressed his opinion. He wouldn't be at all offended if someone else expressed a dissenting opinion. The meeting dragged on for over an hour. Finally, it was decided that the editorial was to be displayed on the school bulletin board with a caption affixed: "This is Jorgen's opinion. What's yours?" No one ever wrote a letter to the newspaper in response.

Even as things were going smoothly for Stig, the Nielsens continued to run into problems in trying to make arrangements for Jorgen in the city schools. For his sophomore year, his parents tried to get him into the magnet high school that Stig would eventually attend. Positions at that high school are assigned by lottery; unfortunately, by the time Jorgen's number came up the sophomore class was filled.

The Nielsens noticed that there were quite a few vacancies in the junior class and asked if Jorgen couldn't simply skip the tenth grade. As it was, Jorgen was a mere one and a half credits shy of being able to qualify for the eleventh grade. In spite of the fact that he had completed Algebra III, Geometry, and Trigonometry at CTY during the summer, the city school system refused to give him the Carnegie credits needed for promotion. Eventually, the city school department referred the Nielsens to the state department of education. Officials there said that the matter could only be resolved on the local level. According to Dr. Diana Whitcomb (who had successfully advocated for Stig's acceleration), Jorgen was a victim of the inflexibility of the system and the fact that no individual within the bureaucracy was willing to step forward and advocate for him. "No one was willing to stick their neck out; you know we all had to have our jobs and say we're not going against the administration. And that was unfortunate."

An odd feature of bureaucratic systems (e. g., all school systems) is that while formalized structures provide individuals with specific rights, including the right to due process, the specific regulations can sometimes hamper flexibility. If an IEP (Individualized Educational Plan) had been prepared for Jorgen before he'd taken the CTY course, in which it had been specified which courses he was going to take at CTY, he would have had no problem getting credit for his work at CTY. Since he was trying to get credit after the fact, it was no go. Of course, who's to say that Jorgen wouldn't have gotten hung up on another obscure regulation had the IEP been in place? As Dr. Nielsen sees it, Jorgen was fouled up by "the attitudes of the people more than just the bureaucratic system itself. If the system had been allowed to work with Jorgen, I think a better solution would've been found, but there were some people who just refused."

Having learned from their experiences with Stig the importance of certifying a child's "giftedness," the Nielsens had Jorgen tested; thus, like his brother, he became entitled to an IEP. The staffing that was held to determine Jorgen's educational future was pointless; the not-so-invisible hands of Mr. and Mrs. Hodgkins were all over the plan that emerged. One of the problems with the IEP process as it currently exists in many states is that local authorities are given too much latitude to decide what constitutes an "appropriate" education. Come September, it seemed Jorgen was going to be right back in the treadmill of futility; as a sophomore at his old school, he was bound to face the same frustrations again.

A Victory of Substance

Jorgen's problems with the city schools were solved when he dropped out, more or less. He simply stopped going to school and enrolled as a "provisional" student at the local university. Whenever a parent places his or her child in an unusual position, there is always a great deal of anxiety. The Nielsens worried that Jorgen would have been left without options if things had not worked out at the university. "When we took that major step with Jorgen," Ingrid said. "I thought: 'wow, what about if I was wrong?'"

In his first semester, he took a full freshman courseload, including the most advanced calculus course that was available and an introductory Russian course. His average at the end of the first semester? An exceptional 3.8. His reaction? "I expected it to be really hard. And when I came, I found that college was like I wanted high school to be."

After his successful semester as a provisional student, Jorgen felt confident enough to apply to the university as a regular student. At first, Norma Barese, the director of admissions, was skeptical. The university's undergraduate program is a high-caliber liberal arts program; most students live on campus, and extra-curricular activities are considered an important part of campus life. "I was very skeptical of him, and from a professional viewpoint, wouldn't have suspected that he would've been able to accomplish what he has."

After a series of interviews, however, she decided to admit him. At fourteen, she felt that "Jorgen was every bit as capable as many of the good seventeen-year-olds that I talked to, in terms of his verbal skills and his ability to put together a thoughtful program .... He's a persuasive kid and not in a manipulative way. He's just grown up in a lot of his characteristics. Nice to talk to and pleasant."

Ms. Barese confidence was not betrayed. In his second year at the university, Jorgen boosted his average to 4.0 and participated in a number of extra-curricular activities. He made lots of friends in the Russian club and acted in Macbeth. He especially took pride in his part-time job as consultant in the university's computerized classroom.

According to Jorgen, attending CTY paved the way for his success at the university. CTY gave him a boost at a time when his morale was the lowest. He wrote in a letter:

> It was really the first time I had gone through a program so fast-paced, and also the first time away from home. When I arrived there, I was happier than, and I do not think I am exaggerating, I had been in my entire life. At once I got along with other students. I seemed to make more friends in a couple of days than I had made in a couple of years. I saw that there were other students out there like me, and even with the same problems, but also with some solutions. The shock did not end when I started classes. We were told to call our instructors and teaching assistants by their first names, as if we were friends! Then I started working and found that the self-paced format fit me fine. I could actually do the work and do it extremely well among the nation's top high-school scholars. Although I felt at the time that I was slightly slower than some others, the fact that I always did so well on my homework and quizzes kept me going. The instructors were always ready to support me and help me. Before I had finished both sessions, I had completed geometry, trigonometry, and Algebra III, the equivalent of two years' work at my high school. I had excellent recommendations and was encouraged to go on to Calculus. It was then, I think, that I realized who I really was and what I had the potential to do if I worked hard enough for it. I was determined to excel, whatever the cost, and I did just that.

Jorgen is presently attending a university in Scandinavia, where he is studying computer science; he is particularly interested in artificial intelligence. He hopes some day to design a machine with an operating system that thinks. "How do we define a life or intelligence?" Jorgen said. "How do we know that the computer upstairs isn't intelligent in its own way? Turning it off doesn't kill it .... It's very hard to conceptualize, and that's probably why there's so much argument about it. Maybe when computers start demanding ... then there'll be a need to start reorganizing your philosophy about computers being more than tools."

The single-minded pursuit of a discipline from an early age allows for the development of "automatic routines," the processes whereby, according to Ochse, knowledge is recombined on the subconscious level and new discoveries are produced. With remarkable consistency, people who have made contributions in any field (whether it be science, literature, the arts, business, leadership) have shown an early interest in their field and maintained their devotion over a period of many years.[3]

It is difficult to predict whether a particular student given the necessary opportunities will end up making a contribution; what can be predicted is that those who aren't given opportunities will not make contributions. From an early age, Jorgen was ready to move ahead in his studies. The obstacles that were placed in his way might have derailed his growth had it not been for the determination of his parents and the vision of those individuals who chose to work with him.

Notes

1. Ochse, R., *Before the Gates of Excellence*, p. 161.
2. Ochse, R., *Before the Gates of Excellence*, Trollope quoted from p. 144.
3. Ochse, R., *Before the Gates of Excellence*, p. 234–240.

Disorganization Skills

Robert Dagleish

"In ten minutes of reading a book, I could have learned everything that I learned in a year of messing around in classes full of people who didn't care about what was being taught and, in a lot of cases, teachers that didn't care about teaching all that much," Bob Dagleish said, summing up his feelings about high school.

Bob is an intense person. When he talks, he rocks or fidgets as if trying to calm some inner fury. A little over average height, he is slim, rough-edged, a bit gangly in the limbs. There is no awkwardness in his speech, however: an excess of ebullience, a touch of righteousness maybe, but mostly one is struck by the conviction with which he expresses his ideas.

Senior year in high school, after his father died, Bob could see no reason to stay in school. For six years, school had offered nothing but frustration and humiliation. His way of thinking, his manner of expressing himself and of doing things simply did not match the pattern of expectations. In part, he had stayed in school as long as he had out of respect for his father — Michael Dagleish, who was, and remains, an idol to his son. His presence lingers in passing references, in photographs, in gestures and ways of thinking.

Michael Dagleish grew up in Arkansas during the depression and had to drop out of school after ninth grade to help support his family. Eventually, he took a GED and went to college. But in many respects he remained an independent, quirky, home-grown sort of intellectual. Among other things, he bequeathed to Bob a passion for literature, astronomy, and photography. According to Bob's mother, Jacqueline, Michael was also a man of many highly developed opinions: "He had some ideas about things that were wrong with society, and he did a lot of writing on the subject. He would write letters to the editor and was active in the union on the base where we worked."

Bob has, according to his mother, inherited his father's tendency to speak his mind about things that bother him — a tendency that has gotten him into trouble on more than one occasion. "Bob holds some pretty unconventional views," said Jacqueline. "But whereas Morgan (his younger brother) has the social sense to keep certain things to himself, ... Bob doesn't do that .... He's more like his father was, except that his father had a way of phrasing things that was very convincing: Daddy was a born salesman."

In a media class in high school, Bob was upset when the teacher regularly turned the class over to one of the students and sat down in the front row to eat his breakfast and read the newspaper. "Bob couldn't keep his mouth shut about what he thought of the man's teaching," said Jacqueline. "I'm sure the school was aware of the situation. But they've got a tenured teacher and they're not going to do anything about it, and they'd just as soon not have it called to their attention."

If Bob had been a model student and if his mother had been ready to raise a stink about the media teacher, something might have come of the complaint. But in high school, Bob was generally viewed as an inattentive underachiever with a big mouth — the kind of person whose opinion counts for very little. To her credit, Bob's guidance counselor recognized his intelligence. "Even when he wasn't doing what he was supposed to be doing, he could make it sound good," she said. "He really could come up and intellectualize a lot."

For an educator, nothing is as frustrating as working with a bright child who seems determined to fail. If that child also happens to be critical, insightful, articulate, conflict is inescapable. Fortunately, Bob's guidance counselor was able to diffuse a lot of his anger and to redirect his energy to constructive undertakings. Still, Bob retains a great deal of bitterness about his high school experience. "I didn't have help," he observed. "I got yelled at every day because I was not paying enough attention in class, and that was the only help I got."

In elementary school, both of Jacqueline's sons — Bob and younger brother Morgan — consistently hit the ceiling on standardized tests and, in her words, went through their classes "like gangbusters." However, both saw their school performance go into a tailspin once they entered junior high school. Bob had problems concentrating on what was going on in his classes. He couldn't seem to get his homework done, and he was constantly in trouble with his teachers.

The experience is not unusual among students who, like Bob and Morgan, suffer from Attention Deficit Disorder (ADD), which according to some sources afflicts as many as 10% of American children.[1] The new responsibilities that come with junior high school — multiple classes with different assignments, the need to work independently, longer reading and writing assignments — can overwhelm an ADD child who may have had no trouble with elementary school.

There is quite a bit of controversy regarding the causes and precise nature of ADD and the related disorder ADHD (Attention Deficit Disorder with hyperactivity). According to the American Psychiatric Association, ADD is indicated when a child displays "inappropriate inattention, impulsivity, and sometimes hyperactivity" for his mental and chronological age.[2] Heredity, organic factors such as central nervous system injuries, and environmental toxins are the most frequently cited causes. According to Edna Copeland and Valerie Love, "most researchers and practitioners consider ADD a hereditary physiological problem."[3] Martha Denkla, M.D., director of the Developmental Neurobehavioral Clinic of the Kennedy Institute at the Johns Hopkins University, attributes the academic difficulties of ADD students to "executive dysfunction." In other words, while they might be quite bright, children with ADD have trouble paying attention, organizing their thoughts, grasping the gist of complex situations, and resisting distractions.[4]

With a combination of counseling, academic adaptations, and, in some cases, medication, children with ADD can succeed in school. For Bob, the struggle is by no means over, but since he entered college two years ago, he has been making steady progress. (This year, he was on the Dean's List at his college.) Along the way, he has benefited greatly from the help and understanding of a number of key individuals (his doctor, his high school guidance counselor and a mentor) but he has also had to overcome myriad obstacles on his own — through sheer determination and persistence.

A Cautious Child

According to Jacqueline, Bob was always "very cautious" as a child. "While he could walk around holding onto things from about eight months on, he never let go until he was about fourteen months old," she said. "And by then, you know, he could have walked a couple of miles just fine. He just never would until he was absolutely certain." The same was true with talking: he was slow to begin, but when he finally decided to talk, he did so in full sentences almost immediately.

Both Jacqueline and her husband read to the boys when they were little. And both boys were extremely curious. "They seemed to absorb everything they were told and really take an interest in it," said Jacqueline. And although she claims that she made no effort to teach her sons to read, both were reading before they started school. "I assume they learned to read from *Sesame Street* and *The Electric Company*," she said.

While Morgan was adept at putting together puzzles and playing board games, Bob had no interest in either. Although his parents were not aware of it at the time, in addition to his attention deficit, Bob has a spatial learning disability. To this day, he has trouble perceiving proportions: he is an accomplished photographer, but drawing even a simple picture is for him an excruciating exercise. "I can see well with my eye," Bob explained. "But when I try to put it down on paper, the stuff gets mixed up."

It became apparent that Bob's spatial disorder was going to be a serious academic obstacle when, in the fourth grade, he encountered long division. "He couldn't get it lined up," said Jacqueline. "He couldn't get it on the paper. Instead of going down, it kind of curved around. He would get so lost in trying to get it on paper that he'd end up trying to do things like divide by the remainder ... I mean, a problem would go on forever. He just didn't know when to stop."

At that point, Jacqueline tried to have Bob tested to clarify the nature of his disorder. To her chagrin, the school's guidance counselor said that they "couldn't test for his kind of disability" — the implication being that his aptitude and achievement test scores were too high to warrant any further testing. Jacqueline was frustrated, but she did not think she had any recourse. "That's something where I could have insisted, but I didn't know the laws and regulations," she observed.

In recent years, Jacqueline has become active with a local advocacy group for learning disabled children. "I wish I had fought harder," she said. "There are a couple of different titles now that you can request. You say my child falls into this category or that category, and this is why I want you to test him." Although advocates have made progress in some states in terms of having ADD recognized as a learning disability, neither federal law nor Pennsylvania law includes ADD as a learning disability. Since Bob was neither identified as learning disabled nor gifted, he was not entitled to any modifications in his educational program under state law.

Jacqueline has since learned that she could have filed a complaint with the Office of Civil Rights under Section 504 of the Rehabilitation Act of 1973 requesting an evaluation and "reasonable accommodation" of Bob's individual needs. Section 504 defines a handicap as "any physical or mental impairment which substantially limits one or more major life activities,"[5] a definition which is broad enough to include ADD. In fact, parents who have invoked Section 504 have won special educational assistance or reasonable accommodations for children with ADD in almost every state.[6]

As Bob's academic problems became increasingly frustrating, he began misbehaving in school and resisted doing his homework. Since no intervention was forthcoming from the school, Jacqueline decided to address his problems independently. She and her husband, Michael, brought him to family counseling, which helped them to cope with some of the emotional issues surrounding homework and behavioral problems. For a while, at the counselor's suggestion, they stopped insisting that he do all of his homework.

At the same time, they made arrangements to have him tutored by a neighbor who was studying special education at a nearby college. The neighbor worked out a system for long division which involved folding a piece of paper so that Bob could keep his columns of figures straight. Instead of insisting that he perform dozens of identical operations, she worked with him patiently — one problem at a time — making sure that he understood what he was doing. This was precisely the type of individualized instruction that Bob needed and should have received at school.[7]

The summer after Bob's fourth grade year, Jacqueline and Michael had him tested privately. The tests confirmed their suspicion that Bob suffered from a spatial disorder. Before Bob returned to school in the fall, Jacqueline went and talked to his teachers, who were generally receptive to the modifications that the counselor had suggested.

In retrospect, both Bob and Morgan feel that they had their best educational experiences in elementary school. "My fifth grade teacher was neat," said Morgan with characteristic succinctness. "She kept things interesting." According to his mother, that was the last time that Morgan was at all interested in school, even though there had been a time when he was so excited by learning that he would make trips to the library to research issues that interested him on his own.

While Bob has managed to maintain more of an interest in academics than his brother has, Jacqueline feels that after elementary school, his needs were never addressed in a meaningful way. "Elementary school, he loved," said Jacqueline. "The teachers were very encouraging." Even though he was having trouble in math, the teachers gave him an opportunity to shine in his areas of strength. They knew that he was good at magic tricks, so to nurture his talent, they let him put on shows when other kids had birthdays. The teachers were also encouraging about his musical abilities. When Jacqueline presented them with the findings from the independent evaluation (which identified Bob's spatial disability but not his attention deficit), they were even willing to make some adjustments: they let him sit at the front of the class; they made sure that he always had clear copies of ditto sheets; and they arranged for him to tutor younger students in math. Tutoring was particularly important, according to Jacqueline, because it allowed him to practice a difficult subject in a non-threatening environment where his knowledge and abilities would be respected. In essence, this modification represented an extremely inventive form of flexible pacing.

Inflexibility

Two years after Bob graduated from high school, his social studies teacher lamented never having been told about Bob's disabilities. "It's like now, two years after the fact, I find out he had a disability. That's sad," he said. His high school photography teacher felt that she also had not been informed: "I was told that he was gifted, but I was never told that he had a learning disability."

Before Bob entered the middle school, Jacqueline made sure that letters from his elementary teachers and test reports were sent along to the guidance department so that people at the school would be aware of his special needs. However, early on she discovered that no effort would be made to address these issues. The assumption undergirding this treatment is widespread in America's secondary schools: everyone is supposed to sink or swim by the same rules. Any modification of the curriculum or teaching methods for a particular student is seen as unfair to the others. Further complicating this situation is a widespread ignorance of the problems which confront students with learning disabilities. Jacqueline described the attitude of the staff at Bob's middle school as follows:

> We'd had him tested and they had the reports, but those are kept in a central file so people can't see. It was just my experience that I might as well be talking to a brick wall. There were no accommodations. I'd go in and I'd say — they'd be taking off whole letter grades for his handwriting. And I'd explain that this is the best he can write. And they'd say, "Oh yeah." And they'd remember it for a couple of weeks and one paper and then it's: "Well, this kid has to learn to write."

After attending meetings where teachers didn't show up or didn't bring the material she had requested they bring, Jacqueline began to feel overwhelmed by a sense of futility. "I think what they try to do is beat you back," she commented, shaking her head wearily. "And I think they succeeded."

Bob's problems in junior high school were aggravated by a peculiar placement policy. Instead of basing students' placement on subject-specific tests or academic performance, placement was made across the board on the basis of scores on a math achievement test. In other words, students with high scores on the math test were placed in high-track classes across the board while students with lower math scores were placed in lower-track classes across the board. It didn't matter how talented they might be in science, history, or English.

On the whole, Bob was frustrated both by the quality of the teaching and the motivation of the other students in his track. "I wouldn't mind being in level two (the lower track) so much," Bob said, "if that still meant that they were trying to teach you .... But if you were below level one — level one they still help, not as much as honors — but if you were below level one, the idea was to shuffle you through ... " In general, he had the sense that the school simply gave up on kids who weren't in the highest tracks. "I think there were a lot of good teachers there (at the school) who were pretty good, but I was in level two and needed help, so they gave us the worst ones, and gave the good ones to the higher classes."

While Bob's frustration at being in the lower track may have contributed to his negative assessment of the situation, his brother — who took classes in a variety of tracks and is generally less impassioned about his education — agreed that the expectations were much lower in level two classes. "In level one courses, if you don't do you homework, you just want to dig a hole and put your head in it. In level two, ... no one does their homework, and if you don't do yours, it's not like you feel stupid or anything. It just doesn't make any difference at all," he said.

After an extensive review of the literature on ability grouping and tracking, Adam Gamoran observed that "grouping doesn't produce achievement, instruction does."[8] In many cases students can benefit from being grouped with individuals of like ability; however, tracking should never be inflexible (i. e., there should always be opportunities for cross-group movement) and ability grouping should not be used to establish a hierarchy of people who receive an education and people who do not. Rather, ability grouping is most useful when used to ensure that students are being presented with appropriate material on a level which is high enough to maintain challenge but not so high it becomes overwhelming and when the highest expectations and standards are maintained at all levels.

Bob became increasingly disillusioned with classes that addressed neither his needs nor his interests. Because he had done extremely poorly on the spatial section of the I. Q. test and because his grades were not particularly good, Bob was never selected to participate in programs for gifted or talented students. Gradually, he slipped into a pattern of under-achievement typical of bright children whose abilities go unnoticed.[9] Bob retains some bitterness about the experience of having been passed up for special programs: "I didn't get to go on field trips or have any enrichment," Bob said. "And for me, a field trip would have been the greatest thing in the world."

Although his performance in math classes was particularly discouraging (he failed Algebra II twice), he was if anything more frustrated by English courses — possibly because he is so talented verbally. "I'm waiting for someone to teach me more English than I knew in eighth grade. Is there anything new?"

For Bob, learning to write the standard five-paragraph essay was a particularly painful experience. He would start on an idea and give up, start on another idea and give up again. He got in trouble with his teachers because he never handed in outlines or because he sometimes handed in papers that had been word-processed. "You've seen the A-B-C outlines they teach you to do in English. For somebody with a spatial problem, there is no way I could write a report trying to follow that. A stream of consciousness is the best for me to start out ... And then I could organize, later."

Even when he was taking medication (dexedrine was prescribed by his doctor when he was in the eleventh grade) that helped him to concentrate, Bob continued having problems with the standard form that his teachers expected. "A lot of English teachers had you hand the outline in with the paper," he said. "But what the heck difference does it make how you got it there if it's good?" From a teacher's perspective, it was undoubtedly frustrating to have Bob in class. To all appearances, he was an extremely bright individual whose performance was spotty, who couldn't seem to pay attention, who was disorganized and easily distracted — a classic underachiever. When asked to describe Bob's academic problems, his guidance counselor said, "He had a good vocabulary and so forth. He seemed to be well-read and very perceptive of everything that was going on around him. So maybe he tended to give people the impression that he was very intelligent. He just didn't follow through then with the effort ... "

Mr. Brown, Bob's high school social studies teacher, put it even more succinctly: "My impression was that he had a lot of ability, but he didn't perform up to it."

Whereas the discrepancy between Bob's apparent ability and his performance in his classes should have been a clear indication to teachers and the guidance staff that Bob needed to have his program modified, an assumption was made that he just had a problem with motivation. Or, as his guidance counselor observed: "I think his teachers felt that he could handle the regular program here. You know, in terms of the difficulty of the work and so forth. I don't remember anyone saying that he should be tested because this work is too difficult for him or he just isn't able to cope with this material."

Mr. Brown wishes that he'd had more information about Bob's disabilities. "There's a communication problem at the secondary level," he said. "Oftentimes, we have no indication of what's going on. And whether it's the parents that don't want that information spread to the faculty or whether the guidance counselors determine that, it's part of a working disadvantage, ... because had I known that there was a problem there, then I could understand the inconsistencies."

Individual differences often aren't addressed in secondary schools because many secondary school educators simply aren't willing to recognize their existence. Although she had no more "objective" information than Mr. Brown, Bob's photography teacher, Ms. Rubcek, discovered that she needed to make a number of modifications in her teaching approach in order to address Bob's needs effectively. She explained:

The one thing we had some problems with was that he was very unsure. If I told him to do something specific ... Let's say that he wanted to make sure everything was exposed correctly, and I explained to him how a light-meter in a camera worked, one explanation would not be enough.

I would have to go over and over. And it was probably mid-way through the first year ... [before] I realized that I just could not give him a lump of information, that I had to be able to break it down into several lumps — small amounts of information — and once he digested those small amounts, he could just move on and on ....

Mrs. Rubcek also recognized early on that Bob learned best in a one-on-one situation, where the material could be explained at a proper pace and where there was a minimum of outside stimuli to interfere with his concentration. While he experienced very little success in high school, Bob did so well in his photography class that Mrs. Rubcek currently employs him to take pictures for her private photography studio. Certainly, Bob's interest in photography fed into his success, but more importantly it was Mrs. Rubcek's willingness and ability to give him individual attention and to break down the barriers that generally impede the development of direct, personal relationships in school.

Quite possibly, Mrs. Rubcek was able to serve (and continues to serve) Bob as a mentor because she'd had the experience of working with a mentor herself. "My mentor was a professional photographer," she said. "He allowed me to go along and do some things with him. Then I shot for his studio .... It's interesting, because I can see Bob following that same pattern."

Getting it Together

One afternoon, sitting in the living room of the Dagleish's low-slung ranch house on a quiet street in suburban central Pennsylvania, Bob, Morgan, Jacqueline, and Bob's specialist — Dr. Jane Shumway* — sat and discussed how one might address the academic needs of students with ADD more effectively.

"I swear if someone gave me some money and some teachers that cared about students, I could set up a better school than the one I went to," Bob said. "If you got students who had my same problems and sent them to me, I'd be happy to help them. Because

---

* Her real name.

it frustrates me to see more people going through the same problems, because I really hated being there."

Morgan is chafed by the length of the school day. "If they just cut out the extra stuff ... If they took out lunch, study halls, and free periods. If the teachers didn't spend all that time just talking about things that aren't even related — if they just got down to the subject and had six half-hour classes — packed them in from nine to twelve ... " Morgan said, shaking his head.

"Definitely," Bob said, picking up on his brother's cue. "If they would cut the garbage out of the day .... People hate going to school because it's eight hours."

Jacqueline believes that kids with ADD can succeed in the mainstream school situation as long as their teachers and school administrators are willing to make some adjustments:

> There's a lot of accommodations that a classroom teacher can make but none of them want to make any exceptions. You know, the attitude seems to be — well, they have to learn how to do this and they have to learn it this way. It wouldn't be fair for me to make an exception for this one child, because there's a problem here. But if they had a physical problem you'd make exceptions for it. I think there needs to be more accommodation in the regular classroom for kids whose learning styles just don't lend themselves to very repetitive work or written work.

Dr. Shumway agrees with Jacqueline, and in the ten years she has been working with ADD children she has developed a number of effective strategies for parents and teachers. "In a sense," Dr. Shumway observed, "what these kids need is an executive secretary or someone to fulfill that role."

Much of Bob's current success is due to his personal courage and determination. The fact is that he never gave up on his education or on learning. He simply found that a lot of his learning had to take place outside of the official channels and that he wouldn't necessarily receive any credit for much of the work that he did.

His relationship to Mrs. Rubcek, his photography teacher, was immensely important to him. She remained supportive and gave him the opportunity to excel in a field where he had a great deal of interest and talent. Jacqueline played an equally important role, providing a sounding board for his ideas and reaffirming his positive impression of himself. Taking dexedrine — in consultation with Dr. Shumway — also had a significant impact on Bob's school performance. "Where before, he couldn't even settle on a topic, after he started taking the medication," said Jacqueline, "he started turning out ten-page, footnoted reports .... His handwriting is even better with the medication."

Jacqueline credits Bob's guidance counselor with keeping him in school senior year when he was contemplating dropping out. "Her door was always open. If Bob had a problem, he could always go down and talk to her," Jacqueline said.

In the spring of his senior year, Bob's guidance counselor allowed him to participate in an apprenticeship program usually reserved for honors students. After signing a contract stating that he would make up the work for any classes he missed, Bob was given the opportunity to spend his afternoons working in a professional photographer's studio. "I did better in my classes that semester than I'd done the whole time in high school," said Bob. Currently, Bob is attending college full-time, majoring in photography with a minor in literature; he is also playing in a rock band with his brother Morgan and working as a photographer at Ms. Rubcek's studio.

Bob's guidance counselor bent the rules to allow him into the apprenticeship program which was usually reserved for students in the honors track. "I think part of the reason things worked for Bob was his personality," said the guidance counselor. "He was willing to be assertive and go after this thing."

It is precisely this type of flexibility which can provide someone like Bob with a meaningful educational experience. If one were willing to try such options with more students with similar problems, one might find that they too would be willing to be assertive and to go after things.

Notes

1. Elliot, Richard O., "Attention Deficit Disorder: Current Understanding."
2. American Psychiatric Association, *Diagnostic and Statistical Manual for Mental Disorders* (3rd Edition), Washington, D. C.
3. For an accessible summary of current understandings of Attention Deficit Disorder, including a lengthy bibliography and numerous appendices see Copeland, Edna D. & Love, Valerie, L. *Attention, Please!*, pp. 57–58.

4. Denkla, Martha B., "Executive Function, the Overlap Zone Between Attention Deficit Hyperactivity Disorder and Learning Disabilities."
5. Section 504 (34 104.35). For a concise summary of the implications of Section 504 see the Learning Disabilities Association of America, "A Guide to Section 504: How it Applies to Students with Learning Disabilities and ADHD," available from the LDA; 4156 Library Road; Pittsburgh, Pa. 15234.
6. Jacobs, Kristi, "Legal Issues and ADD," unpublished paper.
7. For suggestions on how to address the needs of ADD and other learning disabled students in school see Alley, Gordon and Deshler, Donald, *Teaching the Learning Disabled Adolescent: Strategies and Methods.*
8. Gamoran, Adam, "Organization, Instruction, and the Effects of Ability Grouping: Comment on Slavin's 'Best Evidence Synthesis,' " p. 341.
9. Gallagher, James, *Teaching the Gifted Child*, pp. 415–426.4

The Itch to Write

10

Caitlin Rawls

Asked when he decided to become a writer, the great novelist Alberto Moravia bristled. "I have always been a writer," he said, waving a hand to dismiss his interrogator. A question which seems reasonable to the student of education may strike the artist as an object of contempt or derision. To paraphrase T. S. Eliot: with the exception of Shakespeare and Dante, a poet is not master of the word, rather he is its servant.[1]

Discussing her early apprenticeship to words, Caitlin Rawls (who began writing as soon as she learned to form the letters of the alphabet) echoed this sentiment: "I didn't decide: I just wrote. It was just, every free second I had, even as I got older and much more busy ... every free second went to writing." According to Caitlin's father, Dr. William Rawls, Caitlin began to write when she was in the first grade. "She would come home and sit down and write and write and write. She'd write about everything she saw around her," Dr. Rawls marveled. "Tons of stuff all over the place. Papers piled up on her desk." Caitlin's mother, Olga, confirmed her husband's observation. "Her fingers would itch, and she would have to have a pencil in her fingers," she said.

By the time Caitlin entered college, she had published 33 poems, 7 short stories, 4 essays, and a collection of poetry and photographs. As a high school student, she had toured the nation, speaking to school children about writing and had won a dazzling array of awards, contests, and scholarships, including top honors in Scholastic Magazine's Short Story Competition: an honor she shares with the likes of Joyce Carol Oates, Bernard Malamud, and Jean Stafford.

Jim Stahl*, the editor and publisher of *Merlyn's Pen*, a magazine of writings by eighth through tenth graders, describes Caitlin as one of the most talented young writers that he has run across in the eight years that his magazine has been in circulation. "I think her use of language is unusually accurate, specific, and also evocative," said Stahl. "I think that comes because she looks at her surroundings very, very closely. In her poems, there are no wasted words. In fact, normally we ask students to put their poetry through a final revision before we print them in *Merlyn's Pen*. In the case of Caitlin's poems, though, we ran them without revisions. She had already honed them down."

Lena Stanlankovitch, Caitlin's private writing instructor for seven years, concurs with Jim Stahl's assessment: "There is this wonderful, creative style that you work all your life to develop, and (at twelve) she already had it. Fresh images. Beautiful, unusual ways of saying things. And the courage to be creative."

While it would not be accurate to describe Caitlin as a prodigy, in that her writing has yet to earn recognition in a strictly adult forum, she has scaled the summits of accomplishment for young apprentice writers. In her best poems, one notes a sensitivity to rhythmic patterns and the cadence of speech, surprising imagery and original word combinations. Occasionally, there are lines which leap from the page, as when she described the fear of losing her father to illness: "I remember Death / looming in the air like a burnt smell, / like a bad cat, waiting." Her language is sparse but rich in imagery and resonance, and, as Jim Stahl observed, there are no unnecessary words.

If anything, Caitlin's ability as a story-teller is even more impressive. Although much of her fiction deals with familiar domes-

---

* his real name

tic situations, she is not afraid to eschew the conventional wisdom of writing instructors and magazine editors alike — that young writers should write about what they know — and venture into unfamiliar territory, weaving tales about sea voyages, adult relationships, the Vietnam War. While a hint of sentimentality or melodrama may occasionally sneak into one of her stories, Caitlin's work is saved by her eye for convincing details and her ability to empathize without losing ironic distance.

"Usually the kids who have the most success are the ones who stick closest to home in their characters, their themes," observed Jim Stahl, who sifts through 6000 manuscripts a year. "It's unusual to be able to write so well about distant places and distant characters so convincingly at that age." Asked why he found Caitlin's stories convincing, Stahl said: "We think what makes most anything convincing is the degree of elaboration. The amount of time spent on a moment, a place, on an action. And she spends time: she elaborates a moment, she elaborates a dialogue."

Witness the opening to one of her prize-winning stories, a touching tale about friendship and betrayal, written when Caitlin was a junior in high school:

> I'd say at first, if you asked me, that we are all the same inside. That is, we are all inherently good. I'd say we are all alike in the dark, but I wouldn't be right. Some of us drift like vagrant fog off the ocean, and some of us build lighthouses.
> When I was seven, I had a stick-straight genuine bowl-haircut. I had such chubby cheeks that I was dubbed "Pumpkin Head" by my own mother .... and I dressed in the most egregious hand-me-down relics from the late 1960s. But I was a cute, good girl who did "just fine."

The story is a tour-de-force, in which Caitlin exhibits her skill and sophistication. The fog and lighthouse imagery introduced in the opening paragraph are the metaphoric loom on which she weaves her tale. Contrasts between what is bright and what is murky are reprised throughout, but subtly, without exaggeration. In the second paragraph, we witness what Jim Stahl described as Caitlin's trademark ability to step back from a story and describe a narrator in less than flattering terms. It is rare indeed to find an adolescent writer who has the confidence to describe her protagonist as a "Pumpkin Head" in "egregious hand-me-down relics." Most impressive, however, is the story's economy of style: in about 1000 words she creates convincing characters, a compelling conflict, and tells a story which is, in the Aristotelian sense, both "complete" and "of a certain magnitude." The story concludes with a reversal and an insight into human nature; after betraying her friend, the narrator reflects, "... when I say that all people are the same inside, it is wishful thinking."

"I Hate Childrens"

In the early years, before she started school, Caitlin had her parents worried. She was a sunny child, easy-going and sweet, a much-desired, second child born into a close-knit family in a sleepy university town in the South, but she didn't seem to develop or learn things as quickly as her older sister had, and periodically she would become withdrawn, frustrated, and uncommunicative. "She liked being alone a lot," her mother observed. "And she didn't seem to learn all that quickly. She seemed somewhere else. And we didn't know if the somewhere else was that she wasn't normally capable or whether it was something else."

Caitlin's older sister, Renata, was an extremely precocious learner; she spoke and read early, scored in the gifted range across the board when she was given an I.Q. test, and much like Laura Foucher (chapter two) and Stig Nielsen (chapter six) thrived on the challenge of putting together puzzles and playing with Legos and other complicated toys. Renata was, in the words of her mother, "more analytical, more memor(ious), faster learning, quicker to solve a problem" than Caitlin.

While Renata liked the structure that games and toys provided, Caitlin's early play was usually solitary and consisted almost entirely of fantasy. Any toy or game that required a specific outcome — a right answer or a time deadline — frustrated her. "She did a lot of pretending," remarked Olga Rawls, "All that had to do with dolls and those little Fisher Price people who had houses and cars .... She would sit in her room and talk to herself and arrange these people in different settings. Sometimes she would share that, but she didn't need a lot of interaction."

Caitlin's first experiences with educational institutions were almost uniformly miserable. When Caitlin was two and the family moved to the Mid-West where Dr. Rawls took a new position and Olga Rawls enrolled in a graduate program in family therapy, she and Renata were sent to a well-respected Montessori school. And while Renata thrived in the flexible environment, Caitlin was miserable and resisted going to school. When asked why she didn't like it, her explanation was characteristically terse: "I hate childrens."

While Caitlin would grow up to become poised, friendly, and popular enough to be elected the president of her senior class in high school, Olga Rawls feels that this remark reveals an important facet of Caitlin's personality. "Later on, we understood what she meant by this," said Ms. Rawls. "She was a person who really liked her space and she never liked pressure or group activity or being told what to do. Now, at Montessori, there's less of this than there is in a regular school but there was something about that particular environment and those particular children. Apparently, there was a little girl there who always wanted to be with her and followed her around, and that was what bothered her." This conflict between maintaining her privacy and socializing would emerge again later, especially in high school, when Caitlin's friends would have trouble understanding why someone as warm and friendly as she was would want time to be by herself and write, and Caitlin herself would find herself struggling to set limits and create structures that would give her the time and space to work.

When the problems at the Montessori School remained intractable, Caitlin was transferred to a small private day-care center. There, she made friends with the owner's dog and the owner's son, two years her senior, with whom she had long conversations. And although Caitlin never complained about the center, her parents later found out that Caitlin had been terrified of the owner, who disciplined children by hitting them. The extent of the abuse never became clear to Bill and Olga Rawls; Caitlin did not speak about it until they had moved again, this time to the mid-Atlantic region.

Because they believed that children should have freedom to make choices and to interact openly with one another, the Rawlses again enrolled Caitlin in an untraditional school in their new hometown. At the end of the first year, the teachers called Bill and Olga in for a meeting and informed them that Caitlin seemed to be having troubles interacting with the other children. On the bright side, the teachers were impressed with some of Caitlin's artwork: she demonstrated an ability to focus on details, drawing, for example, a pattern on a woman's dress instead of the stick figures that her classmates would draw. Still, they were concerned with Caitlin's social development. They said that she appeared to be withdrawn and was not interested in doing the sorts of things that "normal" children did. Finally, they recommended that the Rawls take her to a psychologist for an evaluation.

Being a therapist by profession, Olga Rawls was particularly sensitive to the teachers' observations. All of her old fears about Caitlin were rekindled, and although she could discern no pathology, she found herself worrying that Caitlin might have some developmental problems that she had overlooked. As it turned out, the evaluation that Caitlin received from the psychologist (an educational specialist) proved to be a key experience which gave Olga and Bill some insight into Caitlin's talents. First of all, the psychologist confirmed Olga's belief that there was no pathology. Secondly, he explained that Caitlin's intellectual profile was very uneven: she was extremely talented in certain areas (creative, associational thinking) and completely unexceptional in others. He suggested that the alternative school was not a healthy environment for her, because it forced her to make too many decisions. The structure provided by a public school, he said, would be much healthier for someone like Caitlin, whose talents needed time to unfold.

On the psychologist's advice, starting with the first grade, Caitlin attended public schools. Learning to write — to form the letters of the alphabet — may be the most important thing that Caitlin learned in school. Otherwise, most of the experiences and the teachers who would have the greatest impact on her development as a writer would be found out of school. According to Jim Stahl, this situation is not unusual for the young writers who publish in *Merlyn's Pen*. "In so many cases, these kids are almost writing in the closet; they're getting no help in English class," said Stahl, himself a former English teacher. "Bottom line, there seems to be an irreconcilable difference between art and institutions .... I don't know if the classroom can really contain the most honest and artistic writing."

For Caitlin, the first clash between art and institutions came in the first grade, when she shared a short story, "The Flat Rat," with her teacher. Instead of praising Caitlin for her efforts and urging her to continue, the teacher circled every spelling mistake in red ink. From that moment, Caitlin decided never again to share her writing with teachers, and with few exceptions she stuck to this rule. Although she did well in school, it became almost a marginal activity for her. "I was never very challenged in school," she said. "But it didn't matter much, because I was involved in so many other things."

Although they had no idea that Caitlin was particularly talented, her parents continued to encourage her, to give her time and space and plenty of paper to write on. Caitlin's mother recognized that writing seemed to help Caitlin to process her emotions when, periodically, they became overwhelming. "She would get into these temper tantrums," said Olga. "She didn't flail or scream. She just seemed overwhelmed, frustrated, and inaccessible .... That's when, in self-defense, after I couldn't talk with her, I said 'well, go write about it, go sit down and write how you feel ...' " In a published essay, Caitlin later acknowledged the importance of these early anger-writings:

> Whenever I was upset with people, I'd write a hate story. It would go like this one, "I hate my Mommy and Daddy. Whey thinck they know something I know its rong. When we went to the zoo My Mommy and Daddy dident know an anmol and I did it was a peeckock ya!" That's how it all began.

It is hard to imagine an exercise more suited to developing the narrative techniques of a young writer; one thinks, for example, of Kafka's letter to his father. According to Olga, what distinguished Caitlin's hate stories, however, was that they usually ended on a more positive note. "By the end of the story she would see the other side: well, maybe it's okay for mom to do this. And maybe she's not so bad." While the initial impulse might have been purely psychological (the stories were a way of venting and processing difficult emotions), from an aesthetic perspective, writing these "hate stories" may have contributed to Caitlin's ability to create narrative distance and to identify with characters whose perspective and interests differ or even conflict with her own.

While school provided very little in the way of structured opportunities for Caitlin to develop her talent, she had an experience in the third grade which proved transformative. Through her state's Artists-in-the-Schools program, she had the opportunity to work with Madeline Tiger, an accomplished adult writer. Unlike most of the regular teachers, who would fail to recognize Caitlin's talent or find themselves at a loss for ways to nurture it, Ms. Tiger was tremendously supportive and encouraging. In a summary of the experience of working with Caitlin's class, which Ms. Tiger wrote for the local school board, she remarked that if ever one could identify someone who displayed an early talent for writing, Caitlin was it. From that moment on, Dr. Rawls began paying much more attention to his daughter's writing.

The family moved one more time before Caitlin finished school — this time to a small city on the East Coast, where Caitlin would choose to attend the public schools instead of going to private school. In junior high school and high school she made lots of friends and was involved in a variety of activities, including field hockey, student government, debate, acting, dancing (jazz and ballet), singing, and, most importantly, writing. Although her high school was a large, inner-city school, drawing students from diverse ethnic and socio-economic backgrounds, it offered enough honors and Advanced Placement courses to keep Caitlin academically engaged, if not entirely fulfilled. In spite of her popularity, Caitlin still felt isolated at times. "I never felt ostracized, but I always had the sense that I was different .... especially when I started getting serious about my writing. I was looking a lot for people to understand me, and I didn't ever feel that anyone did."

In this respect, Olga Rawls feels that attending CTY was particularly important for Caitlin. "For kids like Caitlin, programs like CTY are really instrumental in helping them develop their talent," she said. "No school, no matter how good, could give her what she got in terms of focus on her writing, individual attention, and peer interaction." Caitlin agreed: "These people were interested in going during the summer and interested in teaching me, and the kids were interested in being there .... The atmosphere was just so positive." Attending CTY and having the opportunity to discuss her work in a rigorous workshop setting reinforced Caitlin's sense that she was a genuinely talented writer. "I think it meant a lot to her when one of her teachers said that she might just have the talent to make a career out of writing," Olga Rawls observed.

The Agent and the Therapist

Discussing his daughter's successes as a young writer, Dr. Rawls makes no attempt to contain his pride. "If there was an All-American rating for writing like there is for basketball," he says, "Caitlin would have had it." Speaking with Caitlin, however, one senses that she might have been less enthusiastic about the recognition than her father. When she was in junior high school, she lived in fear that friends visiting the house would notice her poetry in the magazines that were spread on the coffee table. Throughout school, she made every effort to blend in and keep her writing in the background. "In high school, after the book was published, I was basically known as the girl who wrote the book to a lot of people who didn't know me," she said. "And that's weird to have that as your only identity, especially when I was involved in so many other things."

According to Caitlin's mother, Olga, Caitlin has always been motivated more by the desire to write than by the desire to publish. "She just wrote to write. Afterwards, we would read them, and we'd say, 'this is extraordinary; you should send this off,' " said her mother. "In fact, there were a couple of things that were sent off that she didn't think should have been." On one level, Caitlin was thankful that her parents persuaded her to publish; were it not for the efforts of her father especially, she might never have sent off a manuscript. From the time the first poem was submitted to *Cricket Magazine*, Dr. Rawls has served as Caitlin's executive secretary and agent, identifying markets and competitions for her works, keeping her on target for deadlines, hiring typists for manuscripts, and occasionally offering editorial suggestions.

Caitlin is somewhat ambivalent about her relationship to her father. On the one hand, she appreciates the opportunities that he made available to her; on the other, she sometimes resented the pressure that he put on her to revise her works and get them ready for deadlines. Lena Stanlankovitch said that she often worried that the pressure to publish would become too intense, that Caitlin would lose her love for writing. "Her father was always pushing her," she said. "Here's another competition. Enter this one. And I used to get a little bit upset about it, because I thought: 'She's a kid, let her go to dances and plays, and do the things she wants to do.' "

Olga Rawls also worried sometimes about her husband's involvement with Caitlin's writing. "Bill is a very achievement-oriented person," she observed. "He's been successful in his own career through his own talents and hard work. But I think he would have liked to have been a writer himself .... He gets so rewarded by what she does, that he sometimes doesn't draw the line between what's his need and what's hers. Caitlin doesn't like to be pushed."

When Caitlin was in high school and there was always another contest deadline coming up, Olga often found herself intervening, trying to relieve the pressure. But while Olga has managed to maintain a laid-back attitude towards Caitlin's writing, she admits that she put other types of pressures on her daughter. "She says that she wishes that I could just be a Mom and not a therapist," said Olga. "She feels she's absorbed this sensitivity which is great for writing but is not always so great for living. She feels she's too in tune with things: she's too aware of why people do the things they do. And this she attributes to me."

When Bill and Olga Rawls talk about their relationships with Caitlin, it quickly becomes apparent that writing has been the focal point of the relationship between Bill and Caitlin, whereas Olga has concerned herself more with helping Caitlin to develop personally and psychologically. Paradoxically, it may be Bill who has played the leading role in shaping the way Caitlin lives her life and Olga who has influenced her writing most deeply.

People who meet Caitlin are uniformly impressed with her poise and self-confidence. She is articulate and attractive in an unpretentious and direct way. She seems equally comfortable speaking with one person or addressing an auditorium filled with dignitaries. According to one editor who has heard her speak on a number of occasions, she has the ability to win over an audience with her warmth and charm, so that after the first few minutes she could "pick her nose, and it wouldn't bother them." This ability may be partly inherited, but it may also derive in part from the example of her father's professional competence and zeal and from the education that he provided, gradually exposing her to more stressful situations, encouraging her to take on new challenges. "I know that it's a great maturing experience for Caitlin to go out and interact with kids all the way from the first grade to the 12th grade and learn how to lecture, learn to stand on her own feet and be articulate and communicate with different kinds of people," he observed.

After Caitlin left home, much of the tension dissolved between her and her father. Gradually, she has taken more responsibility for editing and submitting her own work: by senior year in high school, she was often submitting pieces without even showing them to him. Ultimately, even Lena Stanlankovitch admits that Dr. Rawls has done more to help Caitlin than to harm her. "I think about all the other talented people who not only don't get any support but get discouraged by their parents, and I think — God All-Mighty — what if Caitlin had come from another household?" she said. "I am fully confident that years from now everybody is going to know Caitlin .... She's going to succeed; I know it." Ultimately, Caitlin herself sees her relationship to her father as overwhelmingly positive: "I think I knew that my father knew what was best for me, and it wasn't much to ask. I wanted to have my stuff published."

While she was willing to accept her father's role as an agent and manager, she had less patience with the editorial suggestions he made and his tendency to try making her work more marketable. The voice and the concerns of her work are not commercial; rather, her writing seems motivated by a deep desire to understand why people do what they do. She rarely writes a piece in which she does not champion the outsider, demonstrate compassion, or wrestle with an important moral issue.

Although both of Caitlin's parents are deeply involved in local politics and volunteer work, trying "to help right some of the wrongs of our society," it seems that her mother has had the deepest impact on her in this respect. Olga Rawls and her parents fled Latvia in the 1940's fearing Soviet rule. They abandoned a 150-acre farm, their animals, and their lives to move to Mississippi, where for three years they worked as indentured servants on a cotton farm. Olga started working in the cotton fields when she was ten years old. She believes that two lessons which she learned from that experience have shaped her life. First, she learned about grace: although they had lost everything, her parents were never bitter. Secondly, she learned about the basic equality between all people. "In these fields were Latvian bank presidents, farmers, and professors. Everybody was leveled, no matter what their accomplishments or wealth had been in Latvia."

In one way or another — through her example, through conversations, or through what she calls "meta-communication" — Olga Rawls seems to have passed these lessons on to her daughters. After graduating with honors from college, Olga's oldest daughter Renata signed up with Teach for America and recently completed a successful year teaching English as a Second Language to migrant children in rural Texas. And Caitlin seems to have absorbed the lessons into her writing, as if she herself had experienced the flight from Latvia and the long hot days in the cotton fields. In a poem in which she describes the experience of moving from one home to another, Caitlin captures something of what her grandparents may have felt: "In the Spring/masses of wildflowers twined and bloomed/calling our names with wide dragonfly mouths./My sister and I would hear them/on those quiet, tree-toad nights,/and once the morning sun cast/Venetian blind patterns on our faces,/we'd put on sandals and run outside."

* * * *

Flannery O'Connor once remarked that all people "start out with some kind of ability to tell a story (which) gets lost along the way." She added that "the ability to create life with words is essentially a gift. If you have it in the first place, you can develop it; if you don't have it, you might as well forget it."[2] There can be no doubt that Caitlin has the gift.

For Caitlin, writing has always been a spontaneous activity. "I'm pretty bad at talking about why I write or where I get my ideas. It's a struggle for a lot of people, and I understand that. But for me, I do it because I just get the feeling; it's mostly a way for me to express myself," she said. "I always write when I have some sort of feeling. I don't just write when I feel apathetic .... It's actually a reliable friend. So, when I write, it's never with other people reading it in mind. I don't write to be published either, because then I probably would have stopped a long time ago."

Caitlin's approach to writing appears to run contrary to the wisdom of the process writing gurus, who emphasize self-conscious decision-making and the application of universal "techniques" to the writing process. Addressing a group of aspiring writers, Flannery O'Connor scoffed at the notion that storytelling could somehow be reduced to a neat universal formula: "I have very little to say about short-story writing. It's one thing to write short stories and another thing to talk about writing them .... The more stories I write, the more mysterious I find the process and the less I find myself capable of analyzing it."[3]

According to her mother, Caitlin rarely revises her work; once she sits down to write it's merely a matter of translating what is in her head to the paper. She sees something, hears a line, or talks with someone, and then she begins working on a story or a poem, without necessarily knowing where the characters are going to take her. Lena Stanlankovitch was astounded when she first discovered this. "When I went to see *Amadeus* and I was watching, when Salieri was looking at Mozart's work and couldn't find a single erasure ... I remember feeling that way ... You look at Caitlin's stuff, and she didn't cross out, no scribbling. She wrote it this way."

While it may appear that Caitlin does not work at her writing, this is not entirely true. She works, but her process may be so deeply internalized that it does not feel like work. In describing the character of optimal experiences, Mihayli Czikzentmihayli noted that such experiences involve a marked absence of self-consciousness. As action and awareness are merged, like the dance and the dancer in Yeats's famous poem,[4] the individual becomes oblivious to the passage of time and even to her own effort.[5]

If she is to continue on her currently successful path, spontaneity will continue to play an important role in Caitlin's development as a writer, but she will also need to continue developing her gift. After participating in workshops, both at CTY and in college, and struggling with editors, she is beginning to view her writing with a stronger critical eye. "I can tell when things are obviously good or obviously bad," she said. "Well, maybe not even that. I'm still pretty close to my work." She is reading more and with greater sophistication, and she is beginning to consider the professional options that will be available to her: "I'll probably write poetry for the rest of my life, but I think my fiction is what I'll try to capitalize on. ... I know that writing is pretty versatile, and if I've decided already that that's what I want to do, I can do it in lots of ways. Right now, I'm not worried about that."

Notes

1. Moravia, Alberto, personal communication. Eliot, T.S., "What Dante Means to Me."
2. O'Connor, Flannery, "Writing Short Stories," in *Mystery and Manners*, pp. 87–106.
3. Ibid.
4. *Among Schoolchildren*
5. Csikszentmihalyi, Mihalyi, "The Psychology of Optimal Experiences."

Conclusion
Part I: Outstanding Features of the American Educational Landscape*

For over a decade, the Center for Talented Youth has been promoting a distinctive vision of education — one which emphasizes serving the needs of the individual student and helping students to take advantage of the vast array of opportunities which exist both in and out of school. Examining the experiences described in the nine preceding chapters in light of CTY's educational philosophy and the findings of retrospective studies on highly successful adults may provide some insight into what constitutes an "appropriate" education for academically talented students. The features discussed below should be considered suggestive rather than exhaustive, aspects of an evolving model. Education is an in-

---

* An earlier version of this chapter was presented at the 1992 Eastern Educational Research Association's annual conference under the title, "Features of an Appropriate Education: Case Studies."

herently dynamic process, varying from individual to individual. While there will always be individuals who soar to great heights of accomplishment and make profound contributions to society in spite of the extreme disadvantages Robert Coles has called "the enormous assaults of the universe,"[1] attempts to delineate some of the factors involved in the development of talent may undoubtedly prove valuable.

The extent to which creative adult achievement depends on natural endowment or environmental factors is a subject of considerable debate. As the titles of early works on the subject imply (e. g., Galton's *Hereditary Genius* and Terman's *The Genetic Study of Genius*), "genius" was for a long time taken to be an inherited characteristic. In the hundred years since Galton began exploring human intelligence, dozens of rival theories have emerged, and the origins and precise nature of intelligence, creativity, genius remain elusive.[2]

From the beginning, CTY has avoided the mire of theoretical abstraction which permeates so much of the literature on giftedness, focusing instead on helping students to develop clearly defined talents in specific fields. Describing the success of CTY's forerunner, the Study of Mathematically Precocious Youth (SMPY) — a program founded by Julian Stanley to address the academic needs of students with exceptional mathematical talents — M.A. Wallach wrote: "What seems most successful for helping students is what stays closest to the competencies one directly cares about: in the case of SMPY, for example, finding students who are very good at math and arranging the environment to help them learn it as well as possible."[3]

Individuals come to the world with certain personality traits and embryonic abilities, talents which will only come to fruition through interaction with the environment. While it appears that only certain individuals are capable of exceptional attainments — the creation of masterpieces, the discovery of basic principles, the setting of records — Bloom estimates that 95% of the people in the world can learn anything that can be learned. And while he may exaggerate, there is certainly great wisdom in his observation that "societies that emphasize only minimal standards of competence are likely to produce only minimal levels of competence and talent."[4] In order for talents of a particular sort to flourish at a given time in a given place, there must be a positive cultural climate. "What is honored in a country will be cultivated there," Plato observed. David Henry Feldman went a step further in arguing that the unfolding of a particular talent is almost entirely bound by "co-incidence." From Feldman's perspective, "... it is an extremely delicate and precise set of processes that leads a child, a field, a stretch of time, a receptive culture, and a set of intellectual catalysts and organizing forces to create the conditions under which extraordinary achievement will flourish."[5]

Each of the factors discussed below appears with some consistency in the literature on the educational experiences of highly accomplished adults and prodigious youth. No attempt has been made to assign values to these factors or to construct a mechanistic model, as the evidence to support such exercises is speculative at best. The process of education is synergistic and indeterminate: certain factors will have played a more important role in the lives of certain individuals. For some, having had the chance to work with a mentor will have been the deciding factor — the event which began the transformation of a bored, uninspired student into an impassioned and creative individual. For another, the discovery of an intellectual peer group will have made the difference. What follows is a discussion of some of the factors that were important in the intellectual growth and academic success of the individuals who were interviewed for this study. For purposes of illustration, reference will also be made to the experiences and insights of some individuals who were interviewed for the study but whose experiences were not recorded in the first eight chapters.*

Significant factors in talent development:
- early and ongoing parental support and intellectual stimulation;
- early commitment followed by intense and continuous work in a specific field;
- a flexible educational environment with opportunities for individualized pacing and continual challenge;
- teachers who serve as role models and mentors, setting high standards, modeling and transmitting values as well as information;

---

* Donna, Sean, Elaine, George, and Howard (not their real names) are students who were interviewed for this enquiry but whose "cases" were not described in the first eight chapters. Their names are italicized to avoid confusion.

- opportunities for interaction with a peer group of similar interests and abilities;
- opportunities for out-of-school learning;
- various forms of environmental or personal stress which serve to focus the individual's energies;
- motivation.[6]

Family Life: Intellectual Stimulation, Values and Stress

Researchers have found that highly creative adults (adults who have made major contributions to society or a particular field of endeavor) generally come from households where there was plenty of intellectual stimulation and learning was highly valued. Cox, Daniel, and Boston reported that parental support played an extremely important role in the lives of the MacArthur Fellows they studied. "... Virtually all the parents let their children know the value supported without pushing .... The parents themselves read, and they read to their children. Most important, they respected their children's ideas."[7] In examining the lives of creative scientists, Mansfield and Busse found three important factors in child-rearing. Parents provided intellectual stimulation, maintained relationships with "low emotional intensity," and fostered autonomy in their children.[8] Similarly, Bloom emphasized the role of parents in transmitting intellectual values, including the love of learning and a belief in hard work, to his sample of scientists, mathematicians, and artists.

Every child and every parent in this study reported that reading together played a significant role in the child's upbringing. Similarly, individuals attached a great deal of significance to trips, visits to museums, conversations, church events, and other family activities. For many children, it was important to feel that they could talk with their parents as problems arose. Llewelyn, Laura, Jorgen and Stig reported that while they were growing up, their parents made sure that the family ate at least one meal together. Many of the parents said that they aspired to this arrangement. "Before we moved to the project," Naomi Green observed wistfully, "I tried to have it so everyone sat down at the table together at least for supper." At the supper table, family members often reviewed events of the day and hashed through problems, although sometimes the discussions were more intellectual, with topics ranging from politics to science.

Bloom and Gustin identified four levels of parental involvement in the middle to high school education of exceptional mathematicians:

> One group restricted their involvement mainly to moral support. A second group made sure their children had materials for their model building and experimentation. A third group, fathers mainly, worked together with their sons on projects and had discussions with them about math and science topics. Finally, the parents of five of the mathematicians were directly involved in arranging special opportunities for them — summer programs or early admission to college.[9]

While the traits exhibited by the individuals examined in this study did not necessarily fit neatly into one of these categories, Bloom and Gustin's observations do provide a useful framework for understanding the various parenting strategies.

Moral support was almost universal; most of the individuals had at least one parent with whom they felt comfortable discussing their interests and concerns. Jorgen stated that being able to talk with his parents helped him through some rough times. "I feel very lucky," he said. "Across the years, my parents have always been there to talk to." And his father agreed: "I feel that we have relationship with him that is very similar to the one that we had when he was two or three years old .... It's the same kind of acceptance and openness, and tenderness." In contrast, *Donna*, an exceptionally talented youngster from a working class family in rural Maine, did not feel that her parents appreciated her talents and interests. Her father was generally indifferent to her activities and her mother sometimes seemed "immature." Yet she felt that her mother was "the only person there for me. She's been good about that."

Materials for projects, computers, books, games were also fairly universally provided. For several years, Tyrell's education consisted almost exclusively of his exploration of his mother's library. Jorgen earned his first computer by getting good grades in school;

thereafter, software, new manuals and gadgets were made available to him and his brother on a regular basis. Michael's father nourished his interest in history with countless trips to museums, battlefields and other historic places. Trips to the local library were a daily ritual, and Michael constantly expanded his collection of books, war strategy games, and computer software.

While Jorgen, Stig, Michael, Laura, and Tyrell all were encouraged to explore their own interests, none were explicitly instructed or supervised by parents in their intellectual pursuits. Llewelyn and Bob, however, both had fathers who acted as their first mentors. Bob's father introduced him to photography and to the life of the mind; in Bob's attempts to make sense of the world, in his creative work, his father remains an important presence. Llewelyn's love of science can scarcely be separated from his interactions with his father: science is quite simply the subject of their relationship.

Bloom's fourth category of parental involvement — "those who were directly involved in arranging special opportunities for (their children)" — encompassed parents who exhibited traits from each of the previously discussed categories. The degree of parental activism ranged from Djuna's parents' reluctance to make any demands of the system to Dr. Rawls's work as his daughter's literary agent to Dr. Pastore's savvy educational diplomacy.

While Djuna had to argue with her parents to gain support for many of the modifications in her educational career — had to prove that attending summer programs or prep school was worthwhile — most parents took the initiative in identifying and pursuing supplemental programs for their children. Paradoxically, in the two families where fathers served as mentors, parents seemed less likely to seek programs aggressively or to apply intense pressure to the system. Had Bob's father lived longer, he might have taken a more active role in seeking appropriate opportunities for his son. Looking back, Bob's mother wishes that she had fought harder to protect his interests. While Llewelyn's parents were willing to make radical modifications to the conventional educational approach in home-schooling him for the first thirteen years of his life, they have looked to the school for a "normalizing" experience and thus have made few demands in recent years.

It is interesting to compare the experiences of the two families in which parents became deeply involved in trying to change school policies. Whereas the Nielsens' experiences might be characterized as a struggle against the system, the Pastores' experiences could be described as a transformation of the system. Children in both families had similar needs, and in both cases parents played active roles in attempting to make the system address those needs. A number of factors distinguished the two families' positions, however. Dr. Nielsen — a visiting professor at the local college, an introverted intellectual with a European manner and accent — was perceived by school officials as an outsider. His family had no strong social ties in the local community. In fact, many of their values and interests were in direct conflict with those of local officials. Dr. Pastore, on the other hand, is a fully integrated member of his community. A doctor with a thriving practice in the center of town, a member in good standing of the local country club, a deacon at a local church, and a neighbor to the Superintendent of Schools, he had every reason to believe that his concerns would receive fair consideration by local officials. Being an insider, and a savvy one at that, he was able to convince local officials that the interests of his son were identical with the interests of the school and the community. In Dr. Pastore's hands, "co-incidence" was not to be left to mere coincidence, but rather to be seized, shaped, and put to his service.

There is some disagreement among researchers about the sort of emotional climate which is most conducive to exceptional individual achievement. Thinkers in the humanistic tradition maintain that creativity is fostered when the home environment is supportive, tolerant and nurturing. On the other hand, Ochse and other critics of the humanistic tradition have found that stress is a common theme in the lives of great scientists, writers, artists, and thinkers. Isolation, bereavement, authoritarian control, rigid discipline, traumatic experiences, brutality, frustrations, deprivation filled the childhoods of many great individuals.[10] In *Children of Crisis*, Robert Coles observed that "many children the world over have revealed a kind of plasticity under far from favorable conditions that make the determined efforts of some parents to spare their children the slightest pain seem quite ironic."[11]

The individuals included in this study were certainly not exempt from suffering. Because he was different, Jorgen was ostracized, teased, and, on one occasion, savagely assaulted by his classmates. Tyrell was abused by a school system more interested in keeping him under control than in providing him with an education. Djuna grew up in a household with a level of stress that would usually be considered unhealthy. By American standards, Djuna's parents were extremely strict: while she was in high school, she was not allowed to receive phone calls during the week, and "disrespectful" conduct sometimes resulted in beatings. Bob, who lost his father while he was in high school, later learned to channel the grief into productive activities: in struggling to overcome a learning disability, he has been inspired by the memory of his father. To some extent, these individuals may have sought solace in their intellectual pursuits, but as Ochse has pointed out, sustained engagement in creative activities and the pursuit of excellence offers "a sense of positive control, mastery, and self-esteem."[12]

It would be absurd and irresponsible to suggest that cruelty — or what is considered cruelty in our society — should have any place in education or child-rearing. Although Djuna was treated harshly by her parents, they did care for her and want the best for her. However, honest research requires an honest examination of the facts, and there can be no doubt that many people raised under far from ideal circumstances have made tremendous contributions in the sciences, the arts, commerce, politics, succeeding where others who had all of the right opportunities failed.

Our failing as a society, evident in what the literary critic Hugh Kenner has called "our inattention" and inescapable, often aimless pursuit of "fun," may be that we are overly enchanted with adolescence.[13] A peculiar narcissism — a delusion of national innocence — propels us to extend childhood to absurd lengths and causes us to chafe at the idea that our task as parents and educators may simply be to challenge our children to take control of their own lives, to support their endeavors insofar as they allow us to do so, and not "to ask merely what is good for them but to ask instead what good might come of them."[14]

Early Involvement, Intense and Continuous Work in a Particular Field

A recent report commissioned by the Department of Labor found that the skills provided by a "liberal education" remain those most in demand in the workplace.[15] Future generations will need to be able to write, read, communicate, analyze and evaluate problems, draw conclusions, and carry out mathematical operations. These recommendations amount to little more than a rediscovery of the components of Jefferson's plan for "An Useful American Education," and as such should be applied to all students.

Reaffirming a commitment to the more visionary aspects of Jefferson's plan will involve creating opportunities for individuals to become engaged in the pursuit of a particular discipline at an early age and providing them with opportunities to develop relevant skills, habits, and thinking strategies. Ochse argues convincingly that the link between precocious development and early burn-out is essentially mythical. Most highly creative adults begin their output early and continue producing until late in life. In *The Structure of Scientific Revolutions*, Kuhn observed that paradigm shifts are almost always brought about through the efforts of scientists "who are either very young or very new to a field and thus not overly committed to its paradigms."[16] While this tendency may not be as evident in other fields of human endeavor, the habits formed in youth inevitably become the framework for the labors of a lifetime.

Writing in 1955, Pressey observed that certain opportunities are needed for the precocious individual to blossom: "expert instruction," "frequent and progressive opportunities for the exercise of the ability," "a close association with others in the field," and "frequent success experiences."[17] David Henry Feldman made essentially the same point when he wrote that "the opportunity to become engaged — to fall in love — with a field [of study] must be offered a child."[18]

In sports and music, we have no trouble recognizing the importance of early specialization. No sane person would think of suggesting that Jennifer Capriati be required to play junior varsity tennis or that Midori, in her childhood, should have been restricted to playing in youth orchestras. On the other hand, teachers and school officials are generally reluctant about allowing students to specialize in intellectual activities. "There is a general belief," wrote Pressey, "that intellectual precocity is somehow not quite healthy, is always a hazard to good social adjustment, and should be slowed down rather than facilitated."[19]

It might be suggested that in framing talents as disorders, educators and psychologists have created an iatrogenic illness known as "giftedness." Instead of being recognized as kids with talents to develop, the "gifted" are seen as patients in need of "treatment." The most common form of treatment, "enrichment," is also the one most likely to aggravate the disorder. One form of "enrichment" involves introducing students to a smattering of different fields without ever giving them the opportunity to explore anything in depth. As one victim of this sort of "enrichment" remarked, "I have learned to count to seven in German, French, Italian, Hebrew, and Spanish. I'm wondering — will I ever learn a language, really learn a language?"

There is of course some danger that one can specialize early only to discover that one is no longer interested in one's field of specialization. *George*, who whipped through three years of high school level math in one summer at CTY, experienced a crisis halfway into his second year of college when he found that he had lost interest in mathematics and computer science. "I was always encouraged to study math and science," he said. "I was never introduced to other ways of thinking." After a dark night of the soul in the computer room, he began taking art and writing classes and transferred to the landscape architecture department. Although he may not necessarily see it that way, as an eighteen-year-old sophomore at an outstanding university, *George* is in a fine position to explore other interests. In general, students with many talents — the type who will be successful in any field they choose — are most prone to this sort of problem.

In his youth, the great chemist Sir Humphrey Davy struggled with this very problem. "In minds of great power," he observed, "there is usually a disposition to a variety of pursuits, and they often attempt all branches of letters and science, and even the imitative arts; but if they become truly eminent, it is by devotion to one object at a time, or at most two objects."[20]

Oddly enough, early specialization may help students to overcome such a crisis of abundance. There is evidence that many of the habits and skills developed through early specialization are in fact transferable. And ultimately, it is always easier to change your mind while you are still young: if someone has started on a specialization early, she is also likely to discover early on whether or not it suits her.

With a few exceptions, most of individuals included in this study were thrilled when they were given the opportunity to delve into a particular field of interest. Llewelyn still maintains that receiving the Science Almanac for his ninth birthday was one of the most exciting experiences of his life. Michael nourishes his obsession with history by reading countless books, attending lectures, and visiting historic places. Ever since he received his first computer, Jorgen's greatest pleasure has been "exploring how computers work — just getting into the operating system and seeing what's going on there."

Caitlin may provide the best example of someone whose early specialization led to later success. With over forty publications in national magazines, she is already one of the most accomplished young writers of her generation. According to Dr. Rawls, she began writing on her own just after she started school. "The first things were written out phonetically. We couldn't read them, so we had no idea how good they were," he said. After a consultant from a Poets in the Schools Program recognized her talent and brought it to the attention of her father, Caitlin received continual encouragement and opportunities to work at her craft, expert instruction from a variety of teachers, and significant, if sporadic, peer support.

"I am certain," Alfred North Whitehead wrote, "that in education wherever you exclude specialism you destroy life." Certainly, if we wish young people to live life to its fullest and if we wish to develop a new generation of artists, scientists, and leaders, we must provide them with opportunities to explore in depth the fields where they show the greatest talent and interest.

A Flexible Learning Environment

At first glance, it might seem peculiar that Japan or Germany would wish to imitate any aspect of the American educational system considering their economic ascendancy and the results of recent international comparisons of achievement which show our students lagging behind in all subject areas. However, since 1984, when Prime Minister Nakasone created the National Council on Educational Reform, the Japanese have sought to strengthen their schools by allowing for more decentralization and flexibility. In particular, the Japanese are attracted to the idea that an education should be tailored to the individual child and are in the process of developing policies whereby high school students may enroll in university courses or even enroll in college before graduating. Similarly, new admissions guidelines adopted by the German university system permit the matriculation of students who have achieved a score of three or better on the College Board's German Advanced Placement Exam and two other A. P. exams.

While many recent reform efforts have sought to homogenize American education, the international community has focused on what has traditionally been one of the greatest strengths of our system. From the seventeenth century when Cotton Mather and many less illustrious figures graduated from college in their mid-teens to the present, flexible pacing, or acceleration (as the practice has also been called), has proven effective, both in its myriad practical incarnations and in a variety of experiments. Terman, for example, found a strong correlation between starting college early and having a career distinguished by superior achievement.[21] Along the same lines, Pressey found that "from 1880 to 1900, 29 percent of those graduating from Amherst at 19 became nationally known, as compared with 12 percent of those graduating at 22."[22] More recently, in an extensive meta-analysis of the literature on ability grouping and acceleration, Kulik and Kulik found that "academic benefits are striking and large in programs of acceleration for gifted students."[23] In light of what has been said above about the value of early engagement and on-going commitment to a particular discipline or field of endeavor, these findings are not surprising.

In *Flexible Pacing*, Cox and Daniel identified a number of strategies which, for the academically talented student, result in appropriate acceleration: continuous progress, compacting, advanced level courses, grade skipping, early entrance, concurrent or dual enrollment, credit/placement by examination. Other options include correspondence courses, mentorships, summer programs, and satellite courses.[24] As we have seen, the students included in this study benefited from various imaginative combinations of these strategies.

During six weeks at a CTY summer academic program, Jorgen completed the equivalent of two years of high school mathematics. When credit for his work and admission to a magnet high school were denied him, Jorgen skipped high school all together and enrolled in a highly selective university, where he achieved a 3.8 average in his first year and a 4.0 in his second. His brother Stig, who at 13 was the youngest student ever to gain admission to the Scandinavian university he is currently enrolled in, skipped four grades, completing four A. P. courses (he earned at least a four on each of the exams) and most of the requirements for an International Baccalaureate in the process. Similarly, Djuna successfully completed a calculus course and a physics course at the University of Chicago while still attending high school. Currently, she is an A student in the honors program at a highly competitive university. Tyrell and Bob, the only students in the study who were not provided with opportunities for acceleration, feel that they were cheated by the system.

The experiences of *Sean* — one of Julian Stanley's original proteges — are an optimal illustration of the case for flexible pacing. In fourteen months of Saturday classes, *Sean* completed the equivalent of four years of high school mathematics (Algebra I, Algebra II, Geometry, and Pre-Calculus); he skipped grades 7, 9, 10, and 12 and graduated from Johns Hopkins at the age of 17. Although radical acceleration initially caused *Sean* a great deal of anxiety, in the long run he is sanguine about his experience: "If it weren't for SMPY," he said. "I wouldn't be where I am today." At just a hair over thirty, *Sean* is already a fully tenured professor at an outstanding research university. "Usually people get tenured at 35 to 40, and they're tired," he added. "And usually you don't see people switch gears and say, 'good, now I can stop working on all this petty stuff and work on the two big problems of social science.' But I think I'm in the position where I can do that — probably because I have more energy .... It's been a big advantage to start my career five years earlier than my peers."

Critics generally attack flexible pacing and the resultant accelerated progress on two fronts. On the one hand, the advocates of "enrichment" claim that acceleration produces superficial, short-term learning. Their arguments are built on rigid assumptions about development and popular misinterpretations of research on "higher order thinking skills." More traditional critics worry about accelerants missing out on important social experiences. Their perspective is a peculiar artifact of the national obsession with adolescence, which might aptly be characterized in the words of social critic Bruce Springsteen as the "glory days" syndrome. While well meaning, these individuals simply cannot see beyond their own nostalgia for homecoming and the senior prom.

There is an overwhelming body of research which suggests that students who participate in flexibly paced mathematics courses, such as those offered by CTY, learn the material at least as well as they would in a normal classroom. Mills and Ablard observed that "despite the rapid pace of progression, these students ... demonstrated mastery of the material covered through both standardized achievement and in-house tests which assess both computational fluency *and* problem-solving abilities. In addition, the essentials of what they learned (was) retained, as demonstrated by subsequent academic performance."[25]

Billy, a National Mathcounts Champion in the fourth grade, had a problem when his teacher tried to make him learn "estimation" skills — one of the higher order thinking skills that recent reforms have emphasized. *Billy* saw no reason to estimate the answers to the problems his teacher gave him when he could just as easily find the precise solution. Why say that five times nine is about 50 when you know that it's 45? Because his teacher had a flexible attitude, she was able to see that there was no reason to dwell on the issue: if Billy ever found himself in a situation where he needed to make an estimate, he would figure it out. As was noted earlier, Stig was less fortunate when he decided to do a book report on *Macbeth* while still in the fourth grade: his teacher simply wouldn't allow it.

Commentators from James B. Conant to Theodore Sizer have suggested that promotion should be based on mastery rather than a rigid K-12 lock-step.[26] An ever-growing body of research suggests that students learn most effectively when the material they are studying is presented just above the level at which they are currently functioning — when they are forced to "stretch."[27] In an article in *The Atlantic Monthly*, Daniel J. Singal reported that a general "dumbing down" of the curriculum has been accompanied by a reluctance to "stretch" students. "In place of 'stretching' students," Singal wrote, "the key objective in previous eras, the goal has become not to 'stress' them .... Placing serious academic demands on them, it is thought, might impede their natural development and render them neurotic."[28]

It is a time-honored cliche that flexible pacing, especially acceleration, leads to social maladjustment. In fact, if anything, flexible pacing tended to have a positive effect on the social lives of the students in this study. For Jorgen and Laura, early college entrance was an exhilarating experience. According to his parents, his brother, and the director of admissions at his college, Jorgen was happier and better adjusted than he'd ever been in school. After his first year of college, the 14-year-old Jorgen said: "When I came to college, I found that it was just like I had wanted high school to be. It was fun and it was a challenge ...." In addition to his academic work, Jorgen participated in a variety of extra-curricular activities: he acted in *Macbeth*, took part in the Russian club, and supervised the University's computerized classroom. And whereas he'd been something of an outcast in school, he made quite a few friends in college.

Sean admits that he might have had a different sort of social life if he had gone through school at a regular pace, but socializing was never a priority. "Maybe I would have fallen in love with a cheerleader," he said. "But I doubt it. I'm very studious. I work hard at my research ... I like to have a few close friends, not a huge circle of friends. I don't feel that I've missed much."

Mentors

Opportunities for flexible pacing arise when the educational climate is such that individuals are encouraged to develop their talents and learning is seen as a continuous process indistinguishable from life itself. Creating an environment of this sort depends on the efforts of both administrators and teachers; in particular, teachers must be able to play the role of mentors for their students, coaxing and prodding, encouraging and instigating, providing guidance and modeling the behaviors associated with success. Like Telemachus's guide, the original mentor, a teacher must have a thorough knowledge of the field that he instructs, but he must also have a sense of the larger context and an ability to adapt his guidance to the individual's needs.

In a study of mentor relations, E. Paul Torrance found that only "nine percent of ... mentors were elementary or secondary school teachers or counselors."[29] In drawing a distinction between teachers and mentors, Linda Silverman inadvertently points out one of the tragic flaws in our assumptions about what a teacher should and shouldn't be. "The difference between the teacher and the mentor is the more personal nature of the interaction with the student," Silverman observes. "The mentor is more of a facilitator of learning experiences than a disseminator of information."[30]

It is precisely because we often expect teachers to serve only as "disseminators of information" that so few function as mentors. If teachers are neither masters of the subject they teach nor willing and demanding guides, then they deserve neither the attention nor the respect of their pupils. "Authority," Rousseau observed, "derives from legitimacy." Children are not hoodwinked by "teacher-proof" curricula and other gimmicks, which perpetuate mediocrity while demoralizing and undercutting the credibility of those teachers who might otherwise have the ability to serve as mentors.

Julian Stanley has described in some detail the role played by a mentor in the classroom: "A mentor must not function didactically as an instructor, predigesting the course material for the mentee. Instead, he or she must be a pacer, a stimulator, clarifier, extender."[31] At the highest levels of study, work with a mentor becomes particularly important. According to Ochse, what is to be gained from working with a mentor is "a style of thinking, a method of working, standards, values, attitudes ... and the *music*" of their discipline.[32] Of course, on the elementary and secondary levels, an effective teacher/mentor must be able to combine direct instruction with "coaching," modeling of skills, and Socratic discussion, depending on the context.

Each of the students in the study has observed the failings of a system in which teachers are neither accountable nor responsible. "You couldn't talk to them," Tyrell observed about the teachers at his junior high school. "None of them knew anything about the place we lived, and none of them cared." Bob told of a teacher who regularly sat in the front of his class reading the newspaper. Jorgen had a teacher who merely talked about whatever happened to be on her mind. Yet, each of these students and each of the students in the study could point to at least one person who had taken a personal interest in him and helped him to develop his abilities. Even though the system had essentially given up on Tyrell, he had an English teacher who encouraged him to work on his writing and helped him to get on the school newspaper. Later, Audrey Rose played a huge role in his life, first by tutoring him and then by introducing him to a variety of new opportunities. Jorgen's Latin teacher used a free period to provide him with personalized instruction. Bob's photography teacher provided both personal and professional guidance — teaching him techniques, helping him to find jobs as a photographer, and ultimately showing him the value of staying in school.

Quite a few students found their mentors outside of school. Caitlin worked closely with Lena Stanlankovitch, her instructor at the art institute, and was deeply influenced not only by her advice on writing but also by her example. For Laura and *Elaine*, attending CTY provided an invaluable opportunity to work with "real scientists." "It was the challenge the teacher provided," said Laura. "The atmosphere of being in a real college course; that's what made it so exciting." "I learned that I love genetics," said Elaine, who went on to do an internship at the National Institute for Health. *Donna* was deeply impressed with her math instructor at CTY. "At first, we'd start out with simple problems and then each lecture would get deeper and deeper. By the end we were doing things that I'd never thought about .... And it said — there was so much you could do with math!" she exclaimed.

What Theodore Sizer has called the "personalizing" of education is an absolute imperative. Administrators must provide an atmosphere in which personal initiative is encouraged and the pursuit of excellence is demanded. Until an atmosphere is created in which teachers are expected to have a thorough knowledge base and enthusiasm for the subject that they teach and until teachers are given the responsibility for what goes on in their classes, the sorts of mentor relationships described above will remain the rare exception in our schools.

Peers

In his memoir, *The World As I See It*, Albert Einstein wrote: "Without the sense of fellowship with men of like mind, of pre-occupation with the objective, the eternally unattainable in the field of art and scientific research, life would have seemed to me empty."[33] Young people especially need opportunities to interact with individuals "of like mind" — people who will entertain unusual questions, who will appreciate new ideas and the intellectual curiosity that generates them, people who will compete with them, challenging and helping them to stretch in the pursuit of excellence.

In recent years, there has been a tendency to view all programs which group individuals with like abilities as elitist. This attitude has grown out of the current devotion to cooperative learning, which many view as the elusive panacea to all of our educational woes. While many of the practices embodied by cooperative learning are both sound and effective, doing away with all ability grouping will produce more problems than it will solve. Students learn most effectively from those whose skill levels are slightly higher than their own: when the gap is too large, the students who are doing the instruction tend to lose patience while the students who are being instructed may become embarrassed or withdrawn.[34]

Students who attend CTY and similar programs invariably rate the opportunity to interact with peers as one of the most rewarding aspects of the experience. Students attending magnet schools or early admission programs or participating in high-powered competitions report similarly exciting experiences.

After being ostracized and bullied by the children at his school, Jorgen was thrilled to find a peer group at CTY. "At once I got along with other students," he observed. "I seemed to make more friends in a couple of days than I had in a couple of years." *Howard*, an introverted science buff, made a similar observation: "I couldn't imagine there was a place where you could talk about cosmological geometry, science fiction, and chess strategy."

Donna's experiences illustrate the frustrations an academically talented and highly motivated student may experience when she does not find an appropriate peer group at school.

> Every time I'll be sitting with my friends at lunch, I'll come up with this remark, and they'll stare at me. And it'll be like what did I say wrong? And they'll think it's really strange. And sometimes I do it just to annoy them. I don't know; it's like there are two halves of me. One half wants to have friends .... And one half just wants to be by myself ....

The sense of being odd, of not fitting in, is widespread among students with talents and interests which diverge from the norm. This can be damaging to the individual's self-esteem. Like Llewelyn, who started using hairspray and cheating on tests so that his classmates would think that he was normal, *Donna* finds herself pretending to be unintelligent. "I've noticed I'm starting to act dumb, just so I won't get the reputation of acting smart all the time," she said. "So, it used to be that I would say these remarks that were smart to them, and they'd look at me for that. Now, they're looking at me because I'm making these remarks that are stupid."

Attending a summer academic program at CTY was a revelation for *Donna*. "I went down there," she said. "And there were people just like me. There were lots of them in huge proportions .... I didn't make friends until halfway through the session, but when I did, we just clicked — like that." *Elaine*, on the other hand, initially resisted attending "nerd camp," professing a preference for sports camp. Now, after attending five CTY sessions, she corresponds with a half-dozen classmates and attends informal reunions every Thanksgiving and Christmas. "We're a very close-knit group," she explained.

While one parent noted that participating in CTY programs had made it difficult for her daughter to accept the social conditions back at her local school, most students reported that they felt better equipped to get along with others after having had the opportunity to make friends. "The next year at school when I skipped a grade," said *Donna*, "I had to make new friends, and that was easier, because I had just done that at CTY .... It was easier to talk to people and all of that."

Out of School Opportunities

Commenting on the plethora of educational opportunities currently available outside of schools, the historian Lawrence Cremin wrote:

> The development of new and more varied forms of education in an ever more extensive range of sites and situations ... expanded the availability of education by making opportunities for teaching and learning more diverse in method, substance, and timing .... Courses in libraries, museums, zoos, planetariums, botanical gardens, historical societies, and national parks ... supplemented the books, exhibits, and presentations that were their common fare, enabling the interested inquirer to gain knowledge and to deepen appreciation and understanding.[35]

Given the nature of opportunities available in society at large, one might reasonably argue that there are many things which are best learned about outside of school. There are numerous examples of highly accomplished and creative individuals whose education was carried out wholly or at least in part in the home: among others, Franklin Delano Roosevelt, Frederick Douglass, John Stuart Mill, Thomas Edison, Nicolas Tesla, Noel Coward, and women writers from the Brontes to Virginia Woolf. The account of Llewelyn's education in the Alaskan bush illustrates amply the rich possibilities of an education which draws on all available resources, skirting the limitations of a conventional curriculum. Describing the experience of homeschooling his children, David Guterson made some incisive observations about the passivity with which most parents approach the process of educating their children. "In a better world," he wrote, "we would see ourselves as responsible and our schools primarily as resources. Schools would cease to be places in the sense that prisons and hospitals are places; instead, education would become embedded in the life of the community, part of the mechanics of democracy, and all would feel a devotion to its processes."[36]

Many of the families considered in this inquiry approached education with the sense of responsibility described by Guterson and a commitment to seeking out the broadest array of opportunities. Caitlin took writing classes at the community art center and traveled with her family to Nepal. The Pastores often designed family vacations and trips to satisfy Michael's interest in visiting battlefields, old ships, and other historic places. The Nielsens regularly attended operas and plays and spent long hours exploring the local parks. Even after Llewelyn had enrolled in school, his parents continued to find ways to make other educational opportunities available to him through travel, visits to museums, and encounters with interesting adults from the community. In essence, families used community resources — theaters, universities, museums, parks, etc. — to develop interests and nurture talents beyond the scope of schooling.

Although they don't always do so, most schools are fairly well equipped to provide a basic liberal education, encompassing those skills needed for productive participation in society. Providing mentors who can assist students to develop higher levels of competence in their fields of specialization remains an elusive ideal on the primary and secondary levels. Many of the students considered in this work had to find mentorship and opportunities for the intensive work required by specialization outside of their schools. Some took advantage of the offerings of local colleges and summer programs like the Talent Identification Program of Duke University, the Center for Talent Development at Northwestern University, CTY, as well as other state and regional programs. A few of the most talented benefited from the information and guidance provided by SMPY (now the Study of Exceptional Talent).[37] Still others had to struggle on their own to create opportunities.

Cremin has pointed out that, in spite of the ever broadening array of educational opportunities available outside of schools, for a variety of reasons large segments of our society continue to rely wholly on the schools for the education of their children.[38] In fact, it is precisely the people who are the most in need of opportunities which go beyond the narrow focus of a lock-step school curriculum, needing to see the relevance of learning to their lives, who have been cut off from the genuine enrichment provided by the cultural institutions and other community resources. Youngsters growing up in inner cities or in isolated rural areas, youngsters whose primary culture or language is not that of the mainstream, are those most in need of the genuine enrichment which must take place outside of the schools.

To address the need for a rational organization of out-of-school opportunities, Dr. Richard Chase, of The Johns Hopkins University School of Medicine and CTY, has designed the Baltimore Learning Network — a coalition of educational resources, including museums, libraries, the National Aquarium, the zoo, theaters, and other cultural, voluntary, government, and business organizations. An interactive computer system, the Baltimore Learning Network will link these organizations and provide children with information about courses, workshops, special events, club memberships, and apprenticeships. Ideally, this system should break down the barriers between various institutions, expanding students' understanding of education and providing them with access to resources they might otherwise never encounter. After piloting the project in Baltimore, Dr. Chase hopes to expand it to other parts of the nation and the world, so that education may once again become an activity which takes place "everywhere and anywhere."[39]

Motivation

"Don't let them see how hard you work," Hemingway once wrote, crystallizing one of the paradoxes of all creative endeavor — that it demands full attention and absolute devotion, yet if done properly should appear effortless, as natural and elegant as the rain or internal combustion.

Virtually every study on successful adults places a great deal of emphasis on motivation; ultimately, it is seen as the factor which separates those who make contributions from those who do not and those who make small contributions from those who create masterpieces or shift paradigms. Unfortunately, the nature of motivation itself is rarely explained in a satisfactory manner.

Mansfield and Busse identify three motivational characteristics which influence the lives of creative scientists: "need to be original and novel," "need for professional recognition," and "commitment to work."[40] However, they do not provide a satisfactory explanation for the sources of these characteristics. Bloom describes motivation in terms of increasing autonomy.[41] In the early and middle years (through high school), parents and teachers play an important role in motivating students, through example, rewards, and expectations. In varying degrees, as the student matures, Bloom sees him or her taking more and more responsibility for work.

In contrast with much of recent thought, Ochse emphasizes extrinsic motivation over intrinsic motivation. Individuals engage in creative endeavors to make money, win fame, or to gain recognition from peers. "Lack of concern for goals would prevent the completion of creative works," she writes, "and creators typically complete a great number of products."[42] According to Ochse, intrinsic motivation — which arises when an individual performs certain tasks without any thought to external rewards or repercussions — is more important for the child who is learning than in it is for the adult who is creating. Her conclusion is that "the motivation to create may be initiated by satisfactions inherent in independent intellectual activity, but it is maintained by expectations of the extrinsic rewards that are gained by using the knowledge and skill . . . ."[43]

If one is to accept the comments of both Bloom and Ochse, one must conclude that motivation becomes increasingly autonomous at the same time that it is sustained more and more by extrinsic factors. Elements of this pattern were evident in the lives of the students examined in this inquiry. Michael's interest in history arose independently and as an end in itself. He made no distinction between reading books on ancient Macedonia and playing video games. While Jorgen needed his parents input to get inspired about his schoolwork, it was the reward he received from them — his first computer — which became the impetus for further motivation. Just as Michael approached the study of history as an end in itself, Jorgen approached the computer and its operating system as end in itself.

Other sources of motivation cited by students included competing with peers, receiving recognition through contests and the Talent Search, attempting to impress a favorite teacher, trying to win affection from parents, and solving a challenging problem. Caitlin's experiences merit particular attention. Caitlin was certainly attracted to writing for intrinsic motives: for whatever reason, she simply enjoyed the act of writing. As her father put it, "writing was what she did with her spare time." Working with a variety of mentors, receiving positive feedback from her parents, teachers and peers reinforced her interest and strengthened her motivation. As her writing became a means of making money and receiving recognition through publication and awards, extrinsic factors began to play more of a role in her continued desire to write. Gradually, Caitlin has begun to rely less and less on her father's assistance in her writing: although he still plays an important role as a business manager for her, he no longer proofreads the manuscripts she sends out. While increased autonomy certainly plays a role in Caitlin's life, she still feels that her motivation to write is as much intrinsic as it is extrinsic.

The distinction between extrinsic and intrinsic motivation is in many respects unsatisfactory — suffering from a problem common to psychological models: the tendency to fragment the human experience into component characteristics or factors. If one is to believe what scientists, artists, inventors and other highly creative people have said about their work, then one must recognize that motivation is a combination of intrinsic and extrinsic factors, inexorably linked. Dostoevski wrote *Crime and Punishment* with the creditors at his doorstep, yet it would be a mistake to think that the writing was done without a sense of mystery.

Addressing the finalists of the 1991 Westinghouse Talent Search, the physicist Frank Wilczek spoke of the "romance of science." Similarly, in an essay in the New York Times Book Review, Octavio Paz described poets as people who listen to "the other voice."[44] This sense of romance, of wonder and awe, bordering at times on mysticism, is not unusual among great creators. It seems that the original impetus, which Aristotle called "the desire to know," helps to sustain the individual throughout a career. As the creative individual matures, however, the desire to make a contribution increases. This desire is nowhere more in evidence than in the writings of Jorge Luis Borges, who imagined all of literature as one and framed authorship as a struggle against the labyrinthine workings of time.

The three forms of adult motivation identified by Mansfield and Busse — the need to be original and novel, commitment to work, and the need for professional recognition may have their precursors in the education of children. The need to be novel and original conceivably grows from the parental relationship, is stimulated by interaction with peers, and crystallizes in the working relationship with a mentor. In a flexible environment, where the student is allowed to progress at his or her own pace and where the artificial barriers between school and other learning environments are minimized, the student can begin to develop a commitment to work and a sense of autonomy. Finally, the need for professional recognition is no doubt developed through parental expectations, competition and collaboration with peers, and through association with a mentor who provides a model of dedication to the highest standards.

Summary

It remains to be seen whether or not any of the individuals whose experiences were described in this inquiry will go on to make valuable contributions in his or her chosen field of endeavor. No attempt is made at prediction. Most have taken advantage of a broad array of opportunities available in the American educational landscape. If one considers their experiences in light of the findings regarding individuals who have gone on to make important contributions, one cannot help but notice certain similarities.

Like many creative individuals, most of the students examined here had parents who valued intellectual pursuits and the hard work associated with such pursuits. They were read to as children and were encouraged to develop their own interests. While the degree of parental support and involvement in these pursuits varied, almost all felt that much was expected of them and that their endeavors were respected. The emotional relationships between parents and children were varied to the point of defying generalization. None of the individuals spoke of feeling pushed by parents; decisions, it seemed, were generally reached through negotiation and consensus.

Educational flexibility was generally valued by all of the individuals included in this inquiry. The students seemed to have a strong sense of what they wanted out of their educational experiences, of what was worthwhile and what was simply an obstacle to their growth. In navigating the intricacies of the school system, attempting to develop optimal educational experiences, many of the students cemented their determination to succeed. For some, various forms of stress — the pain of being ostracized or picked on by classmates or family pressures — may have helped to focus energies on creative pursuits. Already in their early teens each student had at least a general idea of the field they hoped to pursue in adulthood: and many had already achieved notable accomplishments.

Almost all of the students received much of their education outside of school in structured or unstructured settings. And while these opportunities were not always clearly directed at the student's specific needs or interests, they often provided valuable intellectual stimulation and occasionally eclipsed school all together as the source of an individual's seminal intellectual experiences. Many of the students cited experiences at programs like CTY, CTD, and TIP as the most challenging and valuable of their lives. Although the sample used in this enquiry was neither random nor large enough to justify sweeping generalizations, one may still conclude that many students find important opportunities to explore their specialties outside of school with mentors who are not a part of the official educational apparatus. In the future, systems such as the Baltimore Learning Network, described above, will expand the role played by out-of-school opportunities.

Whether they did so in school or out of school, most of the individuals included in this work found mentors who provided them with intellectual stimulation and encouragement and modeled the values and behaviors associated with attainment in their field of interest. More important than any theoretical model of intellectual development were these encounters between apprentice and mentor. These encounters are what set students on fire, gave them inspiration and helped them to focus their lives.

Critics of the recent worsening in social and economic conditions in the United States have pointed to a failure to invest in human capital.[45] If we are to remain competitive as a nation, there is no doubt that we will need to make significant investments in the education of our children. Simply "throwing money" at the problem will not provide any solutions, but the features of an outstanding American education outlined above may provide some guidance to those who seek to improve the quality of our educational offerings.

Every child comes into the world with the desire to learn. A responsible society attempts to create conditions which optimize that potential. Beyond providing everyone with the basic skills necessary to participate productively in society, it is important that we identify those individuals with outstanding abilities in particular areas and provide them with the means to develop them. If we can broaden the scope of our efforts and provide opportunities to students who have previously been excluded from programs which promote acceleration, flexibility, and early involvement with a particular field, we can only stand to benefit. If not, the future presents a bleak landscape indeed.

Notes

1. Coles, Robert, *Children of Crisis: Volume 1*, p. 381.
2. For a concise description of some of the major theories of intelligence see Pendarvis, Howley, & Howley, *The Abilities of Gifted Children*, pp. 44–78.
3. Wallach, M.A. "Care and Feeding of the Gifted," p. 616–617, cited from Stanley, J.C. and Benbow, C.P. "Youths who reason exceptionally well mathematically," p. 1.
4. Bloom, p. 18.
5. Feldman, D.H., *Nature's Gambit*, p. 172.
6. Sources consulted include: Terman, *The Genetic Study of Genius* and *The Gifted Child Grows Up*; Cox, The early mental traits of three hundred geniuses Pressey, "Concerning the Nature and Nurture of Genius"; Mansfield and Busse, *The Psychology of Creativity and Discovery: Scientists and Their Work*; Bloom, B., *Developing Talent in Young People*; Cox, Daniel, and Boston, *Educating Able Learners*; Ochse, *Before the Gates of Excellence*; and Gallagher, "The Gifted, A Term with Surplus Meaning."
7. Cox, Daniel, & Boston, p. 24.
8. Mansfield and Busse, pp. 65–83.
9. Bloom, p. 296.
10. Ochse, pp. 73–77.
11. Coles, *Children of Crisis: Volume I*, p. 323.
12. Ochse, p. 167.
13. Kenner, Robert "Don't Get De-Geniused."

14. Coles, *Children of Crisis: Privileged Ones*, p. 329.
15. Secretary's Commission on Achieving Necessary Skills, *What Work Requires of the Schools*.
16. Kuhn, *The Structure of Scientific Revolution*.
17. Pressey, "Concerning the Nature and Nurture of Genius."
18. Feldman, D.H., *Nature's Gambit*, p. 95.
19. Pressey, p. 125.
20. Bolton, S.K., *Famous Men of Science*, p. 142.
21. Terman, *The Gifted Child Grows Up*, pp. 265–279.
22. Pressey, p. 128.
23. Kulik & Kulik, "Ability Grouping and Gifted Students," p. 191. For a list of other sources on the subject see the Introduction, note 4.
24. Daniel, N. & Cox, J., *Flexible Pacing for Able Learners*, p. 2.
25. CTY Technical Report No. 8, "Young Students' Achievement Follow-up," p. 8.
26. The "Gary System" described by Lawrence Cremin in *The Transformation of the School* is an early progressive attempt at individualizing education (pp. 156–157). Unfortunately, many of the best progressive curricular experiments never took hold.
27. Csikszentmihalyi, M., "Toward a psychology of optimal experience."
28. Singal, "The Other Crisis in American Education," p. 67.
29. Torrance, E.P., *Mentor Relationships*.
30. Silverman, Linda Kreger, "Mentorships," p. 4.
31. Stanley, J.C., "How to use a fast-pacing math mentor," p. 1. See also Lupowski, Assouline, & Stanley, "Applying a Mentor Model for Young Mathematically Talented Students."
32. Ochse, p. 92.
33. Einstein, *The World As I See It*, p. 238.
34. See Mills & Tangherlini, "Finding the Optimal Match: Another Look at Ability Grouping and Cooperative Learning."
35. Cremin, Lawrence, *American Education: The Metropolitan Experience*, p. 647.
36. Guterson, David, "When schools fail children," p. 14.
37. In order to qualify for the Study of Exceptional Talent's services, a student must meet one or more of the following criteria: 1) score 700–800 on SAT-M before age 13; 2) score 640–690 SAT-M before age 13 (females only); 3) score 630–800 before age 13.
38. Cremin, L., *American Education: The Metropolitan Experience*, p. 648.
39. Chase, R.A., "Baltimore Learning Network."
40. Mansfield and Busse, p. 57.
41. Bloom, pp. 515–527.
42. Ochse, p. 139.
43. Ochse, p. 148.
44. *New York Times Book Review*, Dec. 8, 1991.
45. Hornbeck and Salamon, *Human Capital*.

PART II

The Skills Reinforcement Project: A Program for Academically Talented Inner-City Youth

On November 20, 1985, thirty years after the Supreme Court declared in Brown versus the Board of Education that desegregation must go ahead "with all deliberate speed," Judge Leonard B. Sand of the United States District Court in Manhattan, ruled that the city of Yonkers, New York had "illegally and intentionally" segregated public schools and public housing on the basis of race. In his decision, Judge Sand observed a practice of "consistent and extreme" segregation dating back to the National Housing Act of 1949 and continuing "unbroken" to the present. The discriminatory practices of city and school officials, Sand found, "clearly worked to the disadvantage of minority students, who for many years received their educational instruction in generally inferior facilities, from generally less experienced staff, in generally more overcrowded, unstable conditions."[1]

North of the Bronx, across the Hudson from New Jersey, and just south and west of some of the wealthiest towns in Westchester County (one of the wealthiest counties in the nation), Yonkers is both a big city with the gamut of big-city problems and a small town of neighborhoods, driveways, manicured lawns and intricate tribal politics. Suspicion, fear, and the Saw Mill River Parkway have historically divided white from minority, and middle class neighborhoods from the inner city. In 1985, all of the city's 7000 public housing units were concentrated in the southwest, a predominantly black and Latino section of the city. By the end of 1991, 142 units were under construction at five sites on the eastern side of the city, but some members of the City Council and many residents continued to resist the court order so that, in 1992, housing in Yonkers remains largely segregated.

After Judge Sand handed down his ruling, the Board of Education, in contrast with the City Council, acted swiftly to devise a plan for desegregation of the schools. The plan, based in part on the city of Buffalo's experiences, was designed to inspire voluntary participation while serving as a catalyst for school improvement. At the heart of the plan were three basic modifications: re-drawing attendance lines, closing some neighborhood schools, and creating new magnet schools to attract students from all parts of the city. Participation in the magnet schools, as Superintendent of Schools Dr. Joan M. Raymond envisioned them, was to be entirely voluntary.

In April of 1986, taking into consideration changes recommended by the NAACP and the Justice Department (co-plaintiffs in the suit against Yonkers), Judge Sand accepted the essential features of the Board of Education's plan. Judge Sand's revised plan called for quicker implementation, more radical changes in the drawing of district boundaries, and broader use of magnet programs. Judge Sand also suggested a mechanism whereby desegregation could be coupled with choice: school assignments would be based on a ballot filled out by parents on which they would indicate three schools of preference, including at least one choice that would advance the goal of desegregation.[2]

Despite an appeal of Judge Sand's ruling filed by the City Council, the Board of Education went ahead with its desegregation plan when the schools opened in September of 1986. Initially, many students felt out of place in their new schools. Buses were often late, and fights occasionally broke out. In the first two years of desegregation there was some white flight from the schools, with the number of non-minority students declining by 18.5%, but there were never any violent, Boston-style protests. Gradually, the magnet programs gained in popularity, so that by 1988 there was actually a growth in the non-minority population in the early elementary grades. Two years after Judge Sand's ruling, the Yonkers City schools were essentially desegregated, and while busing remained unpopular, students and parents had learned to live with the new system.

While the ease with which the school desegregation plan had been implemented was cause for celebration, certain fundamental problems remained. On September 25, 1988, Pace University Provost Dr. Joseph M. Pastore Jr., appointed by Judge Sand to oversee the court order, told the *New York Times* that a disparity between white and minority achievement was threatening to undermine the process. "The schools are desegregated, but the question is: Are they integrated?" said Dr. Pastore. "When you get a wide range of scores and results within the same setting, it just heightens the hostility between the races," Pastore said. "It reinforces notions of inferiority on the part of minorities and can lead to surface-level conclusions on the part of whites."[3]

The achievement gap between white middle class students and minority or financially disadvantaged students is by no means particular to Yonkers. Whereas providing access to more experienced teachers and superior facilities and conditions should, in theory, result in improved performance, this is unfortunately not always the case.

For years, social scientists have struggled to develop theories to explain the relationship between class, race, and academic achievement. Some have argued that the schools are instruments of the dominant capitalist system, rewarding the cultural experiences and values of the upper classes while penalizing those of the lower classes.[4] From this perspective, schooling amounts to a form of class warfare. In an essay entitled "Social Triage Against Black Children," Andrew Oldenquist takes exception to this perspective, arguing that the academic performance of disadvantaged students has suffered in recent years precisely because teachers and administrators have exerted too much energy trying to accommodate their cultural experiences. He claims that black students in particular have been victimized by the assumption that "hard work and a work ethic, promptness and accuracy, and civility cannot reasonably be imposed on children in black slums, that the 'value systems' of children in black slums require different kinds of traits."[5]

While each of these perspectives is extreme, the importance of institutional expectations in the education of the individual child cannot be exaggerated. In Part One of this book, a number of crucial factors influencing academic success were identified. Among these factors, academically challenging coursework and mentorship relations depend almost entirely on the expectations of teachers and administrators. If a teacher has minimal expectations of a child, he is unlikely to demand her best performance or to ask her questions that will stretch her problem-solving abilities. If a teacher believes that a child is destined for failure, he will certainly not invest the time and effort to develop the deep personal understanding required in a mentor relationship. High expectations alone, however, will no more guarantee academic success than well-lighted classrooms: they are merely a necessary pre-condition for programs which provide rigorous and challenging opportunities.[6]

Jane Smith*, a former teacher and long-time observer of education in the Yonkers City Schools, draws a sharp distinction between desegregation and integration. "Desegregation is just a matter of moving kids around so there's an equal distribution between minorities and non-minorities," she said. "Integration involves changing people's expectations and values, their biases. And that's everybody — from kids to teachers to administrators and central office, to the cafeteria workers."

Ms. Smith recognizes that it would be unrealistic to expect teachers who have spent most of their adult lives in a segregated environment to suddenly shed all of their prejudices. Still, she is alarmed by the extent to which some teachers have internalized certain stereotypes. "I had a colleague who told a parent — 'if I split my class and put all the smart kids over here, and all the not-so-smart kids over there, all the whites would be here and all the minorities would be there,' " Ms. Smith recounted. "I think some

---

* not her real name

teachers have lower expectations of minority kids, and most of them are not even conscious that this is the case."

In 1988, attempting to move beyond desegregation and achieve integration, the new Superintendent of Schools, Dr. Donald M. Batista, initiated Phase II of the Educational Improvement Plan, which includes a multi-cultural curriculum, workshops on human relations for students, teachers and parents, and smaller classes.[7] As Dr. Gladys Pack, Assistant Superintendent, describes it, Phase II is an effort to address the whole range of problems facing minority students.

> "We're looking at some of the other Johns Hopkins programs," she said. "We're looking at *Success for All* which focuses on grades 1–3, and it has possibilities for gifted children and all other children. We're looking at working on a curriculum that's more appropriate for the kids we have. I'm not sure that our curriculum is the most appropriate. And that's again, across the board. Providing additional support services, computer-assisted instruction. You know, direct support services. Better counseling. Better training for the counselors."

Phase II is being implemented with some success, but most people from Yonkers readily admit that much remains to be done. According to Dr. Pack, "there's still very much a gap — an achievement gap."

The Skills Reinforcement Project which has been implemented at the Nathaniel Hawthorne School in Yonkers shares a number of features with other programs that have successfully boosted minority student achievement, yet it is distinctive in many ways. Although a great deal of emphasis is placed on parental involvement and social support, the mainstay of the program is academics. Building on a foundation of high expectations, SRP instructors work with students to develop knowledge and skills in specific academic disciplines. In the tradition of CTY programs, the SRP focuses on English and mathematics, because these are the core subject areas on which later academic success is based.

The Nathaniel Hawthorne School

A yellow brick building with a broad cement staircase, wrought-iron rails, towering pillars, and high-minded mottos engraved on its facade, the Nathaniel Hawthorne School contains two schools within its walls: a magnet elementary school and a magnet junior high school for gifted children, grades 7–9. Inside, there is a warm, homey feeling. The fixtures are old but in good repair. The classrooms are large and sunny. Students move through the halls purposefully, serious about the business of schooling. In spite of its location — a few blocks from some of the toughest streets in southwest Yonkers — because of its reputation for academic excellence, discipline, and high standards, the Hawthorne school has no trouble drawing ambitious non-minority students from affluent sections of the east side. In fact, the middle school has a waiting list every year, with students from all over the city anxious to be accepted.

While the primary function of the magnet program was to create a balance between minority and non-minority students, a number of the teachers at Hawthorne feel that the overall quality of education has also improved. "I'm here eighteen years," said Bill Simon, an English teacher. "I think it's an improvement. More money, more supplies, more innovative programs came into the district because of the court order. How they have been implemented and used, that's a value judgement. But I certainly have been able to work better under the implementation of the desegregation order." Dr. Michael Yazurlo, the principal of the Hawthorne Middle School since 1988, echoes Mr. Simon's sentiments: "We have a tough program at Hawthorne: the expectations are high and we're challenging our students."

Early in his tenure as principal, however, Dr. Yazurlo became alarmed by the high incidence of underachievement and failure among minority students at Hawthorne. "Children at this age are affected by many factors: death, change of address, expectations, sexual awareness, peer pressure," he observed. "It's not cool to be smart: that's the hardest thing to turn around. You see a kid wearing a hundred and twenty dollar pair of sneakers and he doesn't have money to buy a notebook. That's a different value system."

Dr. Yazurlo, the 1990 Yonkers School Administrator of the Year, is aware of the complexity of the issues involved: he confronts them every day. "I don't tell anybody, but sometimes I can't sleep at night, because I go through these crises wondering how I'm going to deal with all these things," he said. It's a side he rarely shows at the office. His power fullback's build accentuated by the sleek Italian suits he favors, Dr. Yazurlo is an aggressive administrator — a hands-on person who keeps the door to his office open and the dialogue (with students, teachers, staff, and parents) going all day long. Whether he's urging maintenance to get the potholes filled in the baseball diamond or joking with a parent, there's no concealing that edgy Yonkers burr. He worked his way up through the ranks: starting as a science teacher, he's held positions as an academic dean, an elementary school principal, and for a while during the seventies (when Yonkers was in the depths of a fiscal crisis) as a mechanic in a garage he ran with his brother.

He may be a populist, but there is an unusual rigor in his thinking. In 1988 when he suggested that physics should be offered in the eighth grade (as it is in most European countries and Japan), the school board dismissed his suggestion. In 1990, Hawthorne sent its science team to the finals in the state's science Olympiad: the question that stumped the Hawthorne kids had to do with quantum mechanics. After that experience, Dr. Yazurlo swore to continue his battle for physics.

Going to school nights, Dr. Yazurlo earned his Ph.D. at Fordham University while on the job. He wrote a controversial dissertation in which he concluded that desegregation had not provided the solution to the academic woes of minority students in Yonkers. Once Dr. Yazurlo grabs hold of a problem, he has trouble letting go. He is a voracious reader, who usually has at least a half a dozen books going at once. But his preferred method of enquiry is face-to-face. "I'm a principal," he says. "I'm not a building administrator. The kids know that my door is always open. At a lot of schools, no one takes the time to talk to kids, to work things out. How else are you going to know what's going on?"

The problem of minority underachievement at Hawthorne is compounded by the selection criteria imposed by Judge Sand. In order to ensure that a racial balance was achieved, separate test score cut-offs were established for minority and non-minority students. While many minority students come to Hawthorne fully prepared to compete with their non-minority classmates in a rigorous academic setting, for a variety of reasons, some need opportunities to develop basic skills. In some cases, they have gaps in their academic background or they have not been exposed to truly challenging work before. Others have never developed effective study skills or work habits. In some cases, they lack self-confidence and an appreciation of academic accomplishment.[8] The same largely holds true for non-minority students from economically disadvantaged backgrounds. In order to make the Hawthorne school a success, Dr. Yazurlo's challenge was to find ways to help all the children in his school to realize their full potential.

The Skills Reinforcement Project

In 1988, when he became the principal of Hawthorne, Dr. Yazurlo decided to tackle the problem of minority underachievement and began spending all his spare time talking to minority parents and children, rummaging through books and journal articles, hunting for possible solutions. Eventually, he came across a reference to the Skills Reinforcement Project, a program designed by the Center for Talented Youth, which had been highly successful in meeting the needs of minority students in the Pasadena and Los Angeles public school districts.

In 1985, CTY initiated the Skills Reinforcement Project to serve the needs of students from racial, ethnic, and socio-economic backgrounds historically under-represented in programs for the gifted and talented. In Pasadena and Los Angeles, minority and financially disadvantaged sixth grade students whose standardized test scores were not high enough to qualify them for "gifted and talented" programs but were high enough to indicate the presence of a great deal of potential (80th to 96th percentile on in-level, nationally normed tests), were selected for participation in a rigorous year-round program in mathematics and language arts. During the school year, they met on Saturdays for three hours, and during the summer, they spent two weeks living on a college campus immersed in an intense academic program modeled on the Center for Talented Youth's academic programs.

In keeping with the CTY philosophy, SRP students take courses in the area where they demonstrate the greatest academic strength — mathematics or language arts. Classes are small and the teachers are subject specialists, experienced at tailoring the program to the needs of individual students. Initially, teachers seek to identify any gaps which might exist in a student's learning and focus instruction on those gaps. Once the gaps have been filled, instruction proceeds at a flexible pace, with emphasis being placed on the development of higher order thinking skills and abstract reasoning within the context of a specific discipline. SRP programs in Pasadena and Los Angeles produced encouraging results, both in terms of measurable achievement gains and improved student attitudes towards education.[9] Astonishingly, students participating in the SRP also showed consistent gains in aptitude, which calls into question the popular notion that aptitude is a fixed, inborn quality, suggesting instead that human intelligence is a dynamic system shaped by the continual interaction of genetic endowment and environmental factors.[10]

Traditionally, programs for minority or financially disadvantaged students have been "remedial" or "alternative" in nature. "Remedial" programs, which emphasize the weaknesses in a child's educational background, often have devastating affects on self-esteem. On the other hand, programs which focus exclusively on developing a student's self-esteem are often equally harmful, because they are based on the false presumption that students from certain racial, ethnic, or cultural backgrounds have different ways of thinking which preclude success in academic disciplines. They ignore the profound contributions that African Americans, indigenous Americans, and Hispanic Americans have made in science, medicine, literature, history, business, politics. Although well-intentioned, these programs do little to provide students with opportunities for ongoing success in academics or life. They raise expectations without nurturing intellectual talent or building a solid base of work habits and academic skills.

In his controversial book *The Content of Our Character*, Shelby Steele distinguishes between entitlement programs and development programs. According to Steele, entitlement programs which aim at equal representation instead of equality of opportunity contribute to minority students' feelings of inferiority and reinforce white students' stereotypes about the abilities of minority students. Steele sees entitlement as a cop-out, based on the white establishment's need for the illusion of innocence. "A preference is not a training program," observed Steele. "It teaches no skills, instills no values. It only makes color a passport."[11]

The popular media have chosen to focus on Steele's premature call for the dismantling of affirmative action programs, brushing aside the more distinctive implications of his work. If one follows his analysis carefully, one reaches a conclusion that poses a much greater challenge: affirmative action must become an upfront investment instead of a guilt-ridden afterthought. Genuine training programs are expensive and difficult to implement, requiring early intervention and sustained effort and providing no short cuts to redemption. However, if we are to right some of what Jonathan Kozol has called the "savage inequalities" of our system, we must be willing to provide minority and disadvantaged children with a broad array of opportunities to develop their intellectual capacities.

There is a significant body of evidence to suggest that programs stressing accomplishment can have a significant impact on the lives of inner-city youth. Headstart, for example, has been shown to improve test scores and raise individuals' chances of succeeding in school and career. Jaime Escalante has shown the impact of high expectations and academic rigor in his classes. Finally, Zweigenhaft and Domhoff demonstrated in their book, *Blacks in the White Establishment*, that economically disadvantaged black youths who attended prep schools through the program A Better Chance flourished in spite of the many social and cultural barriers they encountered.

The Skills Reinforcement Project provides students with the skills and work habits needed to take advantage of the academic and professional opportunities later in life. There can be no doubt that minority and economically disadvantaged students still face many obstacles in our society, but by experiencing early academic success in a challenging program, students gain a sense of empowerment. In attempting to develop a program which would address the needs of minority and disadvantaged students at Hawthorne, Dr. Yazurlo was particularly attracted by this aspect of the SRP model. "We take a little bit here, a little bit there," he said. "Whatever fits in with the overall vision of what we were trying to accomplish. And the basic ideas behind the SRP seemed to fit in well with what we were trying to do."

In the summer of 1990, with a grant from the Jacob Javits Foundation and guidance from the Center for Talented Youth, the Hawthorne school launched its Skills Reinforcement Project. In the first year, 90 students participated — 45 sixth graders and 45 seventh graders divided equally among math and language arts. They attended 20 classes on Saturday mornings during the regular school year and a residential site on the campus of Pace University for two weeks in the summer. Test scores showed improvements similar to those in previous SRP's, with the greatest gains being made in mathematics. Not only did the SRP students show more improvement than a minority control group, they also out-performed a non-minority control group, in terms of effect sizes (the rate of growth in an individual's abilities and achievement) — the implication being that for students participating in the project the gap was indeed narrowing between minority and non-minority achievement.[12] In the first year of the SRP, ten participants made the honor roll for the first time in their lives and two made the high honor roll. One student also distinguished herself on the school's Mathcounts team. In general, parents reported that their children were taking their school work more seriously, were working harder, and were watching less television.

SRP Teacher as Coach

Although it's hard to imagine a more easy-going, gentle individual, Stan Daniels is the type of teacher who does not make a lot of friends in the staff room. "I don't hang around a lot," Stan says. "I'm too busy with preparation. It doesn't leave me a lot of spare time." For Mr. Daniels, teaching is not just an occupation, it's a passion. In fact, he practically bubbles with enthusiasm about his involvement in the SRP program.

"Lenny Goldstein (the other SRP math instructor) introduced me to Mike Yazurlo at a math meet. 'Stan,' he said, 'I've heard a lot about you,' because Lenny and I had met at various meets over the years. And then he told me about the program and asked if I wanted to teach in it," Mr. Daniels recounted. "I had to hold myself back to keep from shouting 'yes!' I was so excited. So I kind of acted calm, like we'll have to see. But I'd already made up my mind."

Mr. Daniels says he enjoys working in the SRP program because the smaller classes and longer periods allow him to provide students with the individual attention he feels they need. Mr. Daniels, who is also a track coach, compares the instructional process to coaching. "You can concentrate with individual students or small groups on developing particular skills," he said. "You can keep on top of them and make sure they're learning." Although he had never taught in an individualized program before, his coaching experience eased the adjustment.

When Mr. Daniels walks into class, his students crowd towards him, waving pencils and pushing papers in his direction, squabbling like fans wanting autographs: "John has seventeen, but I have twelve. Who's right? Who's right?"

One does not need to watch for long to see that Mr. Daniels enjoys teaching or that his students appreciate his approach. As one student put it, "You can ask him a question when you have a problem. And he explains things clearly, which my teacher at school doesn't. And, plus, once you've learned something, you don't have to keep doing it over again."

In Mr. Daniel's class, students spend most of their time working individually with their textbooks or trying to solve problems designed to test their mastery of specific skills and concepts. They work at their own pace, progressing to new material as they master the old. In the meantime, Mr. Daniels and his teaching assistant cruise the aisles, making sure the students stay on task, encouraging, prodding, teasing, and cajoling.

Mr. Daniels also believes that healthy competition can stimulate students' performance. Occasionally, he puts a series of problems of ascending difficulty on the board. "There are five problems on the board," he tells his students. "Probably the most any of you can get is three." Sometimes he'll place a star next to the toughest problem and tell them "I don't think any of you can get this one." The effect is dynamite. "If I just told them to do the five problems on the board, it'd be no way. But this way, except for a few kids, the challenge gets them. All of them want to handle the one with the star."

Although most of his students perform well in his class, in talking about his students, Mr. Daniels tends to dwell on those who are having problems. "You keep asking yourself," he said, "how come I can't get to those kids, too?"

One particularly frustrating student Mr. Daniels nicknamed the Calculator Man. The Calculator Man would come to class on Saturdays with a book bag, pull out a calculator, put it on his desk, and then sit through the class doing nothing.

"You have a calculator," Mr. Daniels would tell him. "Why don't you use it?"

"I don't need it," the Calculator Man would reply.

The Calculator Man's name is Peter. He's a quiet kid, with big brown eyes and a timid smile. Frustrated that Peter was not doing his work, Mr. Daniels began to lean on him. When Mr. Daniels would ask him a question, he would stretch, as if he were bored. Sometimes he was disruptive. "He would forget to bring his book or, when I asked him, instead of saying what he was working on, he'd mumble or just say 'stuff,' " Mr. Daniels observed. "He had hard time focusing and was easily distracted."

Mr. Daniels began watching Peter more closely, and noticed that even when he tried he couldn't do a lot of his work. He would make mistakes performing simple computations, and the other kids would laugh at him. To help Peter save face, after asking him a question, Mr. Daniels would write the answer in the margin of his paper. The nonchalance was a mask, Mr. Daniels had discovered. Peter acted like he didn't care because he didn't want the other kids to find out that he couldn't do the work.

A few days into the summer session, Mr. Daniels pulled Peter aside and talked to him privately. After some initial squirming, Peter admitted that it disturbed him to be so far behind his classmates, but more importantly he asked Mr. Daniels to help him. Although he refuses to make any predictions regarding the overall effect the breakthrough will have on Peter's academic career, Mr. Daniels is thrilled to have reached him. By the end of the summer, Peter was staying in class to work on problems during recess and with each new success, he was beginning to radiate a whole new, constructive self-image. Asked about Mr. Daniels' class, Peter said: "I used to get stuck on division and fractions. But Mr.

Daniels helped me a lot. My regular teacher just sits up at the front of the class and does the problems. But Mr. Daniels helps you when you get stuck, and he tells funny jokes."

Much that has been said about Mr. Daniel's class also applies to Mr. Goldstein's class. Mr. Goldstein is a gentle man, who radiates a vulnerability that creates a fierce sense of loyalty in his students. He doesn't emphasize competition to the extent that Mr. Daniels does, tending to rely more on cooperative activities designed for small groups. Much like Mr. Daniels, however, he builds his class on individual interaction with the effect that his students become thoroughly engaged in their work. "Even though the summer classes go on for five hours," said one of his students, "they never seem too long. It's not like school work. Or I'd say it's like creative and interesting school work."

Readers and Writers

In another life, Anna May must have been a drill sergeant. A powerfully built woman, she speaks English or Sicilian dialect with the same measured authority, her voice throaty and dense from cigarette smoke and experience. Facing an open-ended ring of desks, she centers her students' attention like a great, peaceful anchor. On the first day of summer class, the topic for discussion is beauty. She asks each student to tell her what they find beautiful about themselves. "It doesn't have to be something superficial," she says. "It can be something inside, something that other people might overlook."

Most of the students squirm when their turn comes around. Damon, a large boy wearing round glasses, stares at his hands silently.

"Is there someone in your family whom you consider beautiful?" Anna May prods.

"My mother," Damon says.

"What's beautiful about her?"

"Everything," Damon answers.

After digging for specifics for a while, Ms. May lets Damon off the hook. She asks each child the same question before assigning an essay to be written in class: "What is beauty?" She poses the question, and lets it hang in the air like a great puff of smoke. The silence lingers. Some students start writing; others shuffle their books, papers, pens. At last, Ms. May speaks again. "You can write about someone that is beautiful or some thing. But I want you to get below the surface. What is beauty?"

After about three quarters of an hour, when most of the students have finished their essays, Ms. May asks them to read aloud. These first attempts are, for the most part, short, unfocused, poorly constructed. Ms. May listens closely, complimenting felicitously turned figures of speech, offering suggestions, handing questions over to the class for discussion.

Literature, words, and the ideas of children are important to Ms. May. While outwardly gruff and cynical, she is immensely generous with attention to her students. Much of her time during the next two weeks will be given over to intense individual coaching sessions, in which she will examine student writing line-by-line, providing immediate feed-back and guidance. By the end of two weeks, many of the students will be writing lengthy, engaging narratives, retellings of myths, invented legends.

According to Ms. May and her colleagues, Susan Fein and Louise Bethencourt, their greatest challenge is to turn their students into readers and writers. Each teacher keeps a small library at the back of her class, and students are encouraged to have a novel going at all times. Working in pairs or small groups, students are given exercises that build their vocabulary and teach them about analogies and etymology. Peer criticism techniques are used to help students develop editorial skills. Polished essays and stories are periodically hung on the walls or published in class magazines.

Ms. Fein places a great deal of emphasis on study habits. "I believe it's very important for children to learn how to follow through on their work," observed Ms. Fein. And she has structured her class in such a way that students must continually return to previously assigned work.

For each class meeting, Ms. Fein writes a series of assignments on the board, numbered one through however many there are for that particular day. For example, the following was written on the board when her students entered the class on April 27, 1991:

1. Journal Entry: "Why I wish I lived in the __th century."
2. Check or Complete rough draft of narrative. Write final copy.
3. Scoring high on the M.A.T.'s.
Language lesson #14.
Spelling, page 36.
4. Check Vocabulary from last week
New Work
a. write new word and meaning
b. try applying what you have learned (pp. 42–43)
5. Literature
a. read the poem by Lorraine Hansbury
b. read Lorraine Hansbury's biography
c. read the play *A Raisin in the Sun*: We will do this together.

From class to class, the areas in which Ms. Fein gives assignments remain fairly consistent. Thus, if a student has missed the previous session's vocabulary, before he can begin work on the current assignment, he must complete the previous week's activities. "They don't like to go back," said Ms. Fein. "But I force them. I say — you must finish. If you didn't do an activity for last week, you must go back ... And they go back and they work on it." This approach allows Ms. Fein to maintain some flexibility to individualize the work for students who are either ahead or behind their peers. More importantly, it demonstrates to the students the importance of sticking to a task until it has been completed.

All three language arts teachers in the SRP program are well-prepared, knowledgeable, insightful, and concerned. Yet all three have had some trouble adapting to CTY's instructional model, which places the student at the center of learning and requires a teacher to relinquish some of her control over the class. Easing up on the reins is difficult for seasoned public school teachers even in an environment which is radically different from the one in which they regularly teach. There is always the secret fear that anarchy will break out if discussions are not kept under strict control. There is always the concern that students will use flexibility as an excuse to goof off.

In *The Paideia Proposal*, Mortimer Adler identified three levels of teaching: didactic, embodied by the traditional lecture; coaching, described in detail above; and finally Socratic, which is characterized by "free discussion ... kept on track by a leader."[13] It is the latter instructional strategy which characterizes the writing workshop, the backbone of CTY's approach to instruction in the humanities. All of the Hawthorne SRP instructors use the first two strategies successfully. Their lectures are meticulously prepared, and they take advantage of coaching opportunities as they arise. They allow for some degree of flexible pacing. For certain activities, they break their classes into small groups, allowing students to work cooperatively. Yet they rarely venture into the treacherous territory of open discussion. When they ask questions, they are usually looking for pre-determined answers. In spite of all the successes they've experienced with their students, the teachers seem to retain the suspicion that the students cannot assume full responsibility for learning.

There are certain professions from which we expect perfection: every teacher, every doctor, every writer can always do her job a bit more effectively. The ideal Socratic classroom may exist only in the imagination of theorists. While the Yonkers program has not replicated CTY's instructional model in every detail, there can be no doubt that the students participating in the SRP program have benefited greatly from the patience, diligence and expertise of their teachers. Linda Blake,* whose son is in Ms. May's class, made the following observations:

> His confidence in his ability has improved greatly. He had to be convinced that he had the capabilities to do the kind of academic work, and I don't know that he was always convinced of that .... His class performance has increased ten-fold from sixth to seventh, having experienced the summer program last year and then going through the entire academic program. This year, I can see a difference of about ten to fifteen points in his actual grade scores .... (He) is beginning to understand that reading is something he can do for enjoyment rather than just as a punishment or a lesson. I've seen him get into researching, seeking out information, whether it be in novels or textbooks, or just magazines and newspapers.

Other parents of SRP students noted similar changes in their children. "His grades did improve towards the end of the year," said Pat Manuel, whose son is in Ms. Fein's class. "And he seemed more centered; whereas, before he got into the program, he just didn't seem like he was interested in working."

Elbert Shamsid-deen was particularly pleased with the program's effect on his daughter's work habits. "She seems to be con-

---

* While the names of students have been fictionalized, the real names of adults, unless otherwise noted, are used throughout this chapter.

centrating more on the work," he said. "Whereas before we used to have to chase after her to do the work, basically now we don't have any problem. She goes and she does it on her own."

On lunch break during the summer session, a beaming Dr. Yazurlo shows visitors the tangible signs of the program's success. "Look at them," he says, pointing to a table where seven girls have their noses buried in novels, oblivious to the clank of crockery and silverware and the ice-cream melting on their trays. "If I could bottle that and bring it back to school, I'd never lose sleep again."

Who's Callin' Who A Nerd?

In the summer of 1990, when an article appeared in a local newspaper describing the SRP as a program for students who "have the ability to participate in gifted and talented programs, but whose growth has been stymied by a lack of support or negative influences outside school,"[14] many of the SRP students were furious. "Boy, they didn't take that too well," said Darlene Shamsid-deen, whose daughter was in the program at the time. "I'm talking about the kids. I got a phone call from my daughter. The girl was livid!"

While approximately 40% of the students in the SRP program are on free or reduced lunch, the majority are from working and middle class families. Some are from highly professional families, with parents who are doctors, lawyers, or computer specialists, and though they often live just a few blocks from the projects, they do not consider themselves "stymied." Even the students who come from underprivileged backgrounds generally have at least one parent who believes in the importance of education. "Just the fact that they get the kids signed up for the program and get them to school every Saturday morning, that tells you something," observed Lillian Mein, the Supervisor for Elementary Instruction. "They have the motivation to want something better for their kids' education. They have become actively involved."

In the rush to create a sensational news story or a powerful theoretical generalization, reporters and researchers alike often overlook the views and the values of the individuals they are examining. Adolescents exert a great deal of energy searching and questioning, trying to carve out identities for themselves. To be labeled or pinned down is to be diminished as an individual. Even if the newspaper story was essentially accurate, certain individuals were bound to resent being stereotyped.

John Dewey once observed that "all things are carried out for the sake of education."[15] This is certainly the case for most adolescents. In doing the hard work of shaping their identities and defining their aspirations, they look for allies who understand their struggles, nurture their interests and challenge their abilities. Their judgments of the value of a particular experience — an encounter with a teacher or participation in a program — will inevitably be judged in this broader context.

Balancing the need for social acceptance with academic accomplishment and career aspirations is one of the hardest tasks facing many youngsters. At an inner-city school like Hawthorne, this struggle is complicated by the intense pressure that is placed on many youngsters to rebel against all forms of authority. Even youngsters from middle-class backgrounds experience these pressures. As Zweigenhaft and Domhoff observed, "the oppositional identity that censors academic achievement as 'acting white' ... serves as a magnet that pulls the black middle class back into the lower classes."[16]

"They adopt the street attitude of — it's not hip to be brainy," said Darlene Shamsid-deen. "So even if they have the ability, they don't want to show it, because the other kids are going to call them names." According to sociologist Jay MacLeod, "they form protective peer subcultures" in which "to be bad is to be successful, at least in the limited sphere of one's peer group."[17] Conversely, in the sphere of one's peer group, or a certain limited section thereof, to be successful in school is to be a traitor.

"There is a lot of peer pressure," said Linda Blake. "The desire to be accepted without being called a nerd or whatever. Excellence in education is one of those things that especially young minority males — and being a parent of a male — they're made to believe that any time you excel in something that you're somehow being less than black or less than your peers."

All of the students in the SRP program have struggled with these feelings. Wearing a Mets cap tilted over one eye, Malika is a soft-spoken honor student and member of the Mathcounts team who wants to be a teacher when she grows up. In a voice that is barely audible, she described the pain of being ostracized:

> Well, it's like, people call me a nerd. And in a way I am because, if I pay attention in class, it won't take me that much time to study something, because it's already in my head .... I am a person who will get upset about something that isn't really — that doesn't matter. It doesn't bother me as much as it used to, but when I first started going to Hawthorne that used to really get me that people would start talking.

Malika's SRP instructor Leonard Goldstein feels a great deal of empathy for Malika. "She does very well in school," he observed. "She's different. And it's tough to be different at this age. I mean it's not for me to say. I'm not a psychiatrist, but I mean she appeared suicidal. Not so much that she was about to do it, but she was that kind of person who felt so different, that the world was really, that she didn't fit into the world — that the world was out of whack and she wasn't. I mean, I feel that way too. But it's not fun to be that way in the world .... We were scared for her."

Participating in the SRP program gave Malika a boost in a number of ways. First of all, she discovered a peer group that accepted her talents and admired her for her accomplishments. "Before I attended the program, I didn't know a lot of people. But I made a lot of friends there," she said. Mr. Goldstein was particularly gratified by Malika's new-found acceptance. "A friend of hers was this very pretty, very social girl, who is extremely popular and also happens to be a good student. So, I think socially the program helped Malika a lot," he said. Equally important was the guidance that Malika received from Mr. Goldstein and her other teachers. "I like teachers who are fair," she said. "And they have the same amount of respect for you as you have for them. And they treat their students the same way they want to be treated. Teachers that can give me a challenge in my work, when I'm doing something that I don't know already." Finally, the program was important for Malika because it helped bring her closer to her mother. "My mother likes the program, because she likes to see me moving ahead in math .... So, on Saturday, we'll get up and she'll drive me to school."

A discussion between two SRP students further illustrates some of the issues that concern these children and how they view the program. Irvin, another of Mr. Goldstein's students, loves mathematics and aspires to be a civil engineer or architect. His ambitions stem from a fascination with the New York City subway system, much of which he has traveled and mapped in his own hand. His classmate Sherletha wants to be a child psychologist because "every time somebody says something to me, or if they do something to me, you know, I try to figure out why they would do that. I think there's something behind it."

Irvin — In my class I'd say I'm probably one of the smartest kids, besides the kids that go to Sequential II. Sometimes I do get teased in class, but you know it wears off after a while. You have to accept it, because it's who you are. Like, say, in music, the teacher said I got straight hundreds. So what happened? One of my friends, Edgar, he's like: Nerd, nerd, nerd ...

Sherletha — (laughing) um ... um ... um ...

Irvin — This kid, I think he's jealous. He's in my class this year. I think he still calls me "Nerdvin." And I think the problem is that he's jealous that I'm smarter than him, because ...

Sherletha — (still laughing) I know Edgar. I don't know how he's going to call Irvin a nerd at all. I don't understand that. I don't understand that. But what he said — I don't agree with him when he says I can't help it because I'm smarter. I think that they're smart but they just don't apply themselves. So, you should have said, "I don't know. I just apply myself better." Because I don't know that smart thing. I don't like that.

Irvin — Yeah, I think a lot of people in my class could do it, but they don't apply themselves. Maybe they goof around in class. But if they were actually straight and they didn't goof around, they could do pretty well.

One of the greatest benefits of participating in the SRP, according to Roz Mariani, a counselor in the Yonkers school system and the assistant director of the program, is that it teaches students about taking responsibility for their own learning. "I've seen students who were in the program last summer who've come back this summer with a lot of maturity and more sense of responsibility," observed Ms. Mariani. "They're able to do things on their own. They don't have to be urged — to read or do homework." In particular, Ms. Mariani feels that the students learn a lot about themselves and their peers by living away from home and taking part in the program's social activities. "They're learning to live together, learning to share," she said. It is the combination of personal responsibility and social interaction with an academically motivated peer group, according to Ms. Mariani, that makes the SRP so effective.

With the exception of a few boys who dream of playing for the Mets and a few girls who think they'd like to be fashion models, all of the children in the SRP aspire to college educations and work in fields that require a great deal of professional training. Even the children who are not doing well express an appreciation for the SRP program and the desire to improve their school performance; they understand that their futures depend on it.

Tina is a fairly typical underachiever. In the seventh grade, she was failing two subjects and doing poorly in the rest. She was constantly getting in trouble for talking in class. One of her teachers described her as a student who was "turned off." "She's stopped trying," he said. "I think she basically wants to go to a different school." At the time, Tina recognized that she was not performing up to her potential. "I could do a lot better if I tried," she observed. "I'm not trying hard enough."

Tina likes to have fun, and she hangs with some of the *"baddest"* girls in the school. She likes attention, and she likes to play around. She is also insecure. In class sometimes she sucks her thumb, and she is easily embarrassed. "She does more harm to herself than she does to anyone else," observed Mr. Goldstein who has had her in class a number of times in the past. By the end of the 1990–91 school year, because of her grades and behavior, she was in danger of being transferred from the school. But Dr. Yazurlo decided to give her another chance to prove herself and allowed her to stay in the SRP summer program.

In Ms. Fein's class, Tina flourished. Away from peers who pressured her to goof around and act bad, she made new friends and began taking her work seriously. When the class was broken into small groups for activities, she often assumed a leadership role, soliciting ideas from classmates and negotiating compromises. As often as not, she was one of the girls sitting in the dining room with a book in one hand and a sandwich in the other. In revising a myth about "Crayola, the God of Colors," she worked through break with an intensity which surprised Ms. Fein. "She's a changed person," Ms. Fein said. "What more can I say? I hardly recognize her."

Tina, who wants to be a veterinarian when she grows up, returned to Hawthorne for the eighth grade. And while the SRP may or may not have made the difference in her academic status, it certainly gave her a chance to experience success of which she was extremely proud.

No program can guarantee the success of all participants; however, the vast majority of the Hawthorne SRP students found something positive to say about the experience. They liked the teachers or they enjoyed the social life; they were thrilled to have the chance to get away from home in the summer, to see what life is like on a college campus. In general, they said that they were proud to be a part of a rigorous program which they hoped would help them in the future. "We're getting what we're supposed to get and more," said Anita, a poised and self-assured fourteen year-old. "If we were in a different school, we wouldn't be so advanced." Or as Victor put it: "The teachers are more understanding. And just coming here, it makes me feel proud to be in a school for gifted and talented."

Conclusion

On a sweltering May afternoon, Dr. Yazurlo is having a meeting with A. Donald Duncan and Walter Eddy from the Department of Human Relations, an institution that was developed as a part of Phase II of the city's Educational Improvement Plan to address problems associated with integration.

"How do you absolutely destroy a kid's ego? What are the things you do?" Dr. Yazurlo asks his guests, growling — sounding more like a football coach or a mechanic than a junior high school principal.

No one answers his obviously rhetorical question.

"We have a rule in the building that you're not allowed to wear baseball caps. Some of our teachers will see a black kid wearing a baseball cap and they'll just walk right by him. What are they telling that kid?" Dr. Yazurlo says, pausing for effect. "They're telling him that they don't care about him — that he's worthless."

James Baldwin once observed that a racist is someone who accepts in a black person what he would consider unreasonable behavior in a white. All afternoon the three men have been discussing the state of race relations at Hawthorne. Dr. Yazurlo is frustrated. In spite of the many successes of minority students at Hawthorne, he still finds that too many students are failing or achieving below their potential. He worries that the faculty are losing patience with integration, that a fatal negativity is spreading in the lunch room and the hallways.

Speaking slowly, choosing his words carefully, Mr. Duncan, the Director of the Yonkers Public Schools' Human Relations Department, tries to formulate a strategy. "How many people are there on staff that can have a positive influence?" he asks. "How many are in the middle?" He suggests forming a "brain trust" of these people and using them to influence others. One has the sense that Mr. Duncan has been through this innumerable times before, yet he seems patient, even optimistic. He speaks of "therapeutic" people, teachers who are "flexible, accepting, congruent" — individuals who can make children feel good about themselves.

At the end of the meeting, the three agree to set up some workshops for teachers, parents and administrative staff. The goodbyes are friendly but Dr. Yazurlo remains on edge after his guests leave; neither he nor Mr. Eddy seem content with the meeting's conclusion, which seemed to leave too many issues unresolved.

"It doesn't take much to be a bad teacher," Anna May once observed. The corollary remained unstated: "nothing is harder than being a good one." The same can be said about principals. When Dr. Yazurlo is in a dark mood, he tends to come down hard on his staff, on his programs, and himself. "The SRP is a nice program," he says, "but it's just a band-aid."

Dr. Yazurlo has been in education for too long to believe in miracle solutions. He considers the SRP a "band-aid" because it leaves to many problems unsolved. "Two weeks in the summer just isn't enough," he observed. "It has to transfer back to the classroom, to everyday." He hopes that the students will apply the skills and the habits that they learn in the program, and he hopes that the teachers will raise their expectations and try out some of the techniques developed in the SRP classroom in their regular classrooms.

Mr. Goldstein, for one, does not believe that the techniques he uses in the SRP program are transferable to a regular classroom situation. "I think I would lose a lot of kids," Mr. Goldstein said when asked if he would consider individualizing in his regular classes. "I wouldn't be able to monitor where they were at all times ... I don't think with a regular class that I could take the chance."

Dr. Yazurlo understands the real constraints that face his teachers on an everyday basis: class size, discipline, curricula that have to be covered. Still, he has little tolerance for excuses. He encourages teachers to experiment, to try out new approaches in the classroom. "It's not just a matter of raising test scores and grades," he said. "It's also a matter of smiling, of making kids feel good about what they're doing." He worries about the spread of negativity. "You'll see a new teacher come in excited about trying out new ideas, and in talking to people in the dining hall, wherever, suddenly they've become the same kind of negative force," he said, throwing up his hands. "There's this myth that you can't smile until Christmas."

It is the fragmentary nature of change that continues to frustrate Dr. Yazurlo; reaching some kids some of the time just does not satisfy him. Ms. Mein feels that he is overly critical. "The SRP is a part of a larger process," she observed. "If we give kids something they didn't have before, it's just a part of their natural school development, and they will build on that."

Dr. Yazurlo freely admits that he never envisioned the SRP as anything more than a part of the solution to Hawthorne's problems. Other strategies include keeping a close working relationship with Mr. Eddy and Mr. Duncan from the Department of Human Relations, opening up the lines of communication between minority parents and the school's faculty, and providing ample opportunities for staff development.

On Saturdays, while the SRP students are in class, Dr. Yazurlo and Mr. Eddy meet with a group of minority parents. Most of the parents in the group have been actively involved in such organizations for years. Although one of the group is a member of the PTA, there is a certain degree of dissatisfaction with mainstream channels, a sense that their voices will not be heard in that forum.

The dialogue is open, often friendly, but not without tension. On the one hand, there is a sense that the parents believe in the overall mission of Hawthorne, they trust Dr. Yazurlo, and they feel comfortable speaking to him about the problems they perceive. On the other hand, there are certain key areas where they feel the school could be doing a better job. Like Dr. Yazurlo, they are alarmed at the numbers of minority students who fail courses or do not achieve up to their potential. One parent observes that of the portraits hanging in the library, only one is black — Florence Joyner, a track star. Similarly, of the six teachers involved in the SRP, only Mr. Daniels is black and none are Latino. There is in fact a shortage of minority teachers throughout Yonkers, which can only be partially explained by the school system's low salary scale. Also, there is a general consensus that more could be done to implement a curriculum that is genuinely multicultural. Dr. Yazurlo listens and takes notes.

Parents at the meeting also worry about teachers' attitudes toward their children: they are painfully aware that some teachers do not expect their children to excel. "We want our children to do just as well — better," says one parent, and a chorus of assent erupts. During the discussion of teaching styles that ensues, a few parents voice concerns about specific teachers. Dr. Yazurlo fields some questions.

After a while, Mr. Eddy interrupts. He breaks the meeting into a few small groups and asks each group to lay out some specific goals and some strategies for attaining them. When the whole group reconvenes an hour later, a number of goals emerge, but there is a nearly unanimous feeling that minority student achievement is the priority. The last half hour is spent brainstorming strategies, which range from the utopic to the nitty gritty. A few suggestions result in immediate action: The parents agree to set up a network to share information about effective tutors, useful books, and problems as they arise. Dr. Yazurlo explains the process whereby a parent may request that a teacher stay after school one or two afternoons a week to provide students with extra help. And Walter Eddy agrees to conduct workshops for teachers, parents and children.

Four months after that meeting, one of the participants could report that her daughter had taken advantage of the services of a Latin tutor discovered by one of the other parents, "which helped get her through Latin with a decent grade." In general, Dr. Yazurlo found that a much greater percentage of his teachers were staying after school at least once or twice a week. "They didn't know what hit them," Dr. Yazurlo said, chuckling. "They weren't used to minority parents being so outspoken."

When viewed in the larger context of Dr. Yazurlo's overall vision for the Hawthorne School, the SRP proves to be much more than a band-aid.* For many students it is the high point in their schooling. "It's a lot more fun than school," said Maria, one of Mr. Goldstein's star pupils. "There's no bell and no grades. You don't feel any pressure. You just want to solve the problems because they puzzle you. I don't know. It's great." Parents are equally sanguine. "I think one of the things I find most exciting about the SRP is that it rewards excellence and motivation in minority students," said Ms. Blake. "It is not a tutorial program whereby children are made to feel that they're less than. The emphasis in the program is: you have all these things going for you — let's enhance them."

Elbert Shamsid-deen gives a great deal of credit to the Hawthorne school: "The school itself and the teachers at that school, they're doing a great job. They work at it. They maintain a standard .... This is the kind of environment which is actually needed in the school systems throughout America to help bring about change, because if all the schools were structured like this, with the help that's coming from Johns Hopkins, then possibly we'd see a lot of results like we have with these children."

A school cannot succeed in its mission if it is isolated from its community. Education must be vital and relevant to the interests of the child and it must be consistent with the goals of the child and his parents. While there are certainly cultural differences that separate people of various races and ethnic groups in this country, there are even more profound similarities that link people in hopes, dreams, and ambitions. Any school or any program is successful only insofar as it can help the individual child to develop the skills, the habits, and the sense of personal worth which will allow her to fulfill her vision of herself.

---

* For the 1991–92 academic year Dr. Yazurlo was made principal of a "school under review," New York State's terminology for a school with severe problems. He remains the director of the Hawthorne SRP, and Hawthorne's new principal is supportive of the effort.

Notes

1. *New York Times,* Nov. 21, 1985.
2. James Feron, April 23, *New York Times.*
3. Lisa W. Fodadero, *New York Times,* Sept. 25, 1988.
4. See for example, Bordieu, Pierre "Cultural Reproduction and Social Reproduction," or MacLeod, J., *Ain't No Makin It,* p. 148.
5. Oldenquist, A., "Social Triage Against Black Children," in *The Great School Debate,* p. 260.
6. Nettles, S.M., "Community Involvement and Disadvantaged Students: A Review," pp. 396–97.
7. *New York Times,* Sept. 25, 1988.
8. Lynch, Sharon & Mills, Carol, "The Skills Reinforcement Project (SRP): An Academic Program for High Potential Minority Youth," p. 366.
9. For documentation of achievement gains see Lynch & Mills, "The Skills Reinforcement Project (SRP): An Academic Program for High Potential Minority Youth"; Mills et al., "Recognition and Development of Academic Talent in Educationally Disadvantaged Students"; and Krug, D., "The Skills Reinforcement Project: Math Achievement of Disadvantaged Students." For case studies of students participating in the Los Angeles Skills Reinforcement Project, see Tangherlini, "The Skills Reinforcement Project: Its Effect on Students and their Families."
10. Gallagher, "The Gifted: A Term with Surplus Meaning."
11. Steele, Shelby, *The Content of Our Character,* p. 89.
12. Krug, Damon, "The Skills Reinforcement Project: Minority Achievement in Mathematics."
13. Adler, Mortimer, *The Paideia Proposal,* cited from *The Great School Debate,* p. 191.
14. *The Herald Statesman,* August 3, 1990.
15. Schneider, Herbert W., *A History of American Philosophy,* p. 489.
16. Zweigenhaft and Domhoff, p. 171.
17. MacLeod, p. 145.

The Model Mathematics Project of Appalachia Intermediate Unit 08

13

When Sara started school, she was reading on a sixth grade level and her intuitive grasp of numbers was such that she could add, subtract, multiply and divide. On the recommendation of a school psychologist, she skipped kindergarten and entered the first grade at the age of five. Until the fifth grade, she received her math instruction from her father, a math and physics teacher at the local high school, and participated in a flexibly paced reading group. At age 12, she took part in the CTY Talent Search and scored 640 Math and 630 Verbal on the SAT, which placed her in the top quartile for college bound seniors and qualified her for a National Talent Search award. Before finishing high school, she spent three summers at CTY studying math, biology, and writing and took college courses in chemistry, calculus, and social science. In the fall of 1992, at the age of sixteen, she entered the Honors Program at the University of Pennsylvania with sophomore standing. Sara's experiences mirror those of many of the students whose cases were discussed in the first half of this book; however, her experiences and those of a number of talented students who attended school with her are unique in that they had a profound impact on the educational philosophy and practice of an entire region in Pennsylvania.

Appalachia Intermediate Unit 08, an administrative unit in Pennsylvania's educational system, encompasses four counties, thirty-five school districts, 74,000 students, and area of about 4000 square miles in central Pennsylvania. The area is largely rural, with some mining in the north and some small industry centered around the two largest cities — Johnstown and Altoona. The main highways twist and roll across wooded hills and through fertile valleys, where the landscape is dotted with placid black and white dairy cows. The fishing remains good in many of the streams, and people take their time at stop signs. In the small towns, cars and houses are often left unlocked. "It's a nice place to raise children," said one parent. "There are things that happen, but it's a little more peaceful, a little more sheltered."

Novelists like Sinclair Lewis and Sherwood Anderson have described in exhaustive detail the stifling effects that small-town life can have on the intellect and spirit. The towns in Appalachia Intermediate Unit 08 are hardly the first place one would go looking for future scientists, engineers, mathematicians, or leaders. Teachers talk despairingly about "the central Pennsylvania syndrome." "People don't raise their children to move away from home," said one teacher. "They get intimidated if their kids know more than they do. And there are real pressures on kids to stay put."

In 1985, responding to the needs of students like Sara, Richard Miller, the supervisor of Appalachia Unit 08's Gifted Programs, began developing a Model Mathematics Program based on the pioneering research of Dr. Julian Stanley and the instructional approach used in the Center for Talented Youth's mathematics classes. As a mathematics and science teacher at the junior high school in Roaring Spring — a small mill town in the heart of Appalachia 08 — Mr. Miller had frequently encountered bright students who weren't being provided with adequate opportunities to develop their talents. Throughout the seventies, in the spirit of the day, he had done a lot of work with experiential learning, hands-on experiments, and student-centered instruction. As he continued to test different approaches to instruction, he felt a growing conviction that "more could be done to meet the needs of really talented students." In particular, he was interested in developing programs that would provide opportunities for youngsters to become actively involved in the learning process and remove impediments to their progress.

After being appointed supervisor of gifted programs, Mr. Miller found that he was often confronted with situations similar to Sara's: students with a great deal of ability were being held back, their progress impeded by traditional, lock-step programs. In Sara's case, Mr. Miller provided the family with the support that they needed to convince local school administrators that flexible pacing and individualized instruction were viable options. Sara's case was unique, however, in that her father was an instructor at the high school and her mother was on the local school board. Even then, the modifications (home instruction in mathematics, flexibly paced in-class reading instruction, satellite courses, early enrollment in advanced courses, and cross-registration at a nearby college) met with some resistance from the school's administration. In time, however, Mr. Miller's efforts for Sara began to have a ripple effect in the school district, as other students were allowed with increasing frequency to enroll in advanced courses.

More and more, Mr. Miller found himself confronting similar situations all across the Intermediate Unit. In some cases, he found that he could address students' needs on an individual basis, but he was frustrated by the lack of consistency and the continual effort required to maintain individualized programs.

"It was as if we were reinventing the wheel in every district from the Maryland border up to Tyrone," said Mr. Miller. "The problems were always the same — kids wanting to move ahead in the curriculum and inflexible, outdated notions getting in their way." Mr. Miller was particularly frustrated that his efforts on the part of individual students had such limited effects on the system as a whole. While a certain district might allow a particular student a measure of flexibility, the modifications rarely resulted in shifts in policy. When the student in question graduated or moved to a new district, all trace of the change gradually faded from the system like the Cheshire Cat.

Even when the changes were made on an administrative level, Mr. Miller found that teachers resisted making modifications to address the needs of highly able students. In fact, teachers often presented the greatest resistance to the idea of flexible pacing. "The principal art of the teacher," Albert Einstein wrote in his memoir *The World As I See It,* "is to awaken the joy in creation and knowledge."[1] In recent years, a number of studies have revealed that American students are less accomplished in mathematics and science than many of their European and Asian counterparts.[2] There is every reason to suspect that this is due, at least in part, to the way in which mathematics is generally taught in our schools. Rote learning continues to be the rule. Einstein's "rapturous amazement at the harmony of natural law"[3] is nowhere to be found in the drills, repetition, work sheets, and memorized formulae. On the lower levels, mathematics is often presented as an obscure and somewhat irrelevant ritual by teachers possessing more fear than fascination.

Often, textbooks merely aggravate this situation. In an article entitled, "How Much of the Content in Mathematics Textbooks is New?", which appeared in the September 1987 issue of *Arithmetic Teacher*, James R. Flanders demonstrated that "overall, students in grades 2–5 encounter roughly 40 percent to 65 percent new content, an equivalent of new material two or three days a week. By eighth grade, this amount has dropped to 30 percent, just one and one-half days a week." "There should be little wonder why good students get bored," Flanders continued. "They do the same thing year after year."[4] This phenomenon was by no means unfamiliar to Mr. Miller when he became the supervisor of Appalachia Intermediate Unit 08's gifted programs. Time and again, he had seen bright students lose interest in mathematics because of a limited curriculum and numbing rote instruction.

Thus, in attempting to address what he perceived to be the shortcomings of gifted education in the Intermediate Unit, Mr. Miller decided that he would initially focus his energies on mathematics. Institutional rigidity, uninspired teaching, and an inadequate curriculum were three faces of the beast he would spend the next several years of his life battling. In order to make system-wide changes, he knew that he would have to develop a program that could be replicated in districts throughout the Intermediate Unit. Trouble-shooting for individual students was not only inefficient, it rarely produced any long-term changes.

In hunting around for an appropriate model, Mr. Miller found promise in The Johns Hopkins University's programs for academically talented students. In the summer of 1985, he enrolled in a seminar for teachers and administrators sponsored by the Center for Talented Youth. As a result of this initial contact, Dr. Sharon Higham and Dr. Carol J. Mills of CTY served as consultants, developing procedures for the Model Mathematics Project and assisting in staff training sessions.

Richard Miller is an energetic man with an astounding memory for facts — the names of students, test scores, statistics, anecdotes. He speaks in intense, rapid-fire bursts, winning over listeners with his enthusiasm and wide-ranging knowledge. Colleagues ascribe the wholesale conversion of nine districts in the Intermediate Unit to the Model Math Project to his personal zeal. However, he maintains a more modest perspective. "People have to be in the position to change," he says. "You can't force them to change if they're not ready."

Starting in two districts in Appalachia Unit 08 in the fall of 1985, Mr. Miller and several teachers, chosen because of their flexibility and interest in mathematics, began to adapt CTY's flexibly paced instructional model for a "gifted" classroom situation. Presently, the Model Math Project encompasses nine school districts throughout the Intermediate Unit, where it has been applied with varying degrees of success. Classes in the Model Mathematics Project are closely modeled on CTY's self-paced math courses, but differ in certain essentials. As with CTY math courses, no upper limit is placed on the rate at which students may master material; however, the instructor constantly monitors a student's progress through the curriculum to ensure that the pacing is appropriate.

In Pennsylvania, students qualify for "gifted" programs on the basis of an I. Q. test rather than a subject-specific ability test, so there tends to be a wide range of ability in a given class. Once students are accepted for the Model Math program, they are screened for accelerated work in mathematics through a two-step process: an initial screening using a grade-level standardized test and a subsequent evaluation using an out-of-level ability test.[5]

Based on the test results, a set of goals and educational strategies is developed to match the needs of the individual student. Group Four students are those who score at or above the 97th percentile on the in-level test and at or above the 75th percentile on the out-of-level test. They are provided with a highly modified mathematics program, including fast-paced, advanced instruction; accelerative enrichment; compacting of course sequences;

and early enrollment in advanced course sequences (e. g., beginning to study Algebra in the sixth or seventh grade). Group Three students score above the 95th percentile on the in-level test and at or above the 65th percentile on the out-of-level test. Their modified mathematics program can include fast-paced instruction; enrichment; compacting; and early enrollment in advanced course sequences. However, these students are more closely monitored for understanding of complex mathematical concepts.

Group Two students score above the 95th percentile on the in-level test and between the 50th and the 64th percentile on the out-of-level test. Instruction for Group Two students may include moderately accelerated instruction and greater emphasis on enrichment. These students require a more cautious approach to acceleration — more repetition and continuous monitoring to insure that mathematical concepts have been mastered. Group One students score in the 94th percentile or lower on the in-level test or below the 50th percentile on the out-of-level tests. Mr. Miller and his staff have found that their needs can generally be addressed with traditionally paced coursework and greater emphasis on enriching activities.[6]

While the pacing of the individualized instruction is based in part on test scores, no effort is made to segregate students from the various ability groups; thus, a given class will include students with a wide range in talents. The screening process is not meant to determine rigid guidelines or to put limits on the accomplishments of individual students. If a Group One or Group Two student proves that he or she can maintain a pace comparable to that of a student with higher test scores, through determination and hard work, his or her efforts are only encouraged. In fact, the program shares the unique feature with the Yonkers SRP that it often results in improved aptitude scores. A similar phenomenon has been observed in Japanese schools where programs with "tough standards and strong incentives" consistently raised I. Q. scores.[7]

Two important features of the Model Math Project are its non-spiralling curriculum and the use of diagnostic testing and prescriptive instruction. Most math textbooks spiral through material, perpetually returning to topics that have already been taught. Diagnostic testing allows a teacher to identify the topics and skills that a student may already have mastered and to tailor the program of study to the student's needs. After a student's aptitude level has been established, he is given an achievement test to determine where he should be placed in the course's scope and sequence. Thus, if a child has already mastered certain skills and concepts before the start of a course, he is not required to sit through weeks of pointless review sessions before encountering new material. Diagnostic testing continues throughout the course: part of the teacher's responsibility to monitor the child's progress and to keep presenting new challenges. The advantage of this approach, particularly with highly able students, is that it cuts out much of the redundancy associated with the traditional lock-step approach, allowing the student to progress through material at an appropriate pace.[8] Ms. Peterson, whose son is enrolled in the Model Math Project in Westmont, described the process and its effects most concisely:

> I've been pleased with the fact that my son had the opportunity to participate in the program. He was placed into that type of class in second grade, and he has really progressed at what I feel is a high rate. Of course, I can't really compare him with other, normal 4th graders, but I know that he's working ahead in higher level books — that he's now completing the sixth grade book. And he gets a lot of satisfaction out of that — the fact that he's able to take a pre-test, find out what he's weak in, do whatever work is required to learn those concepts and then to do the post-test and be able to move ahead at his own pace: he just loves it and for him it's very satisfying.

In their book *Flexible Pacing*, Neil Daniel and June Cox reported a number of positive outcomes from the Appalachia 08 Model Math Program, including improved student attitudes towards mathematics, increased progress, self-confidence, and significant gains in achievement.[9] Along these lines, Mr. Miller has noted a marked increase in the number of students receiving regional and national honors on the Mathematics Council of Western Pennsylvania Contest, the National Math League Competition, Mathcounts and the Continental Math League tests since the program has been in place. And it is no coincidence that all but a few high scorers are participants in the Model Math Program. In addition, the past six years has witnessed an increase in the number of students from the Intermediate Unit participating in and qualifying for honors in CTY's Talent Search and also in the average SAT scores of those participants.

Rethinking "Giftedness"

Starting in 1982, with the case of *Green vs. Jenkintown School District*, a series of cases has established a precedent in Pennsylvania for basing the education of "gifted" children on the needs of the individual student.[10] Under state law as it currently stands, all identified "gifted" students in Pennsylvania have a right to an "appropriate" education. The term is nebulous, leaving local school officials a great deal of latitude for interpretation. According to Randall Manning, the supervisor of special education in Intermediate Unit 08, most officials interpret the statute simply as a guarantee of minimum standards. Thus, some school systems continue to argue that once they have provided a student with enough Carnegie Units for graduation (e. g., three high school level courses in mathematics), their obligation has been fulfilled.

A modification that should have had the staying power of bell bottoms and mood rings, the Carnegie Unit has lingered for three quarters of a century, causing as much mischief as any ill-conceived policy in the history of American education. A Carnegie Unit, as originally defined in 1909, represents "a year's work in any subject in a secondary school," which "cannot be accomplished in less than one hundred and twenty sixty-minute hours or their equivalent."[11] For a brief period of time, the Carnegie Unit helped to distinguish secondary from post-secondary education and to establish guidelines for college admission. In the long run, however, the Carnegie Unit has devalued learning, placing hours spent in the classroom before the actual mastery of a subject. The Carnegie Unit has also served as one of the major obstacles to the widespread implementation of flexible pacing at the high school level.

Fortunately, under Pennsylvania state law, all special education students, including the "gifted," are entitled to an Individual Educational Plan (IEP) outlining the "appropriate" course of an individual's education. IEP's are prepared annually or at the request of a family by an "IEP development team," which must include parents, the student's teacher, a certified psychologist, one or more persons knowledgeable about the gifted, and a person familiar with the student's cultural background and its effect on evaluation.[12] While an IEP does give a student certain rights, including the right to due process, Karnes and Marquardt have pointed out that a truly "appropriate" education remains elusive, for districts are only required to provide "training within the confines of their present educational resources."[13]

Richard Miller's definition of "appropriate" educational opportunities is a radical departure from the occasional enrichment classes which are the standard fare of most gifted programs. In Mr. Miller's eyes, a program is not appropriate unless it allows a student to continue to work at her own pace on specific academic material at increasing levels of complexity. One of the reasons that the Model Math Program has taken hold is that Mr. Miller has tied it into the state mandate for "appropriate" education and the IEP process. When a student is enrolled in the Model Mathematics Program, her anticipated progress through the mathematics curriculum is registered on the IEP. If the modifications indicated in the IEP are not put into practice, a student's family has the right to take legal action against the school system.

According to Dr. Tony Trosen, the Director of Curriculum and Instruction in Westmont School District (one of the twelve districts that have adopted the Model Mathematics Project), Mr. Miller has pre-empted the need for costly legal battles by demanding a commitment to flexible pacing from the districts up front. "When we committed to do this in the first through fourth grades, a year back, the superintendent was aware that it was in fact a commitment for the whole district because of the way due process works," observed Dr. Trosen. "Now we just have to make it work." While gaining a commitment to flexible pacing from superintendents hasn't magically transformed institutional attitudes, it has created an environment in which problems can be addressed in a constructive forum. At any rate, in the time that the Model Mathematics Program has been in existence, no family has filed for a due process hearing because they felt their child's progress in mathematics was being impeded by the program. In the past, where school districts had adopted pro-active programs for high ability students, they ranged from substantive academic programs to pull-out programs for the "gifted," with the standard enrichment fare — fieldtrips, worksheets, and games that would be equally beneficial for all students and thus did not address any particular student's individual needs. In general, when Richard Miller took over as the supervisor of gifted programs for Appalachia Intermediate Unit 08, opportunities for flexible pacing were extremely limited.

"Our position within our Intermediate Unit, like the districts in the area, had always been very conservative," said Mr. Miller. "In mathematics, like everything else, we were not very progressive in terms of movement of children." Dwayne Geisler, the head of the math department at Spring Cove High School, was more direct in his appraisal of the situation. "Historically, the kids that we've had that are 'gifted' don't perform as well as kids — the normal kids. So, everybody's saying — I don't want my kid in the program. I want them here — in the regular program."

Never satisfied with the logic that transformed "gifted" children into fabulous monsters incapable of functioning in the real world, Mr. Miller felt that at least part of the problem might be the types of programs that the Intermediate Unit offered. "There were a couple of kids that really gave off lots of signals that maybe we weren't doing what we should be doing," said Mr. Miller. "And it just happened that they coordinated with the flier from CTY and some other readings I'd done."

Paradoxically, in conducting the Model Mathematics Project to address the needs of "gifted" students, Mr. Miller has found that the notion of "giftedness" is rather limiting. He has discovered that testing children with subject-specific achievement tests and observing their performance in a particular field provides a more accurate assessment of their individual needs than general tests of intelligence. Gradually, he and his staff have been looking for ways to provide students not identified as "gifted" with opportunities to benefit from a flexibly paced, individualized curriculum. In so doing, he has come to see ability as a continuum rather than as a demarcation: students are not either "gifted" or "non-gifted"; rather, they have various levels of ability in specific fields of endeavor. "When you look at children and what their needs are," he said, "our bureaucratic way of parcelizing things doesn't always work so well." The point is not to label a student, but rather to provide each with the opportunity to reach his full potential. "Those kids below the top groups," he observed, "have tremendous potential, and once you let these kids move, they just come right up underneath .... The Model Math Project is not a privilege program; it is a program to address the needs of individual students."

Rethinking Teaching

When he initiated the Model Mathematics Project, Dick Miller had a clear sense of the shortcomings of math instruction in Appalachia Unit 08 and some general ideas about the kinds of improvements he wanted to make. However, like Alice in the Looking Glass world, trying to get from square one to square eight so she might become a queen, he was unsure of the obstacles he would encounter and how he would overcome them. Conducting teacher training was sometimes like sitting down for tea with the March Hare and the Mad Hatter: it appeared that ideas were being exchanged, but whenever he went back to check on the program's progress everyone was in the same place where he'd left them, talking the same old nonsense.

"The fact was that the teachers didn't believe that kids could move like that," said Bill Patamowski, the supervisor of Curriculum and Instruction in Hollidaysburg. According to Mr. Miller, some teachers dug their heels in, rejecting flexible pacing and a student-centered approach to learning; others voiced support for his ideas but bogged down in trying to apply them. Still others (secondary school teachers in particular) became territorial, declaring that only they were qualified to teach certain courses or to use certain materials. Some even resorted to constructing obscure and inflexible tests to make demonstration of mastery and continual progress all but impossible. As described by Mr. Miller in the following situation, many teachers simply had trouble with the notion of mastery:

> One teacher comes to mind, and she is excellent. She's an older woman. She taught in non-public schools for a long time; she's creative as can be; she is organized; she is really good. But, she's coming from a very structured background. And we were talking about a little guy in her class. And she was really frustrated .... I had written her up a pacing chart, and I'd told her — "now this may not be realistic, but if he strays too far from it, give me a call." So she called me and said: "you know, he's not moving along because you know he's just so careless. He's missing his ninety percent mastery by a point, two points, six points." So we were chatting, and as we went along, her comment was "well, I know he knows how to do it." And I said, "Mary, doesn't that say it all?"

Flanders attributes this fairly widespread and "exaggerated definition of mastery of mathematical thinking" to G. M. Wilson,

a theorist in the industrial efficiency mold, who in 1926 declared
that "the emphasis on one hundred percent accuracy is an important emphasis and should not require explanation .... Letter-per-
fect results are the only results that are wanted in the business
world."[14] Mr. Miller extends the industrial metaphor a step further: "There are so many teachers who are used to working in a
production-line pattern. They just go: '... This is my standard.
Nobody gets past this.'" In his opinion, such inflexible application
of "democratic" standards is dangerous, because it fails to take
into account individual differences. "With a second or third
grader," he said, "sometimes it's just fine motor skills and organization that gets in the way .... But that's the art of teaching, and
diagnosing — a good teacher can tell when it's obviously an artificial barrier."

Over time, Mr. Miller has developed a profile of the types of
teachers who work most effectively in the Model Math Project.
Flexibility is the key notion. An interest and enthusiasm for mathematics is equally important. Without a fascination for numbers
and an appreciation for the elegance of mathematics, a teacher
simply cannot play the mentorship role demanded by the program. Mr. Miller has found that elementary teachers need not be
mathematics specialists, but they must have a solid background
and no anxiety about numbers. Many of the best teachers in the
program also have training in special education; Mr. Miller attributes this to that field's emphasis on diagnostics and individualization. On the middle and high school levels, the equivalent of
an undergraduate degree in mathematics is absolutely essential,
because once the limits are removed from their progress, highly
able students quickly outstrip the knowledge of non-specialists.

Working with students in the Model Math Project has sent quite
a few teachers back to school for more education. Jane Little, an
elementary math teacher in the Tyrone School District, spends her
summers studying math at Penn State. "If I'm not watching," she
said, "lots of times, especially in the pre-algebra, my students will
be doing things that I haven't done." The teachers who have taken
on the challenge of implementing the Model Mathematics Project
bubble with enthusiasm about the changes it has brought about
in their attitude towards teaching. Joanne Lang, a teacher at Lincoln Elementary School in Tyrone School District, said: "It came
at a good time for me, because I was lacking the motivation to

teach. But it really motivated me to want to teach math. It was a whole new way of looking at the program." Similarly, Linda Dell, an elementary and junior high school teacher in Spring Cove, remarked that "at forty, I rediscovered myself and I decided to get busy and do something with my God-given talent."

Ms. Dell's work in the Spring Cove School District, described in the following section, represents one of the most successful applications of the Model Math Project.

Linda Dell: A Mentor in the "Cove"

In Roaring Spring, Pennsylvania, during the last hot days of school, the air thickens with a bitter pungency which rises from the paper mill in the valley to settle on the hillside streets. To all but the most local traffic up on Route 36, Roaring Spring looks like a patch of fast-food restaurants, gas stations and convenience stores interrupting an otherwise open and green dairy landscape. But for Linda Dell and her students, Roaring Spring's elementary school, better known as the "Cove," is home to a thriving community of young mathematicians.

Set into the hillside, Spring Cove Elementary School is an ancient red-brick structure with a steep cement staircase rising to the front door. Parents of current students speak of their parents and grandparents graduating from the school when it was the high school. Tucked into a corner on the ground level, Linda Dell's classroom is a tiny nook, festooned with posters and mobiles and shelves filled with slide rules, cardboard cubes, tangrams, geoboards, compasses, reference books, math texts (everything from dog-eared Dolciani Wootons to the latest University of Chicago materials). It is an apotheosis of Ms. Dell's perpetual experiments, adaptations, and modifications of curricula and materials.

Fish with mathematical symbols on their bellies swim through the air, inhabitants of some otherworldly realm, governed by the commutative, associative, and transitive properties and buoyed by the ineluctable workings of calculation. Here, mathematics is the language of enchantment and a tool with everyday applications — the Platonic ideal or a question of balancing your checkbook.

Instead of standing at the front of the room, lecturing on a single math concept, Linda Dell floats from desk to desk, coaxing and prodding, asking pointed questions, sometimes saying nothing at all, letting students work out problems on their own. She teaches math to all of the gifted students at the elementary school and the junior high school in the Cove. In her fifth grade gifted and talented class, there are eight students working on seven different levels. Next year, all but two will be ready for pre-algebra.

Today, one of her fifth graders is having trouble figuring out the surface area of a cube, so Ms. Dell has her fetch a cardboard model from a shelf at the back of the class. First, she asks the girl if she can calculate the area of one surface; when the girl nods, Ms. Dell asks her how many surfaces there are. The girl turns the cube over in her hand, smiles furtively at Ms. Dell, and ambles back to her seat determined to solve the problem.

Linda Dell defies all the stereotypes about martyred small-town teachers sacrificing the best years of their lives in Sisyphean struggles against malicious officials and apathetic locals. One would be tempted to call her a professional — but the term is too sterile: a banker's concept implying a mundane trade belittling her artistry and passion for teaching "patterns, relationships and ... the beauty of mathematics."

Linda Dell grew up in Hollidaysburg, Pennsylvania — a twenty-minute drive from the Cove. After receiving a bachelor's degree in elementary education from Penn State, she taught in her home-town for a year. During the nine-year hiatus that followed she taught at the International School in Ankara, Turkey, worked for the Joint Chiefs of Staff in Turkey, and then for seven years ran a small private school for special needs students in the Washington, D.C., area.

On the surface, Ms. Dell radiates a small-town calm: she is forthright and unpretentious. Beneath that surface, however, lies a voracious intellect of cosmopolitan scope. Her varied experiences are manifested in her poise and flexibility. She is a risk-taker but also a consensus-builder. She is soft-spoken but articulate and persistent. She knows the new National Council of Teachers of Mathematics (NCTM) standards backwards and forwards; she keeps up with the research on acceleration and enrichment, learning styles, and cooperative learning. When she meets an obstacle (whether mathematical or educational) she hunts down references, consults with colleagues, or conducts research of her own. She has been teaching for twenty-six years and has never suffered from burn-out. "I get it from the kids," she said. "You look at the faces and see the enthusiasm and you can't help it."

In 1980, Ms. Dell returned to Ebensburg, Pennsylvania, where she worked until 1985, when Richard Miller hired her to help implement the Model Mathematics Program. He chose Linda as the teacher for one of the two pilot sites largely because he knew that Linda had the gumption and vision to make the program work. "Linda is the most outstanding math teacher I've worked with in the twenty-seven years I've been in education," said Mr. Miller. "She is a person who takes ideas and runs with them, expands them, and makes them work."

Ms. Dell saw the opportunity as a calling. "I really appreciate what Dick Miller did for me. I wouldn't have realized what abilities I have in math had it not been for Dick," said Ms. Dell. The year the program started, Ms. Dell enrolled in the local branch of Pennsylvania State University, where she studied nights and full-time during the summer, eventually earning a Master's Degree in Math Education. In the meantime her fascination with math grew into an obsession. "I've developed this totally insatiable desire to know more and more math," Ms. Dell said, chuckling. "My husband complains that I won't go anywhere without my math book: I even take it on vacation."

According to Ms. Dell, before the Model Math Project was in place, there was very little interest in mathematics in Spring Cove. Now, students from the Cove are competing with the best students in the nation on the Mathcounts and Continental Math League tests. "Before the model was in place, we rarely had anyone qualify for honors; now, we have more kids qualifying every year," said Ms. Dell. "This year we had eight, and some of them qualified for multiple awards."

While Ms. Dell is proud of the awards and honors her students have received, she is more interested in teaching her students how to think and solve problems. She believes in introducing students to complex mathematical concepts early: using games and exercises, she teaches second graders about integers and set theory. A problem involving savings accounts and inheritance introduces seventh graders to the notion of exponential decay. "When we did the exponential decay, they found out they were only going to inherit seven cents, and all of a sudden this had an impact on them — it hit them in the money part, where these kids were. And I thought, those kinds of things — they'll never forget them, because it's very real," Ms. Dell observed.

There are no histrionics in Linda Dell's classroom — no star of the show. Although her expertise and confidence are always in evidence, she functions primarily as a mentor: *primus inter pares.* She rarely lectures, preferring to work with individuals or small groups of children — teaching or reinforcing the skills that a particular student needs at the time when he or she needs them. Adapting her presentation to the learning style of the individual child is another of her priorities. "Some children need to see things in order to grasp them; others are ready for more abstract concepts," she observes. "I try to look at these kids and really analyze them as to the type of learner they are, so I know what method of teaching to apply."

The reviews from Ms. Dell's students and their parents are universally positive. "I'm very happy with Mrs. Dell's class," said Rebecca Hazenstab,* who has two children in the model math program at Spring Cove. "I hated math and my kids — that's like their favorite subject in school. They're excited by it, both of them. So, to me, it's amazing." Stewart, a seventh grader, says "I like being able to move at my own pace," and adds with a grin, "and being ahead of other kids." Mrs. Over, whose tenth grade son has been in the program since the second grade, says: "In a regular classroom situation, (he) would have been bored to tears. So this has been great for him."

Ms. Dell believes in keeping parents involved and informed about their children's education. "We run into situations where the parents are finding that they can no longer help their children. And it is very difficult for a child to keep on developing when the family support isn't there." As an example, Ms. Dell cites the experience of David, one of the oldest kids in the program. Presently, he is taking algebra III and trigonometry in the tenth grade. "He'll be the first person in his family to go to college — so it hasn't always been easy for him," she said. "There are certain expecta-

---

* Whereas the names of students have been fictionalized, the names of adults are real.

tions here in the Cove. A lot of people have no desire to go any-where else, and that can be hard to overcome."

In order to keep parents informed about the Model Math Pro-gram, Ms. Dell conducts evening workshops during which she ex-plains her instructional approach and even teaches some math. According to Mrs. Hazenstab, the parents of students involved in the Model Math Project are behind her one hundred percent. "If they were thinking of eliminating this program, there would be protests from every parent who has a child in this, I feel sure," she said. "Like before, when there had been talk of money cut by the state, right away there were letters written and an outpouring of support."

Through a process as inevitable as the lunch bell ringing at noon, Ms. Dell is being promoted to an administrative position next year. However, she is determined to keep a foot in the class-room. "One of the things that I feel very strongly about is that in any kind of an administrative position, particularly where you're telling teachers how to teach, when you remove yourself from be-ing a teacher your credibility sometimes suffers," Ms. Dell ob-served. "Next year I'm going to do more teaching than I will be doing in the following years, but I would like to maintain at least two classes." In spite of Ms. Dell's reservations about becoming an administrator, the position will allow her to have an even great-er impact on math education in the Spring Cove District. Accord-ing to her colleague, Dwayne Geisler, the head of the high school's math department, as the supervisor of the gifted math program in grades K-8, Ms. Dell will provide leadership in the development of math curriculum. "How often do you see a person with a math background in an administrative position?" Mr. Geisler pon-dered. "With Linda in this position, we'll be able to really empha-size content."

Without a doubt, the successes of the Model Math Project in general and of Linda Dell's students specifically have opened the way for her new position. However, she has also been resourceful in making allies of people who were initially skeptical about the value of individualization. "When I came up to the junior high school, the principal met me on the doorstep and said he didn't see why he needed anyone from the Intermediate Unit to tell him how math should be taught in his school," said Ms. Dell. "His biggest concern was 'readiness.' He didn't want to hear anything about acceleration or flexible pacing. He wanted to know if the kids were 'developmentally ready' in the Piagetian sense."

Ms. Dell took the question as a challenge. Years before, when she had run a school for students with learning disabilities, she had become intrigued by the different rates at which children appeared to develop. "I was educated at a time when everyone had to fit into a pigeonhole and everybody was supposed to move at the same pace, and I knew that there was a part of me that was very different. I became attuned to that whenever I was in the classroom. I can't really attribute it to any one person or any one thing — it was more intuitive than anything else," she said. "But I became extremely involved in developmental phases."

After consulting with Richard Miller and her professor at Penn State, Ms. Dell designed a research project to determine whether her students were in fact developmentally ready for the higher level thinking skills involved in the accelerated curriculum of the Model Mathematics Program. Using the Arlan's Test of Abstract Reasoning, she found, to her delight and astonishment, that the fifth grade students she had identified for acceleration ranged from the "transitional" stage to the "high formal" stage — often as many as five years ahead of age-expectations.[15] Presented with these data, the junior high school principal dropped his criticism of the program and has since become one of its staunchest advocates.

Ms. Dell's research on student readiness has also borne unexpected fruit. One of her priorities as the new supervisor of gifted math K-8 in Spring Cove is to identify students who might not qualify under the I. Q. testing requirement. "Next year, we hope to test all students in the fifth grade with the Arlan's Test to see if we can identify more who would benefit from individualized instruction. We want to throw the net wider. We're expecting to have 20 to 25 who can go right into transitional math as sixth graders." Similarly, Ms. Dell expects to have 21 seventh graders who'll skip transitional math and go right into algebra I next year.

It is hard to imagine that someone as ambitious and dynamic as Ms. Dell could also be so unassuming. Between classes, students are continually popping in and out of her room to ask questions, to play with "Fuzzbomb," the hamster which sits in a cage in a corner of the classroom, or just to say "hi." In the transitional muddle between one period and another, when students are trying to hand in completed tests, ask questions about assignments, John, a blond fourth grader, tall for his age, approaches Ms. Dell with two magnets he has dug from a bin along the wall.

"Look, they push each other apart," he says.

"That's right," Ms. Dell says, becoming focused, serious in the midst of the chaos. "Do you know why that is?"

John shrugs.

"Then why don't you do your research project on that? Magnetism. There are some books over on the shelf where you could look it up."

John smiles, nods, and seems to float out of the classroom.

"John is the kind of kid who has all sorts of problems in the regular classroom," Linda explains later. "He has some emotional problems that make it difficult for him to keep focused in a larger group. He can be quite disruptive. That's not to say that he doesn't have problems in my class, but in this setting — with more individual attention — he has really grown."

In *Mentor Relationships*, E. Paul Torrance defined a mentor as "a person with expertise in the mentee's field of interest": an individual who "encourages, praises and prods."[16] It is interesting to note that very few of the individuals in Torrance's study described school teachers as mentors: only "nine percent of the mentors were elementary or secondary school teachers or counselors." In part, this may have to do with the types of relationships that develop in the traditional school environment. Standing at the front of the classroom lecturing to a mass of students, one can never break down the barriers that prevent profoundly personal relationships from developing.

In contrast, Linda Dell's passion for mathematics infects everyone that comes into contact with her. Parents of students in her classes marvel that their children enjoy doing math homework. "It's really a building experience. She never lets them get stuck. They move at their own pace; however, she keeps prodding them too. They're never stagnant," said one parent. "Whenever I have a question about math, I ask Ms. Dell. She's my teacher too."

Because Roaring Spring is a small town, there are only a few identified gifted students. One of the critiques most frequently leveled at the Model Math Project is that it works in small groups, but not in large ones. Sharon Parker's class in Hollidaysburg is incontrovertible evidence to the contrary.

There are 23 children, all on different levels, in Ms. Parker's third grade class at the C. W. Longer Elementary School in the Hollidaysburg Area School District. She has an aide, but the aide is primarily responsible for grading papers and keeping records. Ms. Parker stresses competition somewhat more than Ms. Dell. Twice a week, students in her class practice speed drills and are rewarded for their performance with Disney stickers: Pluto for addition, Goofy for subtraction, Daisy for multiplication, and so on. When students finish a chapter test, they are given the chance to work with math puzzles and games in a giant tee-pee at the back of the classroom. There is a brilliant chaotic buzz in the class; the students are absolutely engaged. All of them are ahead of the students in the regular math classes. Two will finish the fifth grade math book before the year is over. Billy, a National Continental Math League winner, is concise in his appraisal of Ms. Parker's class. "Yes!" he shouts. "Math is great." Tyler, who won a regional award in the contest, missing the national award by one question, also loves the class. "After class," he said, "I think about the problems when I'm walking in the hall."

Active Learners

When he was four years old, Billy's grandmother gave him a book of baseball statistics. While browsing, Billy noticed that some of the statistics were off. According to his father, he was well aware of the relationship between at-bats, hits, and batting averages. He not only noticed that some of the batting averages were wrong, he was able to point out the type of computational error that had been made. "He said — you know, they put these numbers backwards," his father said. "He didn't call it a transposition, but that's what it was. He wasn't content just to say that it was a problem."

The benefits of the Model Math Project to someone like Billy are obvious. Instead of becoming bored reviewing the same old material over and over again, he gets charged up for math class every day. "He's very driven, self-motivated," his mother said. "Competition is good for him. The more pressure, the calmer he gets." Less obvious are the social benefits that Billy has gained from the program. "He was willing to hold back a bit so that he could work with (his classmate) Justin. It makes it more fun for him to have someone he's collaborating with."

In a quiet corner of Sue Tower's fourth grade class in West-mont, Gina and Jenny sit with their desks pushed together, whispering across their math books. Both are soft-spoken and shy, neat girls with long hair and glasses — the one Chinese-American, the other blond, blue-eyed, Germanic. The best of friends, they agree that the opportunity for interaction with peers is one of the finest aspects of the class. When asked how she would feel about being put in a regular class tomorrow, Gina whispers: "I would be un-happy. I would miss the kids." Jenny's mother agrees that the model math program offers the children a valuable social experi-ence. "Ms. Tower encourages them to call their group and see what answers they got," she says. "And just about every night they call back and forth .... And well, Gina comes over to our house frequently to, I guess we can't really call it play anymore. Some-times you can't even hear them. They do educational things when they're together."

Jenny's mother, Mrs. H, who teaches math and computer sci-ence at a local university, is also impressed with the level of prep-aration that the program provides:

> After seeing some of the students I get coming in as freshmen at the uni-versity level, I see some of the areas where the skills are lacking. I see that this program — it's individualized but it does put the responsibility on the student to learn and to do things for themselves. And I think that's majorly lacking with some of my students .... So when I see Jenny doing this stuff, I'm thrilled because I know she won't have problems as she goes on, because she's learning not only the mathematical concepts but the skills to help herself.

Jenny's younger brother, Ricky, is also in the program. Accord-ing to Mrs. H., he enjoys the flexibility but has run into a few problems. Because he is easily distracted, he had some trouble when he took the test that is used to make the initial determina-tions about pacing and ended up with a score that placed him in Group I. Mrs. H. is not convinced that this is an accurate assess-ment and is worried that his pacing rate might be slowed unnec-essarily. According to Mr. Miller, the groupings serve merely as a point of departure for pacing and should in no way limit a child's progress. Thus far, there has not been a problem, says Mrs. H., but Ricky is very competitive. "He's happy with what he's doing, but he's kind of irritated that he's not up there leading the pack." In the long run, Mrs. H. acknowledges that given Ricky's personality the competitive edge may even be helpful. "It just makes him work that much harder," she said.

Jenny's fourth grade classmate, Zachary, was not originally chosen for the school's gifted programs, because, like Ricky, he is an extremely active child who is easily distracted. According to his mother, he has a tendency to tune out when he gets bored. "He gets in trouble," she said. "He wants to be the clown. He wants to get the attention, or tries to think of other things to do to make class interesting for him ... " When he did finally get into the Model Math Project in second grade, it was a godsend. "He is well-suited to independent study .... He does not deal well with repetitive tasks, and giving him the opportunity to move through material when he understands it and go on to something new is ideal for Zachary .... He feels very proud about himself and the fact that he's been able to move ahead."

A strong athletic boy, a soccer and baseball player with an aura of intensity, Zachary has in fact moved ahead: three weeks before the end of fourth grade, he was already finished with the sixth grade book and had scored two points off the top score for the National Mathematics League exam — sixth grade level. Asked whether she is worried about Zachary being out of step with most of his age-mates, his mother shakes her head emphatically. "No," she said, "because if he is bored or asked to do the same thing too many times, he just loses all interest .... I'm not worried about him being out of synch with other kids because he's a different kid."

What does worry Zachary's mother are his organizational skills. "He forgets to take his homework home or forgets to take it back to school or he forgets to do it altogether. We've tried to come up with strategies ...," she said. "Maybe Zachary hasn't decided yet that it's important enough yet to follow through on some of our suggestions. Hopefully, it's a maturity issue."

Sue Tower is occasionally annoyed by the sloppiness of Zachary's work and his unwillingness to show how he has arrived at a particular answer. "I wonder whether I should require him to write out every step," she said. "Sometimes, he'll make a mistake in his computations or something because he's in such a hurry to get the answer. But writing everything out is just too frustrating for him." Her solution is to keep talking to Zachary, to keep asking him for suggestions about how he thinks the problem can be solved.

Leah, a sixth grader who has been participating in the Model Math Project for three years, plans to study business in college so that she can market her own inventions. Although she feels that some teachers have done a better job of applying the model than others, her support for the program is unequivocal. "I like it because I can work ahead of the other kids, because usually I work faster in math," she said. "Because like some of the kids, they do really good work except they don't go as fast as me. Then it's easier for everybody — that they can go their own pace, and I can go my own pace." Leah also relishes the opportunities for interaction that are fostered by the less formal classroom arrangement: "It's real loose. You know, sometimes, like if the teacher's busy, we go up to each other or we go up to somebody who's already past our level .... And if you don't understand something, then you ask."

Ultimately, the Model Mathematics Project changes the way students think about education. In the flexibly paced classroom, students cannot sit back and wait for the teacher to put on a show. They must work in class and they must take responsibility for their own learning.

Conclusion

Tony, a soft-spoken junior at Hollidaysburg High School, was an underachiever until he was admitted to the Model Math Project. The project was especially effective for him because he is an unconventional student with strong opinions about how he likes to learn. According to his mother: "For him, it's probably been good because he tends to work on his own, and he's just a super-advanced kid." Tony agrees: "I really like the idea of teaching myself, because I would sit in normal math classes and it was just so redundant. And this way, if I have trouble with something, I can spend three days on one concept. And if I understand something, I can go through a chapter in two."

Tony has a number of criticisms of the Model Math Project, however. In particular, he does not feel that all of the teachers are equally well prepared. "Our class is the first in the school that's had the program, and most of the teachers really don't know what to do. So we've grown accustomed to walking into the classroom and the teachers are like — 'You know what you need to do. I'm here if you have any questions.'"

Mr. Miller is aware of the fact that there are teachers involved with the project who do not understand the model as well as he would like them to. Some have received inadequate training; even those who have been trained have a disturbing tendency to "regress to the mean," according to Miller. Because of the extensiveness of the program and because the program is no longer funded per se, Mr. Miller cannot possibly hope to oversee the training of every teacher. He finds it particularly difficult to convince teachers that there is a difference between flexible pacing and self pacing. "Some of the teachers get discouraged because they're busy with 28 kids," he said. "So the question is: Are we really being visionary enough? We err on the conservative side and go back to the old pattern. Kids have a natural tendency just to do what they can to get by. Some teachers have fallen into a the trap of allowing kids to dictate the pace."

During its first three years of existence, the Model Mathematics Project was funded by a grant from the Economic Securities Act (Public Law 98-377). In spite of the program's documented successes, once the initial funding period ran out, Mr. Miller and his associates were unable to identify other sources of financial backing. Mr. Miller continued to oversee the program without the support of his able assistant Barbara Thrush, who had to be laid off, and without any funding for workshops, teacher training, research, or staff development. Bill Padamonsky laments this situation but credits Mr. Miller with keeping the program alive. "The teachers were starting to talk. The teachers who were more attuned to the philosophy were able to meet with the others and reassure them — 'Yeah, yeah, you can do it.' And then bingo, the funds were pulled away and we had no more interaction with people from the other districts. So, the project has just become our own projects in each district ... " he said. "But Dick has always been there for us .... He was considered an outsider, so he was able to come in and act as a change agent and say some things that teachers perceived as nasty things but that kept us on track. He took some lumps, but it ended up making our program go ... "

Aware that certain dangers arise when a program is too closely tied to a particular charismatic individual, Mr. Miller has tried to delegate authority to individuals in the districts. He never envisioned the Model Math Project as a teacher-proof program. On the contrary, hiring highly motivated, knowledgeable people has always been one of his priorities. Although the diagnostic testing process and instructional approach is clearly delineated, he believes that teachers should be able to think for themselves, to "take the idea and run with it." He recognizes that for the program to have a lasting impact, the teachers and local administrators must buy into it themselves and continue the work of dissemination. "As an administrator, coming from the Intermediate Unit, I can say lots of things about the model. But when a teacher talks about it, there's a different tone. And I think that's what the other teachers need to hear."

In 1990, changes in the Pennsylvania School Code transferred gifted programs from the Intermediate Unit's jurisdiction to that of the local districts. This change in policy has intensified the situation that Mr. Padamonsky complained about, shifting even more of the burden for the Model Math Project to the local districts. And while this may seem ominous on the surface, Mr. Miller feels confident that the program will survive. He is particularly pleased by the initiatives that have been taken on behalf of the program by various individuals across the Intermediate Unit, indicating that they have made a solid commitment to the program.

In some cases, individual teachers have been forced to modify the program to accommodate the priorities of local systems. In Westmont and Spring Cove, teachers have struggled to keep the project alive in the face of systemic commitments to cooperative learning. According to Linda Dell, cooperative learning can be a valuable instructional tool, but like all tools it has its limitations. "I have been using cooperative learning techniques for years without necessarily calling them that," she said. "It's just, you don't want to use cooperative learning techniques all the time." Once a week she teams students from the Model Math Project with students from regular education for special games and contests which provide all group members with an opportunity to shine. While there are valuable social lessons to be learned from working with children with a wide variety of abilities, there is overwhelming evidence that highly able students make the most progress when they are able to move through the curriculum at their own pace. In some instances, cooperative learning stifles the most talented students by over-burdening them with the responsibility for instructing less able classmates.[17] Teachers in the Model Mathematics Project recognize that ultimately there is no such thing as "group learning"; everyone learns as an individual, and nothing is as precious as the individual's encounter with the moment of understanding.

Fran Bloom's Model Math class at Tyrone High School consists of twelve students from grades 7, 8, 9, and 11. Students work independently but they are also encouraged to use each other as resources when they encounter problems. Mathematics is obviously taken very seriously in Mr. Bloom's class: on a given day, a visitor is likely to overhear heated arguments about heterozygous and pure alleles and equally esoteric subjects. Mr. Bloom freely admits, however, that the model is not as refined on the secondary level as it is in the elementary school. He feels that he is under a great deal of pressure from the administration and the math department to keep his students aligned with regular education. Often, he cannot allow students to advance in the sequence to the extent that Mr. Miller would wish. Instead, he introduces students to unusual concepts and applications that students in the regular educational sequence wouldn't encounter. Statistics and probability are introduced before Calculus. There are computer stations at the back of the classroom and students are encouraged to explore independent projects. Written reports are a common feature of his class, with subjects ranging from concave angles of polygons to the dimensionality of space. Presently, he is in the process of developing a linear algebra course for his most advanced students.

Also in the Tyrone School District, teacher Joanne Lang has set up a parent group to increase community involvement in the project. One of the strengths of the group, according to Ms. Lange, is that it helps teachers to identify problems in the program. "They meet on a monthly basis," said Ms. Lang. "They are a very positive group .... They come with concerns on the math project. And because of that, we were able to rectify some problems that we had .... Sometimes, (parents) see things and kids will share things with them that they won't share with us." Another benefit of the parent program has been a growing interest in the Model Math Project in the community as a whole. "The Math Project's catching on," said Ms. Lang. "Regular Ed teachers are saying — 'Hey, I have this kid and I have to hold him back, and he's suffering.' Now, our curriculum director is saying maybe we ought to take the philosophy here that we're using in the project and apply it ... "

In Spring Cove, Linda Dell has had similar success with workshops she holds for parents and other teachers. "One of the things that I have found," she said, "is that if you can get people in a relaxed atmosphere — if you bring them in and have them be students and take something you know they're going to be successful in ... people start seeing that it works. And what's happened is — you start out with one teacher. And then you get two people. And pretty soon someone is saying, 'How would you go about doing this?'" According to Ms. Dell, the only real constraint on the continued growth of the program is time. "There's a lot of volunteer time there, I think," she said. "But I don't know anybody who's involved in the project, who really believes in it, who wouldn't be willing to volunteer if necessary."

Every summer at six sites across the Intermediate Unit, Barbara Thrush and Mr. Miller run a three-week science program based on the principles of the Model Mathematics Project. Many of the students who participate in the math project also take part in in the science program, which provides them with exposure to subjects like astronomy and archeology which are not available in school. Zachary's mother described visiting her son's biology class as follows: "I walked into biology .... Here are these kids — they have razor blades and they're cutting open pigs and looking at the organs and I'm thinking, he's going to cut his finger off. But he did just fine, and he enjoyed it. He learned a lot in the science experiments that they had an opportunity to do."

In Hollidaysburg, Bill Padamonsky has decided to tackle Carnegie Units. A concerted effort is being made to keep track of students' progress from grade to grade to ensure that teachers are picking them up where they left off instead of forcing them to spend the first half of the year in review. "Wherever those kids are moving," he said, "their folders go along with them and the new teacher just starts them from that point on." Under Pennsylvania state law, local districts are allowed to determine the circumstances under which Carnegie Units are granted. Bill Padamonsky has written a set of guidelines which allow credit to be granted at the moment when students finish a course. This rule applies equally to students who have not yet entered high school. Thus, if a seventh grade student were to finish algebra II half way through the school year, he would be granted credit for that course as soon as he passed the test.

In spite of all the obstacles that continue to face the program, Bill Padamonsky is optimistic. "We now have teachers who are saying a sixth grader can be in the middle of an Algebra One book, and the seventh grade teacher is now going to pick them up at that point. That was unheard of three years ago. I mean, they all had to go back to the first page and prove it all again."

The implementation of a program is a lengthy process; it is difficult to establish the precise moment when a program has been successfully implemented, because a good program is constantly evolving and adapting to address the issues that come up in the school or school system where it is being implemented. Mr. Miller, feeling sometimes like the Red Queen, who had to run as fast as she could just to stay in the same place, wishes he had more time to devote to the project and money to invest in staff development. "Teachers just need the chance to get together and bounce ideas off of each other, to exchange ideas and find out what resources are out there," he said. But the fact is that the influence of the Model Math Project continues in spite of all the obstacles it has encountered. In recent years, administrators from other intermediate units and states have begun to develop programs modeled on the Model Math Project, and due to Mr. Miller's efforts, the state department of education has become increasingly aware of the importance of flexible pacing strategies in addressing the needs of highly able students.

Notes

1. Einstein, *The World As I See It*, p. 260.
2. See for example the President and Governors' Report, Oct. 1, 1991.
3. Einstein, p. 267.
4. Flanders, "How Much of the Content in Mathematics Textbooks is New?" Pp. 20–22.
5. For a more detailed description of the screening process see: Keating, D. P., "The Study of Mathematically Precocious Youth" or Miller, Richard C., "Discovering Mathematical Talent."
6. Miller, Richard, *The Model Mathematics Project: Appalachia Intermediate Unit 08.*
7. Lerner, Barbara, "Good News About American Education," p. 27.
8. Lupowski, Assouline, & Stanley, "Applying a Mentor Model."
9. Daniel & Cox, pp. 63–65.
10. For an in-depth examination of the implications of this case and others see Karnes and Marquardt, *Gifted Children and the Law.*
11. Roush, Robert E., "The Carnegie Unit — How Did We Get It?", p. 73.
12. Pennsylvania State Department of Education, "Checklist for Self-evaluation," p. 4.
13. Karnes and Marquardt, p. 61.
14. Wilson, G. M., "What Arithmetic Shall We Teach?", p. 23.
15. Dell, Linda, "Developmental Stages and the Mathematically Talented." For other research confirming the relationship between mathematical precocity and Piagetian development see Keating, Daniel P., "A Piagetian Approach to Intellectual Precocity."
16. Torrance, E. P., *Mentor Relationships*, p. 8.
17. Mills and Tangherlini, "Finding the Optimal Match: Another Look at Ability Grouping and Cooperative Learning." Also Mills and Durden, "Cooperative Learning and Ability Grouping: An Issue of Choice."

West Virginia's Policy 2419: Voice and Flexibility

14

Ian Craig* began participating in programs for gifted students in the third grade. According to his mother, Phyllis Craig, the students did "fun things" in their weekly pull-out enrichment classes but nothing that addressed their distinctive needs. "Two things I found about the gifted programs," said Ms. Craig, "supposedly the programs were individualized, and yet everybody did the same thing. The other thing, we knew very early that Ian was gifted in math, and yet he never had any math in the gifted program in the public schools."

Currently, Ian is a sophomore at a high school in Kanawha County in West Virginia. Through his participation in a flexibly paced math program that meets one night a week at a high school in another part of the county, he is completing a pre-calculus course this year. Because he was identified as gifted, he has been provided with a Four-Year Plan mapping his educational program through high school, ensuring that he will be able to continue working on the appropriate level of mathematics and to participate in advanced classes in other subjects, including College Board

---

* While student names are fictional throughout this chapter, adult names are real unless otherwise noted.

Advanced Placement courses and dual enrollment at a local college if necessary.

West Virginia is not necessarily the first place one would go looking for solutions to any of the nation's educational problems. With annual per capita income hovering around $13,000, high unemployment, and an often embattled school system, the state remains one of the poorest in the nation. When it comes to the education of gifted students, however, West Virginia has some of the nation's most progressive laws and regulations. It is one of only 10 states which extends to gifted students the rights provided to handicapped children under federal law, including the right to an Individualized Education Program and due process protections.

Public Law 94–142, The Education for All Handicapped Children Act of 1975 (EHA),[1] guarantees handicapped students the right to "a free appropriate public education" in the "least restrictive environment" as specified in an Individualized Education Program (IEP). An IEP, as defined in Public Law 94-142, is "a written statement for each handicapped child" designed to address his or her "unique needs" and developed in a meeting between a representative of the local educational agency, the teacher, the parents or guardian of the child, and, "whenever appropriate," the child. In all cases, the statement must include: "(A) a statement of the present levels of educational performance of such child, (B) a statement of annual goals, including short-term instructional objectives, (C) a statement of the specific educational services to be provided to such child, and the extent to which such child will be able to participate in regular educational programs, (D) the projected date for initiation and anticipated duration of such services, and (E) appropriate objective criteria and evaluation procedures and schedules for determining, on at least an annual basis, whether instructional objectives are being achieved."

While EHA does not extend these rights to gifted students, West Virginia state law does, with certain exceptions. The Education of Exceptional Children Act (West Virginia Code 18–20–1) mandates education for gifted students and establishes Individualized Education Programs (IEP) and due process rights for gifted students in grades 1–8 and for "exceptional" gifted students in grades 9–12. "Exceptional" gifted students are students identified as gifted and displaying at least one of the following characteristics:

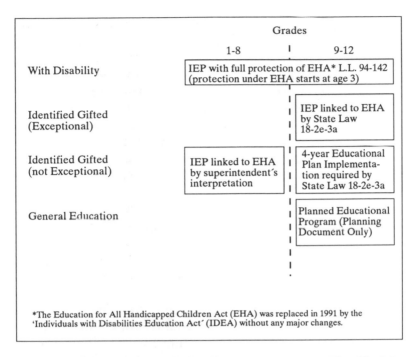

Figure 1. Provision of Individualized Education Programs in West Virginia.

"behavior disorder, specific learning disabilities, psychological adjustment disorder, underachievement, or economic disadvantage." In high school, gifted students not identified as "exceptional" retain the right to an IEP in the form of a Four-Year Plan devised after eighth grade but are not covered by the procedures and policies governing the education of handicapped students.

In accordance with a superintendent's interpretation of 1988, the IEPs of identified gifted students in grades 1–8 and exceptional gifted students in grades 9–12 are tied to federal law (Public Law 94–142) and thus the IEP supersedes all other regulations and documents. For students in grades 9–12 identified as gifted but not identified as "exceptional," the IEP is replaced with a "four-year plan." It is tied to state law instead of federal law, so while it supersedes county regulations and policies, under certain circumstances it may still be subject to state restrictions. The process of formulating the Four-Year Plan is much the same as the process for formulating an IEP; it goes into effect when the student enters the ninth grade and remains in effect through the twelfth grade.

While the Four-Year Plan is reviewed at the end of each year, it may only be revised with the consent of all signatory parties. Although the state code says, in no uncertain terms, that "Schools shall be required to deliver the individualized education program as stated in the four year education plan,"[2] students not identified as "exceptional" do not have the protections extended to handicapped students. Students not identified as gifted also receive four-year plans (known as "Planned Education Programs"; however, for regular education students these serve merely as tools for educational planning which are not legally binding (see Figure 1).

At the heart of most definitions of "giftedness" is the notion of "deviation from the mean."[3] Whether one relies on the classical definitions of Galton or Terman, on more recent psychological constructs, or on the federal government's definition (Marland 1972), giftedness is generally described as an exceptionality, as a characteristic which distinguishes an individual from others to a significant and often measurable degree. Although common sense would tend to support a view of giftedness as anything but a handicap, there are convincing arguments for modifying the educational program of any student whose abilities deviate from the norm. An Individualized Education Program (IEP) provides the means whereby a student's schooling can be adapted to his or her individual needs.

Currently, the State Department of Education in West Virginia considers the IEP (or the identified gifted student's Four-Year Plan) a legally binding contract with precedence over all other educational documents and regulations. Although this interpretation of the IEP had not been tested in court with respect to the education of gifted students, it has been upheld in a number of due process cases and continues to guide educational practice in West Virginia. After a committee consisting of the family and representatives of the school system has agreed upon the appropriate educational services and entered them on the IEP or Four-Year Plan, the county is bound to deliver the services.

Whereas research supports the view that highly able students benefit from differentiated instruction, there remains considerable debate as to what constitutes an appropriate education for a gifted child. In the first section of this work, one approach, frequently referred to as The Johns Hopkins University model or the CTY approach, was discussed in some detail. The policies governing the formulation of IEPs for gifted students in the state of West Virginia are largely consistent with this school of thought in that they emphasize providing gifted students with the opportunity to progress through a rigorous academic curriculum at the appropriate pace. Rather than viewing the development of exceptional talents as something beyond the scope of the regular educational program, the current policy in West Virginia ("Policy 2419: Regulations for the Education of Exceptional Children") focuses on modifying the regular educational program so that it may address the needs of the highly able. In theory, this means that West Virginia is moving away from pull-out programs towards flexible pacing, honors and accelerated courses, and using the IEP as a vehicle.

According to Virginia Simmons, the West Virginia State Coordinator of Gifted Education, the impetus for change originated at the grassroots level. "We had a lot of parents who were dissatisfied with the gifted program," she observed. "It was not defensible, because any time you create a program and you put kids into it, you are not talking about an individualized program and you're not talking about a defensible program .... What we were hearing again and again was that what we were doing for gifted kids is good for all kids."

On the basis of this critical groundswell, in 1986 the State Department of Education commissioned Appalachia Educational Laboratory to prepare a report on the schooling of intellectually gifted children.[4] The resultant document, which would later play an important role in policy decisions, stoked the controversy that was raging in the schools, in that its author, Craig Howley, came out against pull-out enrichment programs and in favor of accelerated academic programs. He also stressed the importance of "active leadership at the state level," mandates for local programs, due process rights, and joint administration with programs for other exceptional children.

Revisions made to the Education of Exceptional Children Act of West Virginia and the regulations adopted by the West Virginia Department of Education in 1988 bear the imprint of Howley's findings. Although Policy 2419, the state's regulations for education of exceptional students, retains enrichment as a programmatic option and includes a number of references to "affective functioning," "process skills," and other trendy concepts, the emphasis is on acceleration. At the core of the program of study lies the following bold statement: "In the student's identified areas of academic strengths, acceleration shall be a primary programmatic consideration."

Nevertheless, current practice varies throughout the state, since some teachers and administrators are having trouble letting go of the traditional enrichment/pull-out approach to gifted education. Dr. Simmons, hired in 1988 by the State Department of Education to supervise the implementation of the new regulations, has taken a moderate stance on the acceleration/enrichment debate, defining enrichment as a transitional stage in an educational hierarchy with acceleration at its summit. "At first," she said, "there was a lot of uproar, because teachers saw the program as leaving enrichment, pull-out, and going totally to acceleration, and they were afraid that wouldn't work to meet the needs of all the identified gifted children, because we do an intellectual program."

Since students in West Virginia are identified as "gifted" on the basis of I. Q. tests and not subject-specific aptitude tests, Dr. Simmons feels that not all identified gifted students are ready for accelerated coursework. She has developed a three-tiered model that provides students with high ability and high performance with opportunities for acceleration, students with high ability and questionable performance with enrichment and some instruction in "meta-cognitive" skills, and underachievers with instruction in meta-cognitive skills, with the eventual goal being to move students into the position where they will be able to take advantage of opportunities for acceleration.[5]

Dr. Simmons's approach to implementing West Virginia's policies obviously represents a compromise between the traditional enrichment/pull-out approach and the more substantive, accelerative approach endorsed by Howley and described in part one of this volume. While questioning the value of teaching "meta-cognitive" skills in isolation and providing gifted students with enrichment (which is often no more appropriate for gifted students than for any other students), one must applaud the general thrust of Dr. Simmons's approach — to prepare students for participation in higher level academic courses. This is particularly evident on the secondary level. Across the state, pull-out programs for gifted high school and junior high school students are being replaced with substantive opportunities for advanced academic study, including Advanced Placement courses and dual enrollment at area colleges and universities.

Implementation: Best Laid Schemes

In an article on school reform, Goldenberg and Gallimore made a distinction between local knowledge and propositional (research) knowledge. "The result of direct experience is local knowledge, which is prior to propositional knowledge," they observed. "Propositional knowledge by definition is 'all else being equal' knowledge. But all else is rarely equal, and there is no way of knowing in advance of direct experience how 'unequal' things at a particular locale will be."[6]

In examining the implementation of educational policies, it is important to keep in mind the tension between propositional and local knowledge. Centrally formulated policies can never fully anticipate all of the local variables that will be encountered by those who seek to implement the policies. One of the strengths of The Education of Exceptional Children Act and West Virginia's Policy 2419 is that while they set forth a philosophical position and a number of basic guidelines, they also provide the means for local authorities, school officials, teachers and families to shape educational practice. An exemplary IEP should draw on the best available research knowledge while reflecting the concerns of all interested parties. Whereas the tools for assessing the individual needs of students are becoming increasingly sophisticated, there is no way of predicting precisely which educational options will match those needs. In theory, an IEP is contract between consenting parties based on a sincere examination of all relevant information and derived from a negotiated process.

Since the revisions to Policy 2419 and the other laws governing the education of gifted children had only been in effect for two years at the time that this study was undertaken, it was impossible to assess systematically the extent to which it had benefitted highly able students across the state of West Virginia. At a future date, it will be important to conduct extensive quantitative research to determine whether the new policies and laws have achieved some of their stated and implicit goals: increased availability of honors and advanced courses in the regular educational program (including Advanced Placement courses), increased numbers of students completing grades K-13 in fewer than 13 years, opportunities for students not identified as gifted to take advantage of strategies proven effective with the gifted, increased numbers of students gaining acceptance to highly selective colleges and universities, and most importantly "increased ... academic achievement and educational performance."

By examining the current status of gifted education in two West Virginia counties, we hope to shed some light on the process of implementation, attempting to gage the extent to which the ideals embodied in the policy are beginning to have an impact on practice. The central questions addressed are: How are policies formulated on the state level implemented (or not implemented) on the local level? How knowledgeable are local officials regarding these policies? What sorts of conflicts have arisen? What are the advantages and shortcomings of centralized policy decisions? What does the policy mean to the students, teachers, administrators on the front-lines? How are various schools and school districts making the transition from the enrichment/pull-out approach to substantive academic approaches to addressing the needs of academically talented students? To what extent is the IEP process providing students with educational programs modified to meet their specific, individual needs? To what extent is the process providing students and their parents with a voice in the educational process?

River County*

In winter, the stark, essential beauty of River County, West Virginia is evasive. Hills of bare-branched hard wood and stands of scrub pine, silted brown flood waters running fast, and the low

---

* The name of this county and all individuals named in this section have been fictionalized.

slung houses with their cement slab porches, metal furniture and fenced-in yards can inspire or provoke a deep and gnawing apathy.

"There are still a lot of people in River County who are waiting for coal to come back. Well, the fact is coal never left. Coal's booming. But it's mechanized, and like it or not, those jobs are never coming back," said one educator, grappling to describe life in River County.

There is no doubt a certain dignity in the peoples' attachment to the land and to a way of life which may soon disappear all together, like the old mining camps which have been vanishing over the past two decades. There is dignity in River County, and people are warm and open. There is dignity, but there is also terrible poverty, hunger, abuse, violence, and apathy.

For a while apathy spares the children; they are playful and expectant waiting for their school buses by the roadside in the morning. And some people manage to stay ahead of it, to catch some wind out of the valley — a scholarship to go back east and study like TJ, the only kid from town in thirty-two years to be accepted by an Ivy League school. Still, if you ask him, he's not even sure it won't catch up with him some day in spite of everything he's done to ward it off.

In the eighth and ninth grades, TJ finished first in the county in the Math Field Day competition. Without ever exerting himself, he has always been the top student in his class. In his senior year, he enrolled in three math courses — Trigonometry, A.P. Calculus via satellite, and another Calculus course at the local college. In his junior year of high school, he won a regional award for his knowledge of U.S. history and founded a literary magazine. Since the school refused to cover the costs of printing the magazine, he paid for it out of pocket. Most of his spare time is spent playing the guitar, writing short stories, reading, and editing the magazine. In the summer between eleventh and twelfth grades, he read 28 books he described as "classics," ranging from *The Good Earth* to *Light in August*. Not surprisingly, he was particularly impressed with Faulkner because, as he said, "when you turn the page, it's hard to tell exactly where you're going to be."

Sadly, TJ feels that his passion for ideas, for literature and learning only serves to isolate him from his peers. "Nobody seems to care about anything around here, except for sports and sex," he said. In the attic of his parents home, over milk and cookies, TJ and his best friend Jerry, his only competitor for valedictorian, talked about friends they'd seen overtaken by apathy and the pressure to give up on academics.

> "You're sitting in one of the biggest sports counties in West Virginia," Jerry said. "If all the kids in Fillmore High School got accepted to Harvard next year it would make less of an impression than winning the state championship."

> "Lee Parker is a shining example of someone who had promise," TJ said. "Now, he does not care about anything."

> "Jeff Roberts," Jerry added, forming the name slowly, a rich drawl engulfing his vowels. "In elementary and seventh grade, he had straight A's, was the only kid identified as gifted from his school. He had an I.Q. of 150. Now he's lucky ... "

> "If he doesn't fail," TJ interjected.

> "Lucky to get a D. He doesn't try at all."

> "He doesn't care about anything."

> "He doesn't care if he lives or dies."

Both boys feel that being intellectually engaged, not having succumbed to apathy, singles them out for ridicule:

> We're despised and hated by everybody," TJ said. "The students hate us. They laugh at us when we get a grade less than an A."

> "And not just the students," Jerry added. "There are teachers too who act the same way the kids do. They feel offended that we try as hard as we do, and they try to just knock you down and stop you where you're at."

Both TJ and Jerry become bitter and sarcastic when they talk about their teachers. They tell stories about out-of-control classes, busy-work, teachers who don't know the subjects they have been hired to teach, and special classes designed to make life easier for football and basketball players. They find a certain dark humor in the workings of the school system's job ladder, in that all of the top administrators at all of the schools that either of them have ever attended started their careers as coaches or physical education teachers.

To illustrate the quality of the educational leadership that this system has produced at Fillmore High School, Jerry tells the following story:

Last year, TJ and I were the recipients of an American History award. It was a nominated award. We raked in a nice plaque, and they put it in the trophy case. Right now, there's a football jersey draped over the top of it being demonstrated for sale. Now, all the football and basketball awards are all nice and displayed, and here's our plaque with a football jersey thrown over the top of it. You don't even know it's there.

Maybe the placement of the jersey was an accident, but for TJ and Jerry, it serves as another reminder of how little the school values their interests and efforts.

Spending a day with Lauren Johnson, a veteran teacher and advocate for the gifted in River County, one gains a sense of just how deeply the resistance to change permeates the educational establishment. Ms. Johnson works as an itinerant teacher of gifted, visiting 7 elementary schools in the course of a week, with responsibility for 39 students. She finds the arrangement deeply troubling. Although she agrees whole-heartedly with the underlying philosophy of Policy 2419 — that highly able students deserve instruction which is adjusted to their abilities — she knows that she cannot provide it in the hour or two she spends with her students each week. "Whenever possible, through regular placement, I try to push for cross- grade placement, this type of thing," she said, "because what I can do with them one hour a week ... is very minimal. Sometimes, I think what I do is just encourage them more."

Elementary schools are small in River County, serving isolated areas, often with no more than a handful of identified gifted children. In the time that is allotted her, Ms. Johnson does her best to expose children to material they won't encounter in the regular classroom. Her emphasis is on mathematics or reading and writing, depending on the needs of her students. Classes usually start with a puzzle or brain teaser, a math problem or a word game. No more than five or ten minutes are spent on this activity, and although it seems to serve more as a transitional device than anything else — a way of capturing her students' attention for the short time she's with them — she always tries to give the problems a context by discussing their implications once the students have finished wrestling with them. Reading, which may occupy the next thirty or forty minutes, is done from children's classics, books like *Heidi* or an abridged version of *Kidnapped* for students in the third or fourth grade. Students take turns reading aloud, and when a chapter is finished, Ms. Johnson opens the discussion. At first, she asks students to recall factual detail, quizzing them on specific events, names of characters, objects described. The students seem at ease with Ms. Johnson; in one class, they joke about a character's name.

"I would sue my mother if she named me Adelaide," says a girl with scrubbed blond hair tied up in a bright red bow.

Ms. Johnson laughs along with the students but doesn't let the discussion lose its focus. Gradually, her questions become more complex, requiring sophisticated responses: definitions of unfamiliar expressions, emotional reactions to characters, interpretations of various actions. At first, there is some confusion regarding a particular character's intentions. Ms. Johnson refrains from correcting her students' interpretation of the situation and makes them go back to re-read the passage in question. Gradually, by asking focused questions, she helps the students to see that there was more to the situation than was immediately apparent: although he seemed to indicate otherwise, Adelaide's father genuinely liked Heidi.

At one school, Ms. Johnson teaches her students basic computer programming skills for the remainder of the class. At Oakwood Elementary, where she has only one student, there is no computer. At any rate, Mikey, a freckle-faced 4th grader with round red cheeks, who hardly speaks above a whisper and avoids looking adults in the eye, has a talent for writing and is interested in geography, history, and dinosaurs.

Ms. Johnson and Mikey meet in the teacher's lounge. After reading and discussing a chapter of *Kidnapped*, Mikey starts a writing assignment. As soon as he has settled down to the task at hand, Ms. Johnson leaves him alone in the room. "I hate having someone sit over my shoulder while I'm writing," she explains. When we return to the class, Mikey has built up a full head of steam; he's chugging along on the second single-spaced page of neat round script, pausing only occasionally to think, puckering and twirling his pencil before diving back down at the page.

Finished, he reads his story. It is not much more than a list of the things he would buy for his family if he were to win the lottery, but it is written in complete sentences and one cannot help being warmed by his generosity. His parents, Ms. Johnson had said earlier, have both been unemployed for years. They live in a trailer up in the woods. In his essay, Mikey lavishes gifts on them — a blue Chevy Blazer for his dad and a white Ford convertible for his mom — but when asked what he wants for Christmas he can only think of one thing: the radio car he knows his parents have already bought him.

Poverty is endemic to River County, and with it hunger, misery, violence. Driving from one school to the next, Ms. Johnson tells matter-of-fact stories about her students' hardships. Lily, a gifted junior high school student with long brown hair and a lively smile, lost her father and her brother to suicide last year. The brother was ten years old. "He had gotten into trouble at school that day," Ms. Johnson said. "So he went home and he shot himself."

To tell this story so casually, to keep driving, then to get out of the car and teach the next class might seem callous. Ms. Johnson is anything but. She cares deeply about her students, but without cherishing illusions. "Anybody with any ambition is long gone," she said. "What we're left with is the people who couldn't get out, or don't know any better."

After complimenting Mikey on his story and discussing a few stylistic points (when to start paragraphs and how to use transitions), Ms. Johnson asks him what he would like to do in the next few weeks. Somehow, inscrutably, the conversation turns to Pompeii.

"Where is Pompeii?" Ms. Johnson asks.

"Near the Gulf of Naples, I believe," says Mikey, his speech oddly measured and mature.

They discuss the history of Pompeii and the volcano; then Ms. Johnson asks Mikey if he's ever been to the sea.

Mikey answers with a characteristically sparse but elegant description: "It was sunny all the time, and the water was cool."

Unfortunately, Ms. Johnson's classes are the rare exception in the county's itinerant gifted program. Other elementary gifted classes consist of the standard pull-out fare, a smattering of subjects in which the teachers have no special expertise: nine weeks on astronomy, nine weeks of a foreign language which the instructor neither speaks nor reads, lots of hand-outs, films, and field trips.

One teacher begins her class with a couple of "brain teasers" — clever word problems which involve keeping track of units of measure and solving Algebraic equations. The first one is easy, and everyone gets the right solution. Only one student answers the second problem, but he cannot explain how he arrived at his solution. The teacher hesitates, about to ask the child to describe his approach to the problem, but it soon becomes apparent that she has not worked the problem herself, that she is only reading the answer from the book. After muddling an explanation (something to the effect that the answer is obvious), without pausing to discuss the relevance of the problem, the teacher hurries onto another topic.

Ms. Johnson is embarrassed and aggravated by the itinerant gifted program. She feels that many colleagues regard it as a cakewalk; because of the small caseload and the infrequent class meetings, they don't take the work as seriously as they should. She questions the value of her own work as well. She feels that any modifications made in a gifted child's studies should be integral to his or her education. And although she attempts to instruct her students at a level that matches their abilities, she does not see their achievements in her classes having any impact on the rest of their school experience.

In River County, attempts to coordinate regular and gifted education have foundered. Justly or unjustly, the regular classroom teachers tend to regard the pull-out program as an unnecessary interruption. Some children and parents tell stories about classroom teachers penalizing children for taking part in gifted classes. "The day the gifted teacher came, they'd suddenly give the kid all kinds of homework, or suddenly there'd be a test to study for," said one parent. "And all of a sudden lots of homework. They wouldn't want the gifted teacher to be there."

Oddly enough, even the students whose pull-out classes are taught by teachers less dedicated than Ms. Johnson, say that their gifted class is the most challenging of all their classes. "If that's the most challenging thing they do all week," observes Ms. Johnson. "I shudder to think about their other classes."

Ms. Johnson is a snappy dresser; she wears suits and wide-rimmed glasses which make her eyes seem large and serious. In class, she is gentle but firm; she uses the same speaking patterns and vocabulary whether she is addressing adults or her students. One has the sense that she regards them as individuals first and foremost. On the wall behind her desk at the Office of Exceptional Children, there is a poster with a quote from Thomas Jefferson, which seems to summarize her educational philosophy: "Nothing is as unequal as equal treatment of unequal people." Born and raised in River County, she is not entirely free of local prejudices, yet she is essentially open-minded and generous. Asked if she's an idealist, she says, "yeah," and pauses before adding, "I suppose you could say I'm stupid."

It was part idealism and part what she describes as her "desire to provoke people" that led Ms. Johnson to become an advocate for gifted students in River County. Even before the changes in the policies and laws governing gifted education came into existence in 1988, she had tried to get permission for some second graders who were reading on the fifth and sixth grade level to be grouped with older students for reading instruction. As she explained:

> Our reading supervisor refused it. I went and talked to him personally. And his question was: if they read the fourth grade book in the second grade, and the sixth grade book in the fourth grade, what are they going to read when they get in the sixth grade? Of course, I almost had a stroke. So, this has been the history of acceleration in the county.

Because of Ms. Johnson's active involvement in promoting acceleration in River County, her supervisor, Dr. Donald Roberts, the Supervisor of Special Education, has delegated a great deal of authority to her. "He backs me up," said Ms. Johnson. "When things get really messy, I know he's going to be there."

Even though Ms. Johnson has her boss and now the law on her side, she still finds herself embroiled in new battles every month or so. In the spring of 1990, Ms. Johnson was the representative from Special Education at the committee meeting where Robin Haciski's four year educational plan was drawn up. Robin, an eighth grader at the time, planned to take a summer course in geometry in a program approved by the state department of education. On the basis of the available assessment materials (99th percentile on all of her standardized achievement tests and an A average), this seemed appropriate to Ms. Johnson. In accordance with the guidelines set forth in Policy 2419, she indicated on the Four-Year Plan that Robin was to receive one unit of high school credit for the summer course, and that she should be placed in an Algebra II course at the high school when she returned to school in the fall.

Robin did well in the intensive six week summer course, but when she returned to River County in the fall, the principal of the Junior High School, Ms. Taliaditti, refused to let her register for Algebra II at the high school (in River County and most of West Virginia, the ninth grade is usually located at the junior high school). The principal claimed that there was no way that Robin could have completed the course satisfactorily in such a short time period. Robin's mother enlisted Ms. Johnson's support, but the junior high school principal would not budge. Eventually, Dr. Simmons, the state's Coordinator of Gifted Education, had to travel out to River County from Charleston to settle the matter. She held a workshop for local administrators on the ramifications of the Four-Year Plan and Policy 2419, and for a while it seemed that there would be more flexibility.

Ms. Taliaditti and other local administrators continued to resist change, however. Instead of informing parents about options for flexible pacing, they made every effort to maintain the status quo. For reasons which remain mysterious, a new restriction was placed on gifted students seeking to accelerate their studies: henceforth, any student taking courses at the high school would have to enroll in at least two courses at the high school. The following year, when Ms. Johnson used the Four-Year Plan to sign twelve gifted students up for a geometry course in the ninth grade, the principal called five of the parents in for a separate meeting and bullied them into changing their plans. Once again, Dr. Simmons had to visit the county to straighten the situation out.

Ms. Taliaditti is a proud woman; a coal miner's daughter with the exuberance of a former athlete, she appears to resent the idea of anything going on in her building which isn't entirely under her control. The very idea of gifted education rubs her the wrong way. In particular, she is skeptical about the effectiveness of pull-out enrichment. "If you have kids who are really challenged and discussing or interacting or really working and you leave them and pick up after a week where you left off, that is not challenging anybody," she observed.

Ms. Taliaditti has another legitimate beef with gifted education: she feels that challenging programs should be provided not only to students identified as gifted but to anyone who is willing and able to do the work. "We've always made allowances for students who try to accelerate, regardless of whether they're gifted," she said. "They don't have to be gifted to go into our honors program: they just have to be interested, make the application, and put out the work that's required for it." On the basis of this statement, one would think that Ms. Taliaditti would have favored Policy 2419 with its emphasis on integrating services for gifted students into the regular program; however, according to Ms. Johnson and a number of parents whose children have attended the junior high school, Ms. Taliaditti has been one of its staunchest opponents.

It is difficult to pin down the motives underlying decisions made by an individual operating in a highly politicized environment, especially when one must rely on testimony collected years after the events in question. Certainly, the administrative hierarchy in River County felt no sympathy towards Policy 2419; thus, to come out strongly for its directives would have required enough commitment to risk future opportunities for personal advancement. Although Ms. Taliaditti does not share Ms. Johnson's zeal for gifted education, this does not explain the extent to which she resisted the implementation of Policy 2419.

Mrs. Haciski, Robin's mother, provides a more plausible explanation. She feels that Ms. Taliaditti was enraged by the criticism of her school's program implied by IEPs calling for higher level courses, some of which could only be offered at the high school. "She made the comment to the parents that her school provided everything," said Mrs. Haciski. "And how dare they leave her school? That her students were not going to take classes (at the high school)."

Although Ms. Johnson and Ms. Taliaditti (each for her own reasons) would be hard-pressed to admit it, the fact is that the junior high school has changed as a result of Policy 2419. A number of opportunities which were unheard of only two years ago are now firmly established. Algebra is currently offered to students in the eighth grade, and geometry is available in the ninth. While this is a fairly normal state of affairs in most parts of the country, and can hardly be considered "acceleration," it represents a significant achievement for Ms. Johnson and the parents of gifted children who fought for it. There are honors sections in English and Social Studies in all three grades — open to anyone who can keep up with the work and described by one gifted student as "really challenging and fun." Appraisals of the school's teaching staff were not universally this warm, but there can be no doubt that progress has been made. For example, students are now permitted to take courses at the high school, and though Ms. Taliaditti is skeptical of the role that Policy 2419 has played in bringing all of this about, she has indicated a willingness to pursue further change. "There's one thing in this school that I'm not pleased with," she said. "We don't do enough for our accelerated kids."

In contrast, Fillmore High School appears at first glance to have bought into Policy 2419 without the slightest resistance. About thirty students are currently enrolled in courses offered by the local college, some of which are taught by the high school's faculty in the high school facility. Some students will graduate having accumulated as much as a whole year of college credit, and some identified gifted students are also receiving credit towards high school graduation through the program. In addition, the school offers an outstanding A. P. English course, A. P. Calculus via satellite, and honors courses in all grades.

Although the local college has been offering courses to high school students for years, it is only through the efforts of Ms. Johnson that gifted students have begun to receive high school credit for their work. Once again, there was a protracted battle, in which people from the state department of education had to be called in to enforce the regulations. To date, county officials refuse to offer dual credit to students not identified as gifted. So while the identified gifted students who have college courses written into their Four-Year Plans are receiving both high school and college credit, other students are receiving only college credit, in spite of the fact that they're doing the same work.

Mr. Stead, Fillmore's principal has mixed feelings about the college courses. On the one hand, he feels "that it's a tremendous opportunity for students to do this while they're still in high school." On the other hand, he worries that offering dual credit will undermine the high school's core program. "Really and truly, we'd like our students to take all their required courses over here," he said. "You know, because we feel we have good courses and we have good instructors. And I think you can understand we feel it's valuable to them, and they're still young. But again a lot of kids are going to college at 12 years old and doing well. So it's a matter of thinking, of the parent and the teacher and the administration. I don't know what's the best at this point. But our teachers feel that they want to keep them here as long as they can, and they want them to take their courses."

One senses that, like Ms. Taliaditti, Mr. Stead feels a certain resentment towards the IEP process and Four-Year Plans. "What is being done in the eighth grade, we have to be involved in and we haven't till now, because it's affecting us on scheduling and everything," he said. In particular, he is worried that lots of students will enter the high school with Four-Year Plans which call for courses that are not currently offered. He has already had to scramble to find foreign language instructors and has begun to worry about the two dozen ninth graders at the junior high school who are currently enrolled in geometry. "We're going to have to get some teachers who can teach the higher mathematics," he said. In the long run, he admits that Four-Year Plans may make scheduling easier. "Now, when we go to sign them up, pre-register, all we need is the Four-Year Plan, and we won't have to talk to them again unless they're going to change it." According to Dr. Simmons, Four-Year Plans are intended precisely to provide schools with an opportunity to "design a curriculum appropriate for the student body's needs."

Throughout the interview with his visitor from out of state, Mr. Stead chews tobacco, pausing every now and then to spit into a cup he keeps on a corner of his desk or to glance at his television which, according to students, he keeps tuned to a sports channel all day long. Maybe this down-home manner is meant to put the visitor at ease, yet it seems to cast doubts upon even his most ardent assertions about the goals he has for his students. A visit to a classroom where a "college-level" course is being taught only serves to heighten these doubts. In spite of the panels missing from the ceiling, ragged books lining the walls, sun browned shades dangling in the windows, graffiti covering the podium at the front of the classroom, one hopes for the best.

The teacher has a warm and straightforward presentational style. During most of the period, he lectures from his notes, but when he is struck by an idea he moves out from behind the podium and paces in front of the class, drawing parallels between the lesson and issues in current affairs or voicing a heartfelt opinion. About half of the fifteen students appear to be taking notes; the other half stare at their fingers or at the teacher in a polite and silent daze. Periodically, he pauses to ask a question, but invariably he answers it himself before anyone else has a chance to think about it — as if he is afraid to engage his students or afraid that they cannot become engaged.

When, on occasion, a student interrupts the presentation, it is invariably to ask whether or not the subject being covered is on the study sheet. After class, the teacher will observe that maybe the class does not deserve the title "college-level" since the students have difficulty learning the material without the aid of study sheets. Although the teacher is well-organized and thoughtful, the observer has the sense of witnessing a farce. It seems that the teacher could take off his clothes and the most attentive student would only ask if nakedness is covered on the study guide. When the bell sounds for the end of the period, one is invaded by a sense of relief and an overwhelming desire to escape from the building.

Conversations with parents, administrators, teachers and students reveal a mixture of feelings about the River County schools. TJ wants out: he is tired of inadequate facilities, indifferent classmates, unengaging classes. Julie Downing, who skipped the sixth grade on the advice of Ms. Johnson and is now a ninth grader aspiring to a career in anesthesiology, loves the junior high school, has only praises for her teachers, and is excited about her Four-Year Plan. Like many bright children whose parents have the economic means, Robin Haciski was taken out of the River County School system after the ninth grade. "I hate having my daughter away at school," her mother said. "This isn't what we wanted. But I can't risk losing a child who's ready to give up, who doesn't care anymore, and is in tears because she hates going to school."

One might argue that the school's difficulties are symptoms of deeper problems in River County and West Virginia. The apathy decried by TJ, Jerry, and Ms. Johnson is, in some respects, an inevitable outcome of economic decline. There are no major cities in River County, no cultural centers. Teacher salaries are abysmal (an average of $21,904 per year in 1990) and in 1987 annual per pupil expenditure was approximately $3000, less than was spent on students in the South Bronx and a quarter of what was spent in some elite suburban areas.[7] Given these conditions, it is difficult to attract good teachers and harder still to hang onto them.

A goal of the current reform movement in American education is to transform the school into an institution which is responsive to its environment but also somehow transcendent. How one goes about creating a dynamic and effective school in an environment of apathy and decline remains open to debate. Jonathan Kozol, in his book *Savage Inequalities*, makes a convincing argument for fiscal equity.[8] Schools in elite suburban areas often spend many times as much per pupil as schools in depressed urban and rural areas. If smaller class-size, better teachers, and superior facilities do not make a difference, Kozol argues, then why do people like the Haciskis make the sacrifices involved in sending a child to an expensive prep school?

As in any enterprise, money makes a difference in education. But the issues addressed by reforms like Policy 2419 — giving families a voice in the educational process and creating challenging opportunities for students — are also important. It is difficult to gage the extent to which genuine change is taking hold in River County. Ms. Johnson and Dr. Roberts both admit to feeling embattled and exhausted. Hardly a week passes when they do not find themselves embroiled in another controversy. "Sometimes I think about retiring," says Ms. Johnson. "My husband and I have put away a little money. My sister lives in Florida; maybe we'll join her." But then something raises her pique again, and before she can stop to think, she's busy convincing Dr. Roberts to square off with the central office about a gifted five-year-old who wants early admission to kindergarten.

Kanawha County: Resistance, Adaptation, and Change*

Joyce Canter, the vivacious, hard-working and sometimes stubborn Coordinator of Gifted Programs for Kanawha County admits that people tend to have strong opinions about her. "They say in the office, had I been going through school now, I'd be

---

* Kanawha County is the real name of a West Virginia county. While the names of children are fictionalized in this section, the names of adults are all real.

ADD, probably hyperactive," she says. Or, "I'm not particularly popular at a lot of schools right now. Not everyone spells Canter the way it's supposed to be spelled."

In addition to coordinating a staff of 80 teachers, Ms. Canter oversees the IEP process for the county's 1700 identified gifted students and personally supervises the writing of Four- Year Plans for every eighth grade identified gifted student in the county: in 1991, that meant 382 committee meetings. An early college entrant herself and the mother of two academically talented daughters, Ms. Canter has a definite agenda for gifted education in Kanawha County. In her words, the new regulations exist to ensure that gifted students are provided with the equivalent of "a good college prep program," and if that has an impact on the whole system, so much the better.

Under Ms. Canter's supervision, Jimmy, an eighth grader with strong verbal and mathematical talents, is enrolled part-time at a high school across town.[9] Ms. Canter advised him to choose that school over his neighborhood high school because of the availability of an advanced level course in computer programming. He takes science and social studies during the first two periods at the junior high school. Then he rides the bus to the high school where he is enrolled in Advanced Tenth Grade English, Algebra II, and the computer programming course. In spite of a county policy which forbids the granting of high school credit for work accomplished before the ninth grade, Jimmy will receive credit because credit was specified in his IEP.

Jimmy's program of study exemplifies the changes Ms. Canter is seeking to effect in the system. The recommendations in Jimmy's IEP were based on a careful assessment of test scores and school performance as well as a lengthy discussion regarding his goals and interests. Ms. Canter uses Policy 2419 not so much as a hammer but as a pair of pliers — to bend county regulations and the wills of schools administrators into a shape that allows them work for her students.

On the other hand, Ms. Canter does not shy from making demands on students. Susan Day, a teacher at Hayes Middle School, speaks admiringly of Ms. Canter's exacting standards. Faced with a gifted student who had a tendency to take days off when he did not feel like going to school, Ms. Canter laid down the line. "Ms. Canter told him that no matter how gifted he was once he hit ninth grade he couldn't keep up .... She just said she wouldn't stake her professional reputation to signing a Four-Year Plan to put him in these advanced classes if he wasn't going to be here more often. She told him she'd be back to check," said Ms. Day.

"She stopped me in the hallway a couple of times," said the student, who did not miss a single day in the first semester of ninth grade and boosted his average enough to qualify for the National Junior Honor Society.

On the whole, Ms. Canter's approach dovetails neatly with the model developed by Dr. Simmons, in which an hierarchical relationship is posited between "meta-cognitive skills," enrichment and acceleration, with each level building on the one before it. Ms. Canter is particularly cautious in assessing the abilities of elementary school students. "Just because you're identified as gifted doesn't mean you go in the accelerated math class .... You must be appropriately placed, and that is done at the IEP meeting," she remarked.

While gifted elementary school students are served in Kanawha County with a variety of programs, ranging from courses in research skills to pull-out enrichment courses to accelerated math, the Four-Year Plans written under Ms. Canter's supervision consistently emphasize substantive academic coursework, in accordance with state policy. "When I sit down with the gifted eighth graders, those children, the parents, the people that are involved at that school, I start writing in Honors English, honors this, honors that, Biology II in a school that may never have had it, Chemistry I in a school that maybe didn't have chemistry. Then those courses are available to anybody. And they have to be offered in the county."

Ms. Canter's strong opinions about what constitutes an appropriate education for an academically talented student are not always shared by parents. One father felt that his daughter was not given enough latitude to make choices for herself. "She wanted to take a sports medicine class, and they told her it was a jock class that she didn't need to take," he said. He admits that his daughter is happy with her program now, but he wishes that she had been given more of a chance to have her interests represented in the IEP. After a pattern of conflicts of this sort, the State Department of Education chose to exclude electives from Four-Year Plans. As Ms. Canter observed: "It's impossible to know four years ahead of time exactly what is going to interest a child. The most important thing is to make sure they have everything they need to get into an appropriate college or to get started on a career."

Many of the schools that serve the students whose Four-Year Plans are prepared under Ms. Canter's supervision do not offer a full range of honors and advanced placement classes. In particular, small rural schools may not have the facilities or the faculty to offer advanced science or language courses. Since Ms. Canter does not have the authority to move faculty or facilities from one school to another, students must make a decision: they may continue to attend their home school without taking the prescribed course or they may commute to another Kanawha County School where the course is offered. Under current arrangements, if the student chooses to commute, the county provides transportation.

With a slightly mischievous lilt in her voice, Ms. Canter describes the pressure this puts on a high school administrator: "You're going to have to make a decision. Are you going to want to ... send your brightest to another school? Or will you accommodate them?"

Although he chafes at the idea of being put on the spot, Mr. Burford, the principal of Hoover High School, a small school in a rural section of Kanawha County, insists that he would bend over backwards to hang onto his top students. "It may be human nature," he said, "but I want those kids here from eight to three, and I don't want anybody to even think that we can't provide what they need."

Mr. Burford good-naturedly entertains the notion that Policy 2419 and the recent legal reforms could have a positive impact on the quality of education in West Virginia, but he maintains the skeptical distance of a seasoned administrator. "In a nutshell, the problem with any new plan is that we never dump the old," he observed. "I like the idea of an IEP; I really do. But I wish the counselors could get out of some of the other things that they're responsible for .... I hate to say it, but at present, the IEP is something we're just getting done."

In pragmatic terms, he feels that the state has not come out as strongly as it could for the IEP/Four-Year Plan process. There are no provisions for relieving anyone on his staff of other duties, and there is no new funding; in fact, the result of recent legislation has been to cut back funding to high schools. Where school systems had previously received three times as much funding for a gifted student as they received for a regular student, now school systems only receive the 3 to 1 payment for students also identified as "exceptional." Under current arrangements, students in honors and advanced courses are funded at a rate of 2 to 1. However, state law also puts restrictions on the number of students enrolled in gifted, honors or advanced level courses for which a county may request reimbursement.

To a certain degree one senses that Mr. Burford and many other principals perceive the IEP as somewhat meddlesome — the tool of central office people who do not have to cope with the everyday realities of running a school. "I'm handed a sheet that says I can have 37 teachers, and it might be that I can't offer a class that's been written into a child's IEP because I don't have a way to hire a person with those credentials, and in some cases I suspect a person with such credentials is not even available," he said, explaining some of his concerns about the IEP process.

The idea behind the IEP is, in fact, to shape the school experience to the needs of the individual student, not to slot the student into the best available option. Although the reality of this exercise can be exasperating, Mr. Burford appreciates the underlying concept. He is even willing to admit that being forced to make accommodations for his top students may not be such a bad idea. "I think we do need to look at individual students and we do need to help guide them through a challenging path," he said. "And certainly we can become more involved with the IEP process."

The Consultative/Collaborative Model

In spite of the reservations of some teachers and administrators, policy in Kanawha County reflects a definite effort to adapt to the changes proposed by Policy 2419 and the Education of All Handicapped Children Law. As pull-out programs become less prominent in Kanawha County, an attempt has been made to integrate special education teachers and teachers of the gifted into the mainstream. To accomplish this end, Kanawha County has developed a Consultative/Collaborative Model.

Ideally, this model provides a framework for cooperation between special educators and regular educators. According to the document outlining the model, a number of factors are central to its functioning: "an equal relationship [between educators], mutual trust, open communication to identify problems, collaboration on the development of strategies, and shared responsibility for implementation and evaluation."[10]

Under this plan, teachers of the gifted often teach classes which are open to students not identified as gifted, as long as at least 60% of the students in the class are identified as gifted. The teachers of the gifted also serve as consultants to regular classroom teachers who are trying to address the needs of gifted students in their classes. In this capacity, they may make recommendations for curricular modification, provide resources, help to plan special projects, and offer assistance.

At first glance, the Consultative/Collaborative Model may appear to muddy waters that are already silted. One of the great weaknesses of the reform movement during the 1980's was the reliance on theoretical models formulated with little consideration of local knowledge. The assumption was that teachers with "teacher-proof" curricula in hand, following a pre-determined series of steps would always attain the same objectives. Like the IEPs, however, consultation and collaboration are anything but "teacher proof," depending largely on the initiative of individual teachers.

Outstanding teachers are distinguished by their ability to recognize what is useful in a model or theory and to adapt it constructively to their own context. What follows are three profiles of exceptional teachers whose work has had a profound influence on students in Kanawha County. Two — Connie Strickland and Susan Day — are teachers of the gifted who have successfully changed their roles to fit the demands of Policy 2419 and the Consultative/Collaborative Model. One, Richard Wilkes, is a math teacher who facilitates a flexibly-paced math course which anticipated Policy 2419 by eight years.

If You Build It, He'll Be too Busy Teaching

In 1962, Richard Wilkes was a rookie third baseman on a San Francisco Giants team in a line-up which included the likes of Juan Marichal and Willie Mays. One month into the season, Wilkes was hit by a wild pitch which shattered his elbow and his dream of a career in baseball.

Thirty years later, the lanky gray-haired former ball player laughs at the experience that changed his life. "If it hadn't been for that pitch," he says, "I'd probably have ended up a bum."

In college, Mr. Wilkes studied engineering, in graduate school, mathematics and education. On the verge of earning a PhD in education, he extricated himself from the program. "They wanted me to train teachers, but that didn't interest me," he said. "What I wanted to do was teach." He still has the gangly gait of an athlete and the sharp, bright eyes of a fast-ball hitter. He's a story-teller and a wheeler-dealer who's as comfortable with the superintendent of schools as he is with a classroom full of kids. Maybe because he has always been good at everything he does, he evinces none of the insecurity which plagues so many educators. "My father was a very successful businessman, on the boards of a number of corporations. I think he was disappointed in my choice of profession. But it's always been what I wanted to do," he said. Richard Wilkes is proud of being a teacher and approaches his work with a zeal which borders on the religious, frequently leaving the school building well after supper-time. "People say there's no respect for teachers. There's respect," he says, pausing for effect, "if you teach."

If one believes his students and the parents of his students, Mr. Wilkes may well be the best math teacher in the state of West Virginia. In the last five years, the state's math field day champions in grades 8 and 9 have all been students from his program. Several years ago, one student earned 7 Carnegie Units through her participation in the program. In 1991, after three years in the program, Heidi B. achieved a perfect 800 on the math portion of the SAT, and one of her classmates finished second in a national math competition for students enrolled in Christian schools. In 1992, Heidi was selected as a Presidential Scholar and invited Mr. Wilkes to accompany her to Washington, D.C. for the award ceremony. Typically, students in his class complete Calculus in their sophomore or junior year. Every student who takes Calculus with Mr. Wilkes must take the College Board's Advanced Placement examination, and none of his students has ever scored less than a four (out of a possible five) on the examination. Former participants in the program are currently enrolled in undergraduate and graduate programs at Rice, Georgia Tech, Harvard, Carnegie Mellon, and Yale.

To an even greater extent than the Model Math Project described in the previous chapter, Kanawha County's[11] individually paced math program is based on the CTY approach to math instruction. In order to qualify for the program, students must take the SAT during the summer after seventh grade and achieve the same scores as the average college bound male senior: in 1991, that was a 500 on the math portion and a 930 combined score. According to Ms. Teel, the Supervisor for Math Instruction in Kanawha County, "one of the reasons that the program has been so successful is that we've insisted on maintaining our standards."

Mr. Wilkes uses tests diagnostically to determine an individual student's strengths and weaknesses then adjusts the curriculum to address specific needs. Instead of forcing his students to review material which has already been mastered, he allows them to move on to new topics. Pacing is individualized, but expectations are invariably high and students typically finish twice as much material in a semester as schoolmates who do not participate in the program.

The class meets for three hours on Monday evenings in Mr. Wilkes's classroom at Nitro High School. Most years, approximately fifteen students from all corners of the surrounding counties, from public, parochial, and private schools enroll in the class. They vary in age from thirteen to eighteen and study material ranging from Algebra I to Statistics, Advanced Calculus, and Discrete Math. In addition to the time spent in class, students are expected to dedicate ten hours a week to the study of math.

"I never thought I'd see my son study ten hours a week at anything," said one mother. "I mean, that is just astounding to me that he would sit down for that length of time. I think it's helped him with his other grades .... And it's self-imposed. For him, it's been good to have a little motivation."

Asked how he motivates students, Mr. Wilkes frowns, arching bushy gray eye-brows. "Motivation is buried in expectation," he says. And then: "I teach children. I don't teach math. That's the way I can have Calculus and Trigonometry in the same classroom. That's what the Japanese are doing."

Students consistently give the same two reasons for liking Mr. Wilkes's class: the opportunity to work at the appropriate pace and Mr. Wilkes's knowledge and contagious enthusiasm for mathematics. "It's incredible that he can keep all that stuff in his head .... I mean, he's teaching all these different courses, but if you ask him a question on any of it, he'll know the answer," said Ben, a ninth grader studying analytical geometry.

Mr. Wilkes politely disagrees with Ben's evaluation. "I get stumped all the time," he said. "I tell them so. But then we just sit down and we work on it. And usually they come up with the answer." It is obvious that Mr. Wilkes relishes problems: a visitor to his classroom will often have trouble picking him out at first, for he spends most of his time sitting amid students, asking questions, posing problems, checking computations, joking, telling stories.

Nitro is an odd town — built in 1918 just before the end of the first World War, it was originally designed to house workers employed in a factory manufacturing nitro glycerin for the war effort. Although the war ended months before production began, the name stuck. Development did not come to the area again until the 1950's when the chemical industry moved to the valley that stretches northwest of Charleston along the Kanawha River. Currently, "the chemical valley" employs more chemical engineers than any other place in the nation, a boon which has not been lost on Mr. Wilkes, who wrangles computers and other equipment from the corporations and frequently invites engineers to serve as guest speakers in his classes.

"None of the speakers talk down to the students," said Mr. Wilkes. "Sometimes, they tell me these students ask them tougher questions than anybody else." Each student is also responsible for writing a biographical essay on an important mathematician which is then presented to the entire class for discussion and analysis, for one of his priorities is to instill in his students a sense of the lives of great mathematicians and the wondrous excitement that comes from solving a problem. "If you expect kids to be great," he said, "you have to present them with great materials and introduce them to the lives of great individuals." Along one wall of his classroom and in his utility closet Mr. Wilkes has accumulated a small library of mathematical biographies and classic works on assorted topics: Godel's theorem, number theory, Euclid, Pythagoras. He is particularly proud of the four volume set *The World of Mathematics*, which he rescued from the trashbin outside of the school library. "Can you imagine," he says, thumbing the pages, "they were going to throw this out?"

His devotion to mathematics runs from the arcane to the high-tech. In addition to the flexibly paced math program and a regular course load at Nitro High School, he appears three times a week on closed circuit television to conduct a call-in math tutorial. His students range from elementary school to college students, and he has never turned a problem away. Lately, feeling somewhat overworked, he has been trying to find someone to take his place, and he can't understand why no one has been willing to step forward.

Like many great teachers, Mr. Wilkes is irreverent. He does not expect anything from the state department of education and feels it is premature to comment on the impact of Policy 2419. "I don't know how much good it will do to have more students taking Advanced Placement courses if they're not taking the exam," he said. He is suspicious of changes in policy and other paper shuffling, knowing full well that serious reform must occur in the classroom. When a policy gets in his way, he makes every effort to ignore it.

One state policy which he takes particular pride in circumventing restricts summer school to remedial purposes. "What is remediation? Either it's teaching or it's not teaching. There's no such thing as remediation," he exclaims then goes on to relate how he snuck some advanced eighth and ninth graders into a "remedial" Algebra II class he was teaching one summer for jocks at a local college.

Mr. Wilkes's rebellion has led to the creation of a program — the Nitro Summer Academy. In 1991, parents who wanted to enroll their children in a summer course modeled on the Monday night program were asked to pay a modest fee to cover Mr. Wilkes's expenses; Paul McClanahan, Nitro's principal and one of Richard Wilkes's most ardent supporters, provided the classroom. By December of 1992, Mr. Wilkes had already lined up a couple of corporate sponsors for the summer program and was in the process of contacting others.

Susan Day: Teaching Children to Write

It's been raining for two days without pause, and the dense brown waters of the Coal River are threatening to overflow. The school buses have been delayed two hours and most of the teachers at Hayes Middle School have moved their cars from the parking lot near the river's bank to higher ground. In Susan Day's classroom, one seems to forget the weather entirely, the mood being defined instead by the constant hum of activity — students writing, reading, talking with their teacher, a sort of luminous presence bustling in the open space at the center of the classroom.

Ms. Day loves to tell stories, and today is no exception. After a student complains that he gets more homework in her class than in all of his other classes combined, Ms. Day launches into a tale from her youth:

> When I was in high school, I had a teacher for Advanced Senior English that everybody in the whole community respected. We all looked up to her as this paragon of virtue .... Well, I was good English student ... so I made four A's effortlessly in Advanced Senior English. Then I went on to Marshall University, where my ACT scores put me in Honors English. And I was the only person in my honors English class at Marshall who had never written a term paper. There was a girl from Letart, West Virginia — a wide spot in the road that I had never even heard of — and *she* had written a term paper. So I looked back on this sweet, pleasant lady who'd been my twelfth grade English teacher and I thought to myself — she didn't prepare me. You know what I'm saying?

"And I hope you won't look back on me and say," Ms. Day says, clapping her hands for emphasis, "Ms. Day should have taught us such and such."

It's unlikely that any of Ms. Day's students will ever look back on her with anything but admiration. According to Joyce Canter, she comes as close as any junior high school teacher to implementing the ideals of Policy 2419 and the Consultative/ Collaborative Model. She teaches Advanced English to seventh and eighth graders, a course entitled Advanced Studies to identified gifted seventh and eighth graders, runs a study "lab" one period a day, and frequently consults with other teachers and staff about how to meet the needs of gifted and talented students. Getting parents involved in the school is also high on her list of priorities: she thinks nothing of picking up the phone to call her students' parents. In fact, one student admitted that Ms. Day had called his mother six times in a semester, and only once because there was a problem.

Ms. Day's Advanced English class is the equivalent of an honors section; in accordance with county policy, at least 60% of the students in the class must be identified gifted students. Usually the percentage is closer to 80%, although Ms. Day readily admits that many of her best students are ones who were never identified as gifted. Writing and reading are the cornerstones of Ms. Day's instructional approach, and the walls of her classroom are covered with samples of student writing. Although Ms. Day emphasizes grammar and mechanics to a greater extent than many of the current advocates of "whole language" and "process writing," she feels that she has combined the best of the new thinking with a more traditional emphasis on rigor.

The portrait of a stern old man hangs in an elliptical wooden frame in one corner of the room. He is, according to Ms. Day, her great uncle A. C. Van Pip and a mnemonic device for the parts of speech. "These kids are a little goofy," she said. "They like funny, corny things. But I think every kid I have all day can tell you the parts of speech."

Every class period starts with a short writing warm-up drill, a provocative quotation or playful suggestion (e. g. — Imagine that you have eaten a cookie which makes you taller or smaller or more intelligent) to help her students get focused. Periodically, Ms. Day tests and drills students on sentence patterns, vocabulary, and grammar, but most of class time is devoted to reading aloud, discussing literature and student writing, and completing independent work. In class, students work on weekly writing assignments or "reading contracts," which include exercises to develop vocabulary, comprehension, and writing skills. Students choose the books they read and often the subjects of the essays that they write.

Ms. Day also makes a point of assigning papers which require research and a long term commitment. For the most part, her students seem to appreciate the responsibility that she demands of them. Explaining the importance of long-term assignments, an eighth grade boy said: "Well, the assignments are based on as close as you can get to what we'll be doing in high school, so we have to get used to and know how to do it, so we'll be able to do it." A seventh grader elaborated on the same theme: "she treats everybody like they're intelligent, that's what's so good about her."

Students also appreciate the fact that Ms. Day provides numerous opportunities for them to read successful stories and essays aloud to classmates and to display them on the walls of the classroom. In some instances, Ms. Day has even helped students to publish articles in the local newspaper. Joe, a quiet ninth grader who initially seems uncomfortable speaking with adults, becomes animated when he tells of getting his work into print. "It was exciting," he says, his voice knotted with pleasure. "I got to take home a copy and brag about it to my older sister."

Considered in light of an educational philosophy which emphasizes acceleration and mainstreaming of gifted students, the Advanced Studies course may be more difficult to justify. All of the students who participate in this course have been identified as gifted, and the curriculum retains elements of Kanawha County's traditional enrichment program. However, Advanced Studies is by no means a pull-out course, for it meets for a single period every day just like all other courses at Hayes. In essence, it is a demanding elective for gifted students which combines the humanities, social sciences, and educational planning.

Much of class time is spent practicing forensics and preparing for academic competitions. Ms. Day's students regularly win statewide awards in the Optimist Club Oratorical Contest and Delta Kappa Gamma Speech Contest. Over the last four years, the Hayes Academic Team, comprised mainly of students in the Advanced Study classes, has gone to the county finals four times and failed to become champions only once. During one nine week period, they participate in a "mini-course" in economics taught by a volunteer from a local business. Occasionally, Ms. Day invites graduates of Hayes Junior High School to speak about their further educational and career experiences and introduces students to the many educational options that they will need to consider in constructing Four-Year Plans. Planning for college also plays an important role in the class: Ms. Day shows films about various colleges, passes out brochures for browsing, and gives students time to work with SAT preparation software. As in all of Ms. Day's classes, there are a lot of writing assignments. On the whole, Advanced Studies seems to be an engaging class, but there is no reason to believe that it would be any less appropriate for students not identified as gifted.

Ms. Day welcomes the time that Policy 2419 has given her to work with underachieving gifted students. Second period on Wednesdays all identified gifted students who are not maintaining at least a 3.0 average must present themselves for a mandatory study lab in her classroom. During this period Ms. Day discusses study strategies, checks student assignment notebooks, and helps students to analyze any problems they might be having. In the fall of 1991, six of eight students enrolled in the mandatory lab made the honor roll after nine weeks. Describing the mandatory lab, one student, whose average rose from a 2.19 to a 3.39 (out of 4.0) said: "She nags. We had to check up with her, to make sure everything was done .... But it helped." Another remarked: "I'm unorganized, very unorganized and this helped me write down what I had to do and then do it when I go home in case I forgot. It was an easier way for me to remember what I had to do."

Sam Lee, the principal of Hayes Junior High School, is a dynamic individual, strong-willed, opinionated, warm, hard-working. He is respected by his staff even though they may not always agree. In keeping with much of the current literature on the effects of grouping students by ability, Mr. Lee is not certain that the initiatives which have been brought about through Policy 2419 are in the best interest of students. "I've been unable to find any significant studies in the last ten years that encourage us to group students at the seventh and eighth grade level," he said. "Related to gifted, I've seen it. But related to math, science, English, social studies, and the general, I have not found a single article of research and have looked in each and every reader's guide to periodical literature and been unable to find one."

The reason that Mr. Lee has been unable to find any articles discussing the merits of ability grouping for average to above average students is because the research has not been done. On the one hand, there is solid evidence that ability or achievement grouping is effective for highly able students when they are grouped for classes where the instructional materials and approach is significantly modified. Mr. Wilkes's math classes and Ms. Day's Advanced English classes are fine examples of effective use of grouping as a precondition for acceleration and subject-specific academic enrichment.

Critics of ability grouping, such as Robert Slavin and Jeannie Oakes, tend to equate grouping of any sort with tracking and point to the pernicious effects that these practices have on students placed in lower tracks. They demonstrate — quite convincingly — that students in lower tracks are not exposed to challenging materials and are often given inferior teachers with disastrous effects to their self-esteem and achievement. Cooperative Learning, in its various incarnations, has been advanced by Slavin and others as an alternative to tracking. Slavin's research on cooperative learning and ability grouping shows that students considered to be of average and below-average ability show great gains when they are grouped with higher ability students in structured cooperative settings. Furthermore, he demonstrates that above average students do no worse than they do in the traditional classroom setting.[12]

Advocates for the academically talented argue that the level of achievement expected in traditional classes falls far below that which many students are capable of attaining. Mediocrity, they tell us, is not an acceptable standard. It is unfortunate that Cooperative Learning and ability grouping are often pitted against each other in a zero sum relationship, for each technique is well-suited to achieving certain educational goals. Working in cooperative groups does teach students to collaborate, share ideas, and value peers with diverse backgrounds and capabilities. But differences in ability do exist, and it is often necessary to group students in order to address the needs of individuals with specific talents.

Students at Hayes tend to support this contention. When asked to compare Advanced English with other English classes they had taken at Hayes, gifted students invariably preferred Advanced English. Kyle, who had Ms. Day in seventh grade, had to take a regular English section in the eighth grade. "Last year, that was pretty good how we had writing assignments and stuff," he said. "And this year we have to start out with like 'what is a noun?'

'what is a verb?' because most of the kids in my class don't know. They can't pick out a prepositional phrase. So I just get 100% in that class because there's not much challenge to it .... We have an assignment and she says turn this in within two days, and I'm usually finished with it that period. Everybody else is saying 'how do you do that?'"

Another student, Rosa, complained that her hand hurt from writing paragraphs in her regular English class. Asked whether her hand hurt as much when she was in Ms. Day's class, she said: "No .... It was fun. We did creative writing and stuff." Comparing the two classes, Felicia remarked: "We did a lot of writing (in Advanced English) and didn't start out with 'what is a noun?'" One particularly perceptive student, Edgar, commenting on the boredom he felt in the regular English class, was unwilling to blame his teacher. "We had Ms. Z., and not because she isn't good, but it was like she'd have to slow down for kids. And she'd make the assignments easier so that they could get it too. And it was like an easy A class."

The question one must ask is not whether Ms. Day should lower her expectations but rather whether the expectations should be raised in the other English classes at Hayes. Maybe the school could benefit from having two "Advanced" sections. As Edgar rightly observed, however, there will always be students who need more time to master the same material. The solution is not remediation or lowered expectations, but rather flexible pacing.

Mr. Lee is too sophisticated to accept Cooperative Learning or any other single approach as an educational panacea. "We have to be eclectic," he says. Then he goes on to expound on the virtues of the math program at Hayes. "We have a unique math program at Hayes Jr. High School that will meet not only (the gifted) students' needs but every students' need in the junior high, whereby we group the kids not according to grade level but according to sequence of skills." At the end of each school year, all students are tested for skill mastery so that they may be appropriately placed in the following year. "We've had several 7th grade students who have placed into the first year Algebra course, and that means that by the time they have completed the junior high, they will have sequentially completed Algebra II," Mr. Lee added.

"We keep reinventing the wheel — don't we? — in public education," says Mr. Lee. "And cooperative learning just happens to be the trick right now."

Connie Strickland: A New Role for the Teacher of Gifted

Connie Strickland, teacher of gifted, grew up just north of Hoover High School in the narrow valley that hugs the banks of the Elk River, twenty miles upstream from Charleston where the Elk runs into the Kanawha, and a hundred miles from Point Pleasant where the Kanawha empties into the Ohio. There's some farming in the valley, but the hills are too steep and the valley floor too crowded for anyone to make a living at it. Unemployment is high. An oil refinery, the only local industry of note, shut down in 1985. Most people commute to Charleston for work, but Elkview and Clendenin, the high school's two feeder towns, are certainly more than bedroom communities. According to Mr. Burford, the principal of Hoover High School, people live by the Elk because they like the country or because they've always lived there. Driving through the valley, one cannot help recalling the solitary tug of lines by that great river poet from the other side of the Ohio, or James Wright's measured voice:

> It can't be the passing of time that casts
> That white shadow across the waters
> Just offshore ...

Most of the students at Hoover High School have no intention of entering college. Football, partying, and deer hunting are more immediate, over-riding concerns. In recent years, there has been a slight increase in the numbers of students going on to post-secondary education, from 25% up to about 33%. But it's still rare for anyone to go out of state. Between 1968 and 1980, according to Mr. Burford, only one student from the area became a doctor, and of the 111 youngsters who graduated from high school with him in 1968, only three finished four years of college. "Lots of kids that go to college are the first people in their families to even attend college," he observed. "There's a lot of anxiety. I could cite you lots of examples of kids who severely limited their options because they weren't willing to go away from home."

In May of 1991, Connie Strickland had serious reservations about Policy 2419 and the changes in West Virginia's laws as they pertained to gifted education. A teacher of gifted students since

1974, the chair of the committee that designed Kanawha County's gifted program, and, in the words of a colleague at another school thirty miles away, "the dean of gifted teachers in the county," Ms. Strickland resented the insinuation that her work was expendable. For the sake of cost-cutting, or so it appeared, everything she had struggled for was going be swept away like so much debris in the flood waters of the Elk. Oddly enough, this attack from the legislature and the state department of education was coming at a time when everything else was going right in her career. Over a three year span, she had labored tirelessly to set up what she considered a first-class program for gifted students at Hoover High School. She had won the support of her principal and thousands of dollars in grants from government and private sources for a satellite dish, televisions, VCR's, computers, and software. Through her satellite program, students were taking courses in Japanese, German, Russian, A. P. U. S. Government, A. P. Physics, and A. P. Calculus. Two mornings a week, an hour before regular classes started, she was meeting with (a dozen) students to teach a college English course, with dual credit offered through a local college. Her students were winning contests county-wide, state-wide, even nation-wide. Three of her graduating seniors were National Merit Scholars, and one was headed to Harvard on a full scholarship. To top things off, she'd been chosen by the Reader's Digest Association as one of ten "American Heroes in Education," an honor accompanied by $ 10,000 for her school and a $ 5 000 personal stipend (all of which she spent on her students).

Seven months later, Ms. Strickland's program was still in place and her attitude towards the reforms in gifted education, although still reserved, had warmed a bit. Strictly speaking, because of the numbers of identified "exceptional" gifted students at Hoover High School, Mr. Burford could not justify hiring her as a full-time teacher of gifted. Ms. Strickland feared that she would be forced to spread her efforts over more than one school or to teach six regular sections of English. But she had underestimated Mr. Burford's support. "Connie's program has been the best thing we've done, as far as I'm concerned, head and shoulders above everything else," said Mr. Burford. "I don't think the community would let us drop this. It's one of the few things that this community has gotten behind other than athletics for a long time." Through some creative management, a bit of hard-headedness, and a lot of cooperation from Kanawha County's Assistant Superintendent of Schools, he arranged to hire Ms. Strickland as a half-time teacher of gifted and a half-time regular educator. This allowed her to maintain the satellite program and academic teams, while assuming expanded responsibilities as the coordinator of a variety of in-depth and accelerated independent study programs.

It may seem contradictory to highlight a program run by a teacher whose practices are firmly rooted in the very traditions of gifted education this work has so consistently appeared to argue against. The curriculum that Ms. Strickland participated in designing and implementing placed a great deal of emphasis on academic competitions, highly theoretical models of learning, and courses in which "cognitive, affective, creative processes" and learning skills are taught in isolation from substantive academic content. However, it is important to distinguish the reality of Ms. Strickland's practices in recent years from the theoretical model presented in the county's earlier "Program of Studies for Gifted."[13] In fact, a close examination of the program Ms. Strickland supervises reveals that her practices are largely consistent with Policy 2419 as it was revised in 1988 and with the major themes developed in Part One of this work. Her program is built on academic rigor and challenge, opportunities for specialization and accelerated work, out-of-school learning, autonomy, a combination of competition and cooperation, flexibility, and most importantly attention to individual differences.

Administratively, classes for the gifted at Hoover High School are no different from any other classes; anyone may sign up for them, and, with the exception of some of the satellite courses, all of Ms. Strickland's classes meet every day at the same time for a single period, just like all of the other academic courses at the school. The fact that none of her classes can be characterized as pull-out classes reduces friction with other teachers and lends legitimacy to her work. More importantly, if one examines her schedule for the 1990–91 and 1991–92 academic years closely, one cannot help but notice that, with the exception of a few students who were taking an independent study on "current events" and those who were preparing for various academic contests, all of her students were enrolled in honors or advanced academic courses. For example, in 1990–91, her course offerings included: Latin II, Writing for Publication, College English, World Cultures,

Philosophy, and, via satellite, Russian I & II, Japanese I & II, A. P. Economics, A. P. U. S. Government, Latin I, German I, and Honors World Geography.

At first glance, preparation for academic contests might seem like enrichment of the least defensible sort; however, closer scrutiny reveals that Ms. Strickland uses the contests as a vehicle for specialized independent study. At the beginning of the school year, students who are interested sign up for academic teams. The course is counted as an elective. Ms. Strickland has developed and assembled a variety of materials — flash cards, study sheets, specialized, primary sources and reference books — to drill students on the various subjects. Although all students continue to study all subjects, each student is encouraged to develop an area or areas of expertise on the basis of demonstrated interest and ability. The contests are not seen as ends in themselves, but rather as a means to encourage students to undertake advanced, independent study of particular subjects.

With the exception of "Future Problem Solvers," a contest based on Guilford's multivariate model of intelligence,[14] preparation for all of the contests in which Ms. Strickland's students participate (Academic Decathlon, Quiz Bowl, Knowledge Master Open, etc.) involves developing skills in the context of specific content. Thus, in the classes which include students preparing for competitions, one student may study history, while another studies art and music, and two others study science. There is considerable evidence that knowledge and skills developed within a particular discipline are transferable;[15] it is the practice of mastering new material and honing specific skills that teaches the automatic routines necessary for high-level, creative performance.[16] And although Ms. Strickland may not be entirely qualified to serve as a mentor in each of the subjects being studied, she recruits teachers from various departments to help her develop materials and she routinely enrolls as a student in the satellite courses she supervises. Throughout it all, she emphasizes teaching students to think clearly and to make connections between the various disciplines, as she explained:

> They're inter-relating their knowledge, their art, their music, their English, their social studies .... At first, that wasn't true. When we first started doing it, it was all pure facts and regurgitation — that kind of thing. But now they're able to do that, and I see it particularly with the

kids that are in problem-solving, because .... I teach them something one day, or they learn it in government, and three weeks later, I see it come up on one of the problems they've written ....

June and Susan, veterans of Hoover's gifted program, are sanguine about the impact it has had on their lives. June, who plans to make a career in business, was particularly impressed with an economics course she took via satellite, which provided her with an opportunity to practice business skills. The class sold donuts and earned $1300 in profits, which they used to buy a laser disc player for the school library. "That was the most I have ever learned in a social studies class," she said. "We started a company and worked hands-on." Susan, the editor of the school newspaper and a member of various academic teams, was similarly impressed: "You cannot learn nearly as much in a regular class, because, with a teacher just standing there telling you what to do, it gets quite dull and boring." She particularly enjoyed the contact with students from different parts of the country provided through the distance learning program. "We'd call in," she said, "and you could hear people from like Mississippi calling in."

One of the greatest strengths of Ms. Strickland's program, according to Mr. Burford, is that exposes students to people and experiences which previously could not be found in the valley.

> "Regardless of how you feel about Senator Kennedy, they were having the hearings of the Senate caucuses. Was that this year or last year? And they got the word out like a week or two in advance that they would have a live hook-up with this A.P. government satellite class. So, I went up there and one of our girls actually talked on the phone with Senator Kennedy and some of the other senators, on t.v. The senator was asking them about the satellite course and how they felt about it. And it really made an impression on them."

Mr. Burford feels that experiences like these have gone a long way towards making academics "cool" at Hoover High School. "Now, it's cool to be smart," he said. According to both Susan and June, however, it's not always easy to be a part of the gifted program.

"Jealousy runs rampant," observed June.

"I've heard people say: 'I wish I could be like June — she's so pretty, she's smart, she's popular,'" Susan added. "And then you hear people say: 'I hate her because she's pretty, she's smart, she's popular.' "

Sometimes, June finds herself making excuses to her friends. "Some people, like if you're going to an academic competition, they're like — 'oh, going to a brain-child meeting?' And you just have to say something like — 'hey, it's going to get me to Disney World.' "

One feature of the gifted program that may help to make it cool is the fact that all courses at Hoover High School are available to all students, and although most of the students who sign up for courses with Ms. Strickland have been identified as gifted, students with unidentified talents have provided many pleasant surprises. Tom, for example, is not the sort of student whom a teacher would nominate for special programs. He is quiet and reserved. He does not distinguish himself as a student and suffers from a learning disability which makes it difficult for him to write. Mr. Burford admits that he had reservations when Tom decided to enroll in a Japanese class via satellite. In his second year of Japanese, however, Tom is experiencing remarkable success, which Ms. Strickland feels is beginning to spill over into his other classes. "I do see a carry over there," she said. "He is rubbing noses, and shoulders with these other achievers and it is rubbing off. They've formed like little study groups, and if they form it for Japanese, they use it for English, or they use it for history, so he becomes a part of that study group that goes sort of throughout."

Sean's experiences provide similar evidence of the flexibility of the gifted program at Hoover High School. Sean enrolled in Chemistry I instead of a required World Civilization course in his sophomore year because he wanted to take A.P. Chemistry via satellite in his junior year. In order to accommodate this wish, Mr. Burford allowed him to make up the World Civilization course in an independent study with Ms. Strickland during his junior year. It is Ms. Strickland's flexibility that makes such arrangements possible; during a given period, she is apt to have students studying as many as five different subjects in her class. Primarily, she sees herself as a facilitator and resource, encouraging students to take the leading roles in their own educations.

Don, who participates on a number of academic teams, might never have been identified for gifted programs had the process depended on teacher recommendations. Scruffy, wearing an old Red's cap, a flannel shirt, faded blue jeans and cowboy boots, he considers himself a "redneck." "I never was in gifted," he said. "I didn't figure out I could do anything — I thought I was dumb all through elementary school." According to Ms. Strickland, one of Don's friends brought her to his attention. "He brought Don in and said, 'Ms. Strickland, you might like to meet this young man.'" In a few short months, Don earned himself a place on the "A-team," the school's top quiz bowl team as the history specialist. Ms. Strickland feels that gradually he's changing the way he views himself and his abilities. He has taken it upon himself to develop study materials for his classmates, and his grades are starting to rise. "That's something Don's running into now," Ms. Strickland said. "That's why his grades are coming up, because he knows I can't take him out of classes (for competitions) unless he's performing."

Ms. Strickland continues to worry about the state's distinction between gifted and "exceptional" gifted students. Like other educators in rural West Virginia, she believes that most of the students she works with are culturally disadvantaged in many respects. She feels that it is particularly difficult to identify students who qualify as "exceptional" under the "economically disadvantaged" clause. She suggests that in Appalachian culture there is a degree of shame attached to being poor, and most individuals do not wish to be singled out for special services because of their economic circumstances. This manifests itself, for example, in the fact that many students who might eligible for free lunch simply do not sign up. "They won't count these kids even though I know that they're culturally deprived," she said, obviously aggravated. "There's no test that's going to show they're culturally deprived."

In the meantime, Ms. Strickland has reached what might be characterized as an uneasy truce with the new state laws and policies. Choosing not to dwell on them, she continues to focus her energies on moving forward with her programs, identifying problems as they arise and directing her energies towards solving them. Oddly enough, many of the adjustments that Ms. Strickland has made in her programs mirror the changes being made on the state and county level. The extent to which this is intentional and the extent to which it is serendipitous is difficult to say, even for Ms. Strickland herself. A number of county policies adopted at the same time as Policy 2419 and the changes in state law summarized above seem to have eased the transition.

An energetic and outgoing woman, she has sought from the beginning to integrate the gifted program into the mainstream of Hoover High School. In accordance with the Consultative/ Collaborative Model, she now has one period a day which is dedicated exclusively to consultation and collaboration with other teachers. Through conversations with the regular education faculty she keeps tabs on gifted students and makes recommendations as to how they might best accommodate the students' individual needs. She also provides other teachers with materials for study skills courses, helps them to write grants, and recruits other teachers to supervise satellite courses and help her train the academic teams. Her ability to serve the students in her independent studies has also been enhanced through collaboration. Because of her constant interaction with teachers in the regular education program, she has been able to convince them to provide syllabi and other materials for students such as Sean, who are making up regular coursework in independent studies. Undoubtedly, Ms. Strickland would have been involved in such undertakings, but the Consultative/Collaborative Model has accelerated the process and lent institutional legitimacy to the practice.

In order to support the changes that have come about as a result of 2419 and the general move towards mainstreaming of exceptional students, Ms. Strickland hopes to teach a graduate level course on the special educational needs of highly able students to her colleagues on the Hoover High School faculty. There can be no doubt that teaching a course on-site has huge advantages over the traditional approach. In her dual role as instructor and consultant, Ms. Strickland can provide other teachers with immediate feed-back while maintaining a dialogue on the relationship between theory and practice. And unlike some professors at education schools, she is deeply invested in the success of students at Hoover High School and thus has an added incentive to make sure that all of the teachers in her classes really learn what she teaches.

Ms. Strickland willingly admits that Policy 2419 came at time when West Virginia was ready for a change in its approach to gifted education. Her own students described elementary and middle school pull-out programs plagued by the usual problems: irrelevant games, inconsistent instruction, lack of clear goals, and lack of rigor. "The group cut its own throat," she said. Then, with a combination of wistful resignation and indomitable optimism, she quotes Joseph Renzulli: "if you don't affect the regular curriculum, you haven't done your job."[17] This sentiment echoes Virginia Simmons's emphasis on "defensible programs." Ultimately, Ms. Strickland's programs are converging with the goals of West Virginia's new policies; nay, are demonstrating an exemplary approach to implementation — a marriage of some of the best practices in the tradition of gifted education with some of the most important features of the American educational tradition as delineated in part one of this volume.

Conclusion

Critics have remarked that the fundamental shortcoming of the school reform movement in the 1980's was its failure to focus on the institutional context of our nation's educational problems. In their book *Politics, Markets, and America's Schools*, John Chubb and Terry Moe argued that "existing institutions cannot solve the problem because they are the problem."[18] In their attack on the prevailing organizational structure of public schools in America, they painted a picture of a classical Weberian bureaucracy incapable of responding to the needs of a diverse student population. In their words, public education in America is "too hierarchical, too rule-bound, too formalistic."[19] This line of criticism is certainly not new; already in 1970, Feyereisen, Fiorino, and Nowak observed that "the central problem in school administration is how to cope with change and innovation in organized structures which were not designed to respond to changes in the larger environment but which were, in fact, designed to ignore them."[20]

According to Chubb and Moe, attempts at reform which do not produce "new institutions of educational governance"[21] are bound to fail because they will inevitably lead to "new legislative or district policies, administered by the educational bureaucracy."[22] They conclude that the only way to break free of the stifling bureaucracy is to provide families and schools with choice — that is, to replace a system governed by democratic institutions with one governed by the market.

Since a choice system is fraught with problems of its own, and it is unlikely that such a radical measure would ever garner enough support to be enacted, we must seek ways to change the existing structures so that they are better suited to addressing the problems which confront America's schools. In particular, we might do well to consider approaches which circumvent existing regulations and redefine institutional relationships, undercutting the hierarchy, replacing compartmentalization with collaboration, and encouraging personal interactions.

This case study of the implementation of West Virginia's recent reforms in gifted education demonstrates some of the difficulties associated with attempting to make a closed bureaucratic system more flexible and responsive to its environment. In River County and to a lesser extent in Kanawha County, we saw that administrators view the IEP process as something meddlesome, a means whereby the State Department of Education imposes its priorities on local schools. Whereas some of the parents, teachers and administrators interviewed reacted negatively to IEPs and Policy 2419 on an immediate, gut level, when questioned more closely, most were able to recognize certain advantages embodied in this approach, including:

- more opportunities for students and parents to become informed about and participate in the educational decision-making process;
- placement of students in appropriate courses on the basis of accurate assessment of abilities and needs;
- increased use of flexible pacing alternatives such as grade skipping, course compacting, mastery-based promotion, Advanced Placement courses, and dual enrollment;
- opportunities for students not identified as gifted to participate in advanced level courses and to benefit from strategies proven successful with identified gifted students;
- facilitation of long-term planning.

In the two counties examined in this study, Policy 2419 is beginning to have an effect on education in West Virginia largely because it circumvents the bureaucracy. Central to its functioning is the Superintendent's decision which makes a gifted student's IEP take precedence over all other educational documents, thus insulating gifted students from inflexible regulations. By placing deci-

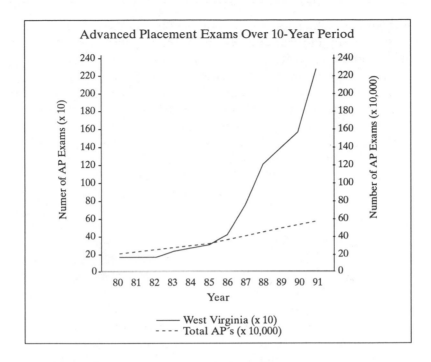

Figure 2. Comparison of Rate of Growth in numbers of Advanced Placement Examinations Taken Annually: West Virginia versus National Sample. (Source: The College Board Summary Reports 1980–1991)

sion-making authority in the committee which designs the IEP, the State Department of Education has in effect divested itself of authority. Policy 2419 sets the parameters for the discussion of an individual student's program, but the individual student's IEP results from a negotiated process. All concerned parties — the district, the school, and the family — are represented at the IEP meeting and its content is determined through consideration of the best available assessment data and constructive dialogue. Ideally, under this system, an education is transformed from a standardized, often inappropriate service into a program agreed upon by consenting parties, regulated by a contract and protected by due process.

Some promising data is already beginning to appear. The rise in the numbers of honors and advanced courses across the state is encouraging. Another fortunate outcome has been the increase in the number of teachers being trained to teach Advanced Placement courses, which has resulted in increases in the number of students enrolling in these courses and receiving certification on the College Board's Advanced Placement Examinations. Over the last five years, West Virginia's compound rate of growth of participation in the Advanced Placement program has been four times the national average. Since the implementation of Policy 2419 in 1988, the number of students taking A. P. Examinations in West Virginia has almost doubled (see Figure 2). Whereas West Virginia ranked 47th among the states in numbers of A. P. exams taken annually in 1986, by 1991, it had risen to 32nd. Whereas the percentage of students scoring 3 or above on exams usually lags behind growth in the numbers taking exams, this has not been the case in West Virginia, where the rate of growth of scores of 3 or above is also almost four times the national average.

Quite a few obstacles remain in the implementation of Policy 2419. Many parents are still poorly informed about the implications of the policy and the importance of voicing their concerns at the meetings where IEPs and Four-Year Plans are formulated. School administrators need to recognize the potential value of IEPs and Four-Year Plans as long-term planning devices, and teachers need to continue expanding the collaboration between regular teachers and teachers of gifted. Ultimately, Policy 2419 will only have a sustained impact on the quality of education in West Virginia if it engenders genuine change in the classroom. As one parent put it, "Any program is only as good as the people you have behind the program teaching." Individuals like Susan Day, Ms. Johnson, Ms. Strickland, and Richard Wilkes will be effective teachers regardless of the manner in which the bureaucracy is configured; however, the use of IEPs and Four-Year Plans as specified by West Virginia's new laws and regulations is beginning to eliminate some of the barriers that prevent students from benefiting from genuinely flexible opportunities. As one student put it: "The plan gives you an idea of what you're going to be doing ahead of time. I'm going to take as many advanced classes as I can."

The planning process, in demanding collaboration between local schools, the district, and families, helps to break down the constraints of the bureaucratic system, providing an opportunity for the types of personal interaction so frequently absent in the public school setting. However, where changes have occurred, it has been largely through the efforts of individual activists, such as Ms. Johnson and Ms. Canter. While the accomplishments of these individuals are admirable, there is a risk involved in not spreading responsibility for the implementation of reform; if the individual retires or is replaced, new issues may become the priority. Fortunately, it appears that at least in some instances the changes are beginning to take hold. Teachers and administrators are beginning to recognize the advantages of providing students with flexible options instead of generic pull-out programs. And most importantly, parents are becoming more involved in the process. As one mother told how she has become more savvy about the process: "My son just brought papers home. And it was written in there — what do you want to choose for your child? And he pretty much made his idea of what he wanted. So we went along with it, but ... I think I'll have more input with my other two children."

Notes

1. Public Law 94-142 was replaced in 1991 by the Public Law 101–476 "The Individuals with Disabilities Education Act" (IDEA); however, no changes were made in any of the provisions discussed in this chapter.
2. West Virginia Code §§18–2E-3b Cum. Supp. 1989, pp. 365–66.
3. Pendarvis, Howley, and Howley, *The Abilities of Gifted Children,* p. 4.
4. Howley, Craig, "Intellectually Gifted Students: Issues and Policy Implications," Howley, Craig.
5. Simmons, Virginia, "The West Virginia Model for Academic Instruction," West Virginia Department of Education, 1991.
6. Goldenberg, Claude & Gallimore, Ronald, "Local Knowledge, Research Knowledge, and Educational Change."
7. Teacher salaries from the New York Times, March 9, 1990. Per pupil expenditure for West Virginia from the 1987 Census of Government, Vol. 4, No. 1: Finances of Public School Systems, Bureau of Census, United States Department of Commerce. Per pupil expenditure for The South Bronx and elsewhere, from Kozol, Jonathan, *Savage Inequalities.*
8. Kozol, pp. 123–24.
9. For over twenty years, Kanawha County has had a policy of open-door enrollment, which allows students to enroll in any school in the county.
10. Kanawha County Department of Education, Consultative/Collaborative Model, p. 1.

11. The individually paced mathematics program is supported by Kanawha County and the Regional Education Service Agency.
12. Slavin, R. E. Ability grouping and student achievement in elementary schools.
13. Kanawha County, "A Model for Education of the Gifted," 1986.
14. Guilford, *The Nature of Human Intelligence.*
15. Bruner, J., *The Process of Education.*
16. Ochse, *Before the Gates of Excellence.*
17. Renzulli, J., *The Enrichment Triad Model.*
18. Chubb and Moe, p. 3.
19. Ibid. p. 26.
20. Feyereisen, Fiorino, & Nowak, p. 27.
21. Chubb & Moe, p. 11.
22. Ibid. p. 18.

15

The Optimal Match: A Program for Recovering Our Children from the System

At a school in a dusty little town in the Southeast, we spoke with a group of ten or eleven sixth graders, mostly Mexican-American and mostly the children of migrant farm-workers. These were children whose teachers felt that they were capable of superior academic work but who had not been identified for the school's gifted program or for any other advanced classes. In spite of the fact that the state in question has a progressive testing policy, which allows students to take tests in their native language or to gain acceptance for programs on the basis of a score on a sub-test of the I. Q. battery, none of these students had qualified. Yet they were all high achieving students: thoughtful, articulate, and insightful in conversation. One of the students, a serious girl with short brown hair and a slightly Mexican accent, said she liked school but that she sometimes got bored because her classes were too easy. When asked why she and the other students in the room hadn't qualified for the gifted program, she explained in a tone that was almost indulgent, as if the matter were self-evident: "we're smart but we're not intelligent." She did not say where she had learned that formula, but it was one that we would hear from other students in the town. Later, we discovered that it was the phrase used by the school system's educational psychologist to reassure students not selected for the gifted program. In a town where only sixteen students of 5 000 were identified as gifted, the phrase sounded oddly tantalizing; it gave the sensation of standing in water to the neck but being unable to drink it.[1]

The phrase is simultaneously nonsensical and profoundly disturbing. Considering it, one feels as if one were standing too close to a painting and, overwhelmed by brush strokes, colors, textures, could perceive neither pattern nor purpose. Later, when one steps back and examines it in all of its simplicity and oddity, one cannot help feeling that something has been revealed. The effect is vertiginous — as if one had opened the chest of a frog to peer at its beating heart — for here is one of the fundamental problems of American education, intact and robust in spite of a decade of frenzied attempts to reform the nation's schools. Instead of asking what the child needed, the school was looking for the right procedure. Instead of using the information that the test provided as a starting point for an individualized and flexible course of study, the school supplied a mystery.

Readers of Edgar Allan Poe will be reminded of the case of the purloined letter — the mystery that stumped Monsieur G., the Parisian Prefect of Police, precisely because its solution was so simple. In explaining why the Prefect was unable to find the missing letter, in spite of a systematic examination of the thief's apartment where the letter was openly displayed in a card-rack hanging beneath the mantelpiece, the great detective Dupin made certain observations about the prefect's methods which might, without too much modification, be brought to bear on the operation of the bureaucracies which have run our nation's schools for much of the twentieth century. "The measures," said Dupin, "were good in their kind, and well executed; their defect lay in their being inapplicable to the case, and to the man. A certain set of highly ingenious resources are, with the Prefect, a sort of Procrustean bed, to which he forcibly adapts his designs. But he perpetually errs by being too deep or too shallow, for the matter in hand; and many a schoolboy is a better reasoner than he."[2]

In his efforts to apply his methodology with rigor and precision, the Prefect failed to consider what was most important — the individual who had hidden the letter. The previous twelve chapters have provided ample evidence that when school systems adhere too rigidly to bureaucratic procedures, they lose track of the individual children whom they were created to serve. Sitting at her desk in the neon glare of the classroom, the student becomes invisible precisely because she is so much more obvious than the haze of requirements, reports, and regulations which surround her.

If we are to reform the schools, let us reform them in such a manner that the child is recovered from the process. Let us mobilize the tremendous energies which are now being wasted in the perpetuation of the system and put them at the service of the child. Let us recover the notion that schools exist to provide students with a useful education, and let us expand upon that notion. Let us imagine schools whose purpose is to engage the intellect and to nourish the drive to mastery. Let us imagine schools which recognize that all students can attain excellence, but that not all students will master the same concepts and skills at the same time or in the same manner. Let us imagine schools that are flexible enough to accommodate individual differences, and brave enough to celebrate them. Let us imagine schools which teach children the value of social interaction, cooperation, and community, but let us also imagine schools which encourage healthy competition, which reward individual initiative, which recognize that equity and excellence are not mutually exclusive — that it is in fact absurd to speak of one in the absence of the other. Now, let us imagine how to get there.

This chapter is an attempt to frame the findings from the case studies presented in this volume in the context the educational reform movement. With a few exceptions, past attempts to describe appropriate educational programs for the academically talented have suffered from their insularity and indifference to the problems of educational reform as a whole. Traditionally, the debate among educators of the gifted has focused on how to create better *programs* for the gifted and not on how to improve the schools. But this sort of intellectual provincialism is no longer tenable.

If one examines the case studies summarized in this volume in light of the research on effective schools, one finds that most of the obstacles encountered by academically talented students grow out of systemic problems which will never be solved by a retreat to insular, pull-out enrichment programs. This is not to suggest that academically talented students do not have distinctive needs, rather to suggest that these needs are best addressed through modification of the regular program. If a school is to work for its brightest students, the instruction offered in the core courses — English, foreign languages, science, mathematics, history, geography, and the arts — must meet the toughest international standards and must, by definition, be enriched. Instead of hour-in-class requirements, we must develop standards based on much higher expectations than are currently the norm. For example, upon graduating from high school, all students should be able to express their ideas clearly and concisely in Standard Written English. More specifically, all graduates should have the capacity to write a term paper of significant length (e. g. 10 type-written pages) in which they construct a coherent argument, support their ideas with relevant details, and demonstrate a sensitivity to the basics of usage and style. Furthermore, understanding and analyzing complex texts — whether literary, historical, scientific, or technical — should not present any problems to high school graduates. They should be conversant in America's literary and artistic tradition and the various traditions which have had the greatest influence on it — African, Asian, and European. In the course of their studies, graduates should acquire a fluent reading knowledge and basic conversational ability in at least one foreign language. They should be confident in their ability to apply skills learned in algebra, geometry, trigonometry, and analytical geometry to solve authentic problems involving many steps. It would not be unreasonable to expect a working knowledge of the basics of calculus and statistics as well. Furthermore, familiarity with some of the uses of computers — word processing, spread sheets, and elementary programming applications — should come as no surprise. In social studies, we might do well to model our standards on the College Board's Advanced Placement Examinations. Before graduating from high school, students would be expected to pass A. P. style tests in U. S. History and Geography, European History and Geography, African History and Geography, and Asian History and Geography. The A. P. standard might also be applied in the sciences, such that one would anticipate every graduating senior to be able to pass an advanced placement examination in chemistry, biology and physics.

In all subjects, students would earn their diplomas by demonstrating mastery of skills and the ability to apply those skills to solve problems and answer questions. The Advanced Placement Examinations are the only existing instruments with a proven national track record, and while recent research on alternative assessment has produced some promising new developments,[3] a return to a long-neglected tradition may prove even more fruitful. In order to allow students to demonstrate the ability to think on their feet and apply skills to authentic problems, we would do well to supplement conventional paper and pencil examinations with the centuries old, European practice of oral examination.

While the standards outlined above might sound unreasonably high, they are precisely the sorts of standards aspired to by the Japanese, the Hungarians, the Belgians, the Malaysians, the Germans, and the best schools in the United States. Obviously, we will not attain these standards simply by overhauling our high schools; raising the standards in our elementary and middle schools will be just as important. To start with, the tremendous redundancy of the elementary school curriculum must be eliminated. Most students are ready to begin studying Algebra in the fifth grade. The standard for English set forth above is, if anything, too lenient; if a school is truly rigorous, its students will learn to write coherent and compelling essays by the age of fourteen, having gained fluency in their writing and mastered the basics of grammar in the early years of elementary school. Similarly, to attain the standards set forth above, one would need to integrate the study of science and history into the elementary curriculum. There is no reason for twelve-year-olds not to know the names and locations of the capitals of all the countries in Africa. Nor is there any reason not to expect research papers from ten-year-olds. As Mike Yazurlo suggested, the rudiments of physics should be introduced five or six years earlier than is currently the norm. In most European countries, nine and ten year-olds study the basics of mechanics, electricity and magnetism, and gravitation.[4]

While the majority of students will require 12 to 13 years of schooling to attain the standards outlined above, the case studies give reason to expect that the most talented students would complete the requirements, especially in their fields of strength, by the age of 13 or 14. Flexibility would further be enhanced if promotion were based on a series of examinations (oral and written), covering three-year intervals (early elementary, upper elementary, middle school, and high school).[5] With the implementation of examinations of this sort, promotion would depend on learning instead of artificial notions of age-appropriateness. As students would begin to reach higher and higher levels of attainment at much earlier ages, it would be up to local schools to provide further opportunities and to assist students in finding options in the community or at institutions of higher learning.

In any event, improving the quality of the core curriculum should be the fundamental goal of all reform efforts. Once that is assured, flexible pacing strategies, opportunities for in-depth exploration of specific subjects, and study with mentor/teachers will prove to be simple, cost effective approaches to improving the educational experiences of the most talented students.

The program for educational reform advanced in this chapter derives from the case studies and an examination of the research on effective schools and the issues raised by the current debate on school reform. The discussion is primarily directed at the general educational program of American schools. Whenever it is relevant, however, particular attention is paid to the manner in which the suggested changes might affect academically talented students. The chapter is divided into four sections, each containing a discussion of a particular problem and a number of suggestions for change. Section one focuses on systemic issues. It includes a discussion of the effects of massive bureaucracies on education and suggests a mechanism, the Individualized Education Program (IEP), whereby the administration of school systems may be decentralized for the express purpose of making the needs and abilities of the individual student the focus of the educational process. Systemic changes of this sort are the cornerstone on which all other reforms must rest. The second section focuses on redefining the role of the state in a decentralized system and suggests various strategies for consolidating and eliminating intermediate bureaucratic structures. Section three is concerned with school organization and the implications of effective schools research for the principals, teachers, and community members who must run the nation's new generation of schools. Section four addresses the changing role of teachers and explores a number of crucial issues related to classroom practice. Finally, an attempt is made to integrate the strategies for reform set forth in this chapter with the eight features of an appropriate education discussed in chapter nine.

America's educational reform movements have always come cloaked in Messianic rhetoric: from colonial times, agents of change have sought the educational grail — the one best system which might deliver us from all evil. Although a number of suggestions for educational reform are presented in this chapter, these are by no means intended to be canonical or exhaustive. The goal quite simply is to frame the case studies in the context of the school reform movement and to suggest a number of strategies to individuals and communities who are grappling with the problem of designing schools to provide all students with an optimal match between their individual needs, abilities, interests and their educational programs.

Voice, Ownership, and the Optimal Match: Decentralization with a Purpose

In the April 1990 issue of *Phi Delta Kappan*, Chester Finn, a principal designer of the Edison Project for the Privatization and Profitization of Schooling in America and former U.S. Assistant Secretary of Education, described the changes being wrought by the current educational reform movement as a shift in paradigms. According to Finn, where the old paradigm consists in viewing education in terms of processes, the new paradigm emphasizes results — particularly, measurable gains in learning. While cynics might dismiss Finn's enthusiasm for the new paradigm as merely another apologia for the no-new-spending approach to public education, there is a seed of educational revolution in his analysis which transcends ideology. "Our understanding of 'compulsory education,' " Finn wrote, "will come to mean engaging in some form of systematic study until one attains a specified level of knowledge and skill, rather than sitting in school for a set number of years." This vision of a decentralized and profoundly flexible educational system is as consistent with the features of an appropriate education presented in chapter eight of this volume as it is revolutionary. Unfortunately, given the current structure of America's school systems and the character of the various proposals which have been advanced to replace or change this structure, Finn's vision is also utopic.

If the public policy debate surrounding educational improvement has produced any consensus, it is that the administration of the nation's schools needs to be decentralized. Research on the last decade's reform efforts indicates that schools are most effective when they have clear goals, strong leaders, opportunities for teachers to "make decisions, and community support: in sum, when there is local control."[6] In their various reports and policy statements, including America 2000, the president and the nation's governors have affirmed their commitment to decentralization. More importantly, the changes beginning to occur on the grassroots level at schools all across the nation are proof of popular sentiment favoring increased local control.

What is absent from Professor Finn's proposal and many other plans for educational reform and decentralization is a mechanism to place the needs of the individual student at the center of systemic change. Before embarking on a discussion of the potential for Individualized Education Programs to fill this gap, it may be valuable to describe in some detail the nature and origins of the systemic problem as well as the shortcomings of the approach which is generally accepted as the only alternative to current arrangements.

Most of the problems which currently plague our schools derive from the last great school reform movement (or paradigm shift) which gripped the nation at the turn of the century. While the reformers had the admirable intention of providing an efficient educational system for a rapidly growing school population, the centralized bureaucracies they created to run the schools have lost America's children in their machinery. One might argue that the situation is not surprising, that our schools are afflicted by the classic problems which result from huge impersonal bureaucracies: insularity and irresponsiveness to the environment, a rigid hierarchical management structure, inflexible adherence to rules and regulations, a counter-productive separation of line and staff workers, and alienation of line workers (teachers) who see themselves not as professionals but as proletarian cogs in a vast industrial machine and often behave in accordance with this perception. More than anything else our school systems appear as caricatures of the decaying heavy industries on whose management structures theirs are based. Even school architecture suggests containment and production organized along Tayloristic principles of order and efficiency, with little room for asymmetry, improvisation, individuality, or community.

If the case studies reported in this volume are any indication, public support for decentralized decision-making is wide-spread. In spite of the omnipresence of massive bureaucracies and the never-ending volumes of regulations which govern the nation's schools, local initiative has never disappeared entirely; instead, it has become a form of maverick activity. Individuals who take the initiative to skirt the rules and ignore the system's implicit assumption that they are not capable of making decisions are often tremendously effective and receive support on all sides. One thinks of Richard Wilkes sneaking advanced younger students into a "remedial" Algebra II course for college kids, Jorgen Nielsen's Latin teacher tutoring him during her free periods, Audrey Rose risking her career to help Tyrell Green shed an improperly assigned label, Mike Yazurlo telling parents how to get teachers to stay after school, or Richard Miller using IEPs to provide students with Carnegie credit for coursework completed in less than the required number of hours.

Decentralization is not a new idea, nor is it good in and of itself. In criticizing the problems characteristic of the current educational system, one must take care not to romanticize what came before. One room schools and their urban counter-parts had the advantage that they gave local citizens a greater say in running the schools, they allowed for cross-age tutoring, ungraded classes, flexible promotion, and immediate accountability,[7] but they were also subject to manipulation by unscrupulous local politicians. Teachers had nothing but their wits to protect them from the assaults of their constituents, and job security was virtually nil. The qualifications for teaching positions were minimal: teachers rarely had more than a high school education. Drills and drudgery often filled the school day. Finally, a pervasive provincialism often resulted in contempt for the study of subjects lacking in immediate practical value, indifference to the concerns of minorities, and willful disregard for all non-local sources of expertise.

In the popular debate, schools of "choice" have been framed as the only alternative to the current centralized arrangements.

Chubb and Moe, the most widely cited advocates of "choice," describe excessive bureaucracy and centralization as the inevitable result of "institutions of democratic control" and a voucher-based system as the only viable substitute.[8] While their analysis of the shortcomings of the bureaucratic system is insightful, their observations lack historical perspective. Bureaucracy and centralization did not arise from institutions of democratic control, they were consciously imposed upon the schools during the latter part of the 19th century and the beginning of the twentieth century.

In portraying a market driven system as the only alternative to bureaucracy, Chubb and Moe disregard some of the potential shortcomings of a system of choice, which include: a continued concentration of disadvantaged students in particular schools and neighborhoods when advantaged schools refuse to accept them; the elimination from troubled schools of activist families who might voice complaints and spearhead change; the waste of energy expended in the search for the "perfect" school; opportunities for unscrupulous profiteers to take advantage of the uninformed[9]; massive resistance from professional educators' associations and unions; and the loss of the inherent strengths of genuinely public schools.

Schools of choice no doubt have a role to play in the transformation of American education. With the proliferation of private institutions, public schools may begin to feel pressure to change their practices in order to hold onto students, particularly in states like California where funding is linked to attendance. Furthermore, private schools often enjoy greater ability to experiment with novel approaches to instruction which, if proven effective, may challenge the public schools to improve their programs. In the future, one might even hope for greater collaboration between private and public institutions, as local schools band together to share resources and explore opportunities in the community. For example, a public school might provide the laboratory and a private school the teacher for an advanced science class, which neither might have had the resources to offer alone.

While there are many promising avenues being pursued in the private sector, it would be a mistake to give up on public education. Despite Chubb and Moe's analysis, "institutions of democratic control" are not the fundamental problem with American education. Public school bureaucracies as they are currently configured are essentially anti-democratic, in that they marginalize individual initiative and do not provide a forum for competing ideas about the nature and aims of education. This does not mean, however, that public schools cannot succeed in educating students. On the contrary, some of the most successful schools in the nation — the ones which have produced the greatest number of Nobel Laureates and which continue to produce most of the finalists in the Westinghouse Competition and most of the members of the U. S. math and science olympic teams (which are among the best teams in the world) — are public schools. The solution to the problems of the nation's schools does not lie in privatization alone, but rather in the discovery of a mechanism which will activate the tremendous resources of the public education system which are currently being wasted and help to catalyze the shift in paradigms.

Although children have no explicit right to an education under the United States constitution, laws in every state include provisions for some form of public education. Currently, federal law guarantees individuals with disabilities the right to a free *appropriate* public education as specified in an Individualized Education Program (IEP). There is no reason why other children should not expect the same. In its simplest form, an IEP consists of an assessment of a student's needs and abilities, a program of studies based on that assessment, a list of educational goals, and provisions for evaluation of the services provided. The idea behind the IEP is to place the student at the center of the educational process — to make the child's education "appropriate" for her individual needs and abilities. As demonstrated in chapter eleven, the use of IEPs has had a tremendous impact on the education of gifted students in West Virginia. There is no reason to believe that the many "smart" kids who will never be identified for special programs under current policies might not reap similar benefits if their educational programs were designed to address their individual needs and abilities.

IEPs are not proposed as a panacea, but rather as a key element in the reform process. In order for IEPs to be used effectively, a number of other changes must accompany their implementation. First of all, the IEP must be recognized by the state as the primary educational document with precedence over all other regulations, rules, and restrictions. Secondly, an individual or individuals must be assigned explicit responsibility for overseeing the planning and assessment processes. Thirdly, the IEP must be linked to a system of flexible placement and promotion. Finally, teachers, parents, and individual students must be given a say in the formulation of the IEP. The goal of the IEP committee should always be to prepare a document which will be useful to the teachers and other individuals who must decide how to help a student attain the stated goals and objectives.

In the past, IEPs have come under fire from teachers, guidance counselors, and principals who have perceived them as burdensome and intrusive. In the context of unexceptional schools, where students are expected to sit passively while the teacher delivers a pre-fabricated curriculum, this attitude is not surprising. However, in a context where flexibility and optimal learning experiences are goals for all students, IEPs become the primary educational document. This has long been the case in effective programs for students with disabilities. Linked to a system in which promotion is based on proven mastery, as described above, IEPs would provide teachers with information on pacing, learning styles, behavioral issues, and individual strengths and weaknesses essential to planning a student's course of instruction.

Linked to a system of flexible promotion, an IEP, as described above, represents the single most important initiative that any state can take to correct the problems which plague school systems governed by top-heavy bureaucracies. First of all, IEPs can be used to assign power previously vested in the bureaucracy to families and the local authorities who comprise the IEP committee. Secondly, if IEPs take precedence over all other educational documents, they can provide the means for circumventing Procrustean restrictions and regulations. Furthermore, the IEP process provides parents and students with an opportunity to voice directly their concerns and interests regarding the individual's course of study and to negotiate its content. Finally, the IEP serves as a contract, delineating specifically the school system's obligations to the individual child and her family. Goals and desired outcomes are explicitly stated as are the means for assessment. When an IEP is in place, accountability is no longer a mystery.

In the current scheme of things, the decisions about a child's education have usually been made before the child ever enters the school, indeed before the child is born. No effort is made to ask the child about his interests, goals, and expectations or even to discuss with him the value of education. School is presented, quite simply, as a given, compulsory activity, like brushing your teeth or changing your underwear. If a child's abilities are assessed and a decision is made on the basis of an assessment, the explanation is frequently dismissive or oddly tantalizing, as in "you're smart but not intelligent."

Unlike certain reformers who would put an end to testing, advocates of the IEP process simply believe in using data derived from tests in a new manner. Instead of serving as tools to identify students for specific pre-fabricated programs, tests are used to assess growth, to evaluate instruction, and to diagnose student achievement for the formulation of IEPs. If anything, in cases where test data is inconclusive or ambiguous, the IEP committee might request further testing. The extent to which an IEP will provide an individual with an appropriate education is largely dependent on the accuracy of the assessment. To this end, decisions should never be made on the basis of test data alone. Insights from parents, teachers, and other individuals who have worked with the child must be given equal weight. Finally, the child's desires and expectations should always be considered. Regardless of how conscientiously one conducts the evaluation, there will always be unanticipated events in the life of any individual which will make assessment problematic. An IEP is meant to be flexible; at the start of each year or as new information becomes available, it can be re-negotiated at the request of any of the signatory parties.

Under current arrangements, schooling is seen by many families not as a right but rather as something imposed on them by the state. Financially disadvantaged parents and some minority parents are particularly suspicious of the intentions of schools. As we have seen, this is because their interests generally receive little or no consideration in the formulation of school policies. This is not an accident. Whether one views a bureaucracy as a "closed system" or adopts the more current "living organism" analogy, one cannot escape the conclusion that the primary function of any bureaucracy is to perpetuate itself. The ability of an organism to perpetuate itself depends in large degree on its ability to protect its environment from hostile intruders. Squid have ink, porcupines have quills, and educational bureaucrats have jargon, rules, and regulations. No threat of bodily harm, no display of territorial force intimidates and confuses the uninitiated parent quite as much as a reference to a policy number followed by a barrage of edu-speak.

Even parents who do take on the bureaucracy frequently find that their efforts are useless. In the words of Mrs. Dagleish, "They just beat you back." Anyone who has tried to place a phone call to an official at a school system's headquarters knows what she means. It always difficult to find the person who is responsible for a particular issue. And when you think you've finally gotten hold of the right person, he slips through your hands. The goal of the individual bureaucrat is to blend in with the system. Because the primary concern of the bureaucracy is to protect itself, it is difficult to find anyone who will take responsibility for an unusual action. If one is to progress within the hierarchy, one must be willing to toe the company line. Thus, as Jorgen Nielsen found, although there were a number of people in his city's school bureaucracy who felt that he had a legitimate gripe with the system, none were willing to stick their necks out. Similarly, no matter how much sympathy Ms. Taliaditti felt with West Virginia's policy of providing flexible pacing options for the academically talented, she was unwilling to take on the county hierarchy. Just as the body will isolate and reject a foreign body which is introduced into it, so the bureaucracy will expel anything that it perceives as a threat to its survival.

Chapter Eleven included an examination of the role played by Joyce Canter as the coordinator of gifted education in Kanawha County and provided a germane contrast. As the person responsible for representing the state's interest in the formulation of IEPs for gifted students, she has been provided with the means to battle the bureaucracy and to make judgements about the relevance of regulations to particular circumstances. She has a direct stake in the education of each child whose IEP she helps to formulate, because her signature appears on each of these documents. In the event that a problem arises, the child's parents know exactly whom to contact; they have a copy of the IEP with her signature on it. Whereas the incentives for taking personal initiative are virtually non-existent in the traditional bureaucratic system, the IEP process places a premium on individual initiative, hence Ms. Canter's frequent visits to the county's schools.

One of the beauties of the IEP process is that it forces the bureaucracy (or a person representing the bureaucracy) to come face to face with the parent, the child, and a representative of the school to negotiate the content of the IEP. In effect, this requires the system to recognize that each child has distinct needs and to place meeting those needs ahead of the bureaucracy's need to perpetuate itself. It also breaks down the artificial separation between staff and line workers, in that it takes decision-making powers out of the hands of the isolated, central bureaucracy and places it in the hands of the IEP committee. Thus, expertise is no longer framed as something remote and unquestionable, and experts are forced to deal with real people and real issues instead of abstract models and theories.

The careful reader will have learned from the case studies that the ease with which modifications were made in the regular educational program to meet an individual's needs was strongly related to the ability of parents to serve as advocates or diplomats. This observation is consistent with Albert O. Hirschman's findings on the mechanisms whereby institutions in decay (such as our nation's schools) may be revived. In his research on third world economies and systems in decline, Hirschman found that for any institution which provides goods or services there is "an elusive optimal mix of exit and voice" which will result in the mobilization of "hidden, scattered or badly utilized resources" and the delivery of higher quality services.[10] Examining services for which demand is relatively inelastic, such as transportation or education, Hirschman found that increased choice often has an unexpected negative effect on the quality of services. When customers have too much choice, they have no reason to pressure a firm or system to improve the quality of its goods or services: the incentive is simply to jump ship.

America's public schools have never been particularly responsive to this sort of pressure. In fact, the case studies seemed to indicate that if schools respond to families at all, it is when they voice their opinions and not when they exercise choice by leaving. Dr. Pastore could arrange tremendous opportunities for his son Michael because he had direct and easy access to the superintendent of schools. After her junior year in high school, Laura Foucher was able to take advantage of a variety of flexible opportunities because she cultivated a similar relationship with the superintendent in her district. Had a mechanism been in place whereby Ms. Green could voice her opinion about the content of

Tyrell's education, then maybe he could have benefitted from similar opportunities. Conversely, there is no reason to believe that the quality of education in New York City Schools was improved by Tyrell's departure. Yet one cannot help suspecting that there was just as much slack in the New York City School system as there is in any other system — resources which, given the proper application of pressure, could be mobilized to improve the quality of services. While some improvements might result from policies which force schools to become more responsive to families exercising the choice option, genuine long-term improvement of the public schools will depend on the development of mechanisms which provide families with a voice in educational negotiations and reward them for pressuring the system to mobilize their full capacities.

Providing families with access to expertise and a voice in the forum in which decisions are made about the individual's education is one of the most important functions of the IEP process. This process serves to legitimize the school's activities in that it gives families the sense that their opinions can have an impact on educational policy. Instead of being something that a school does to one's child, education becomes a negotiated process, the result of shared discussion, analysis, and compromise.

All this would mean very little if it weren't for the fact that an IEP is a legally binding contract. In a number of cases which have come before the Supreme Court, the right to a public education has often been framed in terms of property rights, in that students are guaranteed the right to due process.[11] In most businesses, it is customary that any exchange of goods or services is delineated by a contract. Historically, the contract between schools and families has remained implicit. The problem with such arrangements is that they provide no means of guaranteeing accountability. How can you tell if the goods have been delivered if you don't know what they are? One of the crucial functions of an IEP is to specify the nature of the educational goods and services.

The idea that there are certain advantages to be gained from making the ownership of individual rights explicit derives from R. H. Coase's work on liability and social cost. At the heart of Coasean analysis is the idea of negotiation. Most complex exchanges of property or services are shaped by negotiations which produce contracts delineating the rights and responsibilities of the concerned parties. According to Coase, negotiations between competing interests naturally tend to produce a situation in which net social gains are maximized.

In contrast, under current arrangements in public education, the assumption is made that negotiation is too costly; thus, rules are substituted for negotiations.[12] While individuals retain a legal right to education in a formal sense, the absence of negotiation produces a de facto loss of ownership of the educational process. As we have seen in the case studies, more often than not the absence of negotiation results in a situation in which the interests of the student and the student's family are subordinated to those of the system — the assumption being that the interests of society are represented by the system. In his analysis of liability law, Coase demonstrated quite convincingly that there is no guarantee that the inflexible application of general rules to specific circumstances results in a net social gain. In fact, there is evidence that this type of strategy, when considered in light of its total effect, often proves as destructive to the public good as it is to the individual.[13]

A number of questions arise from the application of Coasean analysis to public education. First of all, one must ask whether the potential benefits of negotiating educational services do in fact outweigh the costs. If, in light of the evidence presented in the case studies, this is assumed to be the case, one would need to identify an efficient process to implement negotiations. Choice is generally advanced as the simplest solution to this problem. While providing vouchers would symbolically restore ownership, vouchers do not necessarily foster negotiation. As a rule, private schools do not enter into negotiations with customers; rather, the package of educational services is presented as a finished product — take it or leave it. Under a system of unlimited choice, energy and resources that might best be expended on negotiations to bring about improvements in the quality of services may be wasted as consumers flit from school to school in search of the elusive perfect institution. If ownership is to become more than a symbolic gesture, a mechanism will be needed whereby families can gain ownership not only of the services per se but more importantly of the right to negotiate for those services.

A system based solely on choice provides no incentive for families to become involved in their schools; the act of choosing a school implies an acceptance of the school's authority. If a problem gets bad enough, the family will simply choose another school. In a system where the emphasis is on *voice* and *ownership*, there is a tremendous incentive to become involved. By providing each student with an individual assessment, the system indicates that it values his or her distinctive needs and abilities. Similarly, by allowing families to participate in the formulation of the IEP, the system legitimizes its activities. Finally, there is a tremendous amount of evidence that when Americans feel they own something, they take much better care of it, investing time, effort and money. Ultimately, providing students with IEPs may be the best way to preserve America's public schools and to inspire parents to become genuinely involved in their children's education.

Consolidation and the Role of the State

The state has a legitimate interest in every child, to guarantee that each is provided with an education which will equip him or her for productive participation in society and for full enjoyment of the rights guaranteed by the United States Constitution. It remains the state's responsibility to ensure that the schools provide students with mastery in the core areas of academic study which are needed both for continued study and employment. Furthermore, it is the state's responsibility to ensure that all students have equal access to programs of the highest quality.

The state's legitimate interests not withstanding, the compulsory nature of schooling remains problematic. A number of recent efforts at reforming the nation's schools have merely aggravated this situation. Although most states only compel children to attend school through the age of sixteen, American society is structured in such a manner that anyone who leaves school before graduating from high school is essentially disenfranchised. During the 1980's the school reform movement was dominated by plans to toughen standards by raising graduation requirements and the amount of time that students must spend in school. Not surprisingly, these efforts to raise standards were not particularly effective, especially when viewed in terms of their cost.

The fundamental problem with these reforms is as old as the Carnegie Unit.[14] Instead of defining standards in terms of skills mastered and information acquired, the reforms fell back on the old bureaucratic crutch: days spent in school, hours spent behind a desk. Absent any notion of quality. If the reformers had really wanted to improve the quality of education, they would have delineated explicit standards for the courses required for graduation and created tests, similar to the New York State Regents' Examinations or, better yet, the College Board's Advanced Placement Examinations, whereby students could certify that they had met those standards. The result might have been to provide students with an incentive to graduate earlier instead of later, having spent less time in school but having mastered more material.

Historically, the biggest problem with the states' involvement in education has been their failure to address the fundamental issues, such as excellence and equity, which are precisely their domain. At the same time, state bureaucracies have been all too willing to become embroiled in the micro-management of minutiae. Although they have often acted with the best of intentions, the regulations, standardized curricula, and behavior codes they have imposed have merely undermined the authority of local schools and made education increasingly rigid and unresponsive. The effect of the various intermediate and district bureaucracies has generally been the same. In their unwillingness to share authority with families and schools, the state authorities have shown contempt for the decision-making capabilities of their citizens and bred resentment in the same.

The use of IEPs in West Virginia demonstrates that this need not be the case. While the state must set goals and lay down basic ground-rules, there is no reason why state officials should not endeavor to delegate responsibility for the means whereby the goals are to be attained to the local schools. In fact, there is ample evidence that doing so would tremendously increase the effectiveness of schools. In a system based on voice, ownership, and local control, the state would confine its authority to the following fundamental issues:

– *Setting standards for promotion and graduation and administering examinations to certify that students have mastered specific skills and content and can solve authentic problems at the appropriate level.* To break the traditional age/grade lock-step and allow students to progress continuously through the curriculum, examinations might cover three-year increments. Promotion would be by subject area. As soon as a student could demonstrate mastery of a subject on a particular level, he would begin working towards certification on the next level. Gradually it would become the norm for students to work on different levels in various subjects on the basis of their abilities.

In designing new tests, states would do well to emphasize authentic problems involving many steps as well as essay and oral examinations which have long played central roles in the European system. Again, the College Board's Advanced Placement examinations might provide a model for integrating traditional concerns such as reliability, validity, and objectivity with the current interest in authenticity and applicability. Furthermore, as with the College Board's Advanced Placement Examinations, results should be scaled: that is, there should be an indication of whether an examination was passed, passed with honors, or passed with distinction. On the high school level, passing with distinction would be equivalent to earning a "5" on an Advanced Placement Examination. At all levels, provisions should be made for placement and credit on the basis of successful completion of the examinations. Ultimately, the goal should be to eliminate hours-in-class and years-in-school types of requirements. The use of examinations for promotion and graduation would provide the means to circumvent such requirements.

– *Protecting the rights of minorities and the rights of individuals to due process.* The state must provide every individual and every minority group with the means to seek redress for infringement of their rights.

– *Creating guidelines for the formulation of Individualized Education Programs, setting forth the responsibilities of the IEP coordinator, the role of each of the parties on the IEP committee, and affirming the state's commitment to providing a free appropriate public education to every child.* The guidelines should be a concise document, widely distributed, written in plain English with a minimum of jargon. West Virginia's Policy 2419 might serve as a model were it not for its many violations of the last requirement. The document should specify that all students have a right to an appropriate education: one in which an optimal match is created between their demonstrated ability and achievement levels and the content and pace of instruction. Decisions regarding the specific content of any individual's education program should be left to the local school.

– *Conducting standardized testing and distributing the results to the schools and all members of the community.* In a clever essay, an opponent of testing compared standardized tests to thermometers.[15] What would happen, she asked, if hospitals were only allowed to use thermometers to decide whether a patient was ill or well? Obviously, many sick patients would go untreated. However, the essayist's conclusion — that all standardized testing should be abandoned — is equally absurd. What would happen if thermometers were banned from hospitals?

States should administer (or contract private firms to administer) at regular intervals norm referenced and criterion referenced standardized tests. The results of such tests would help communities to gage whether their schools are on target and to focus their attentions on problem areas. The tests would also provide important data needed for the formulation of IEPs and for students applying to various out-of-school programs.

– *Overseeing the consolidation of the various bureaucracies (state, intermediate, district) and the redistribution of expertise to the local school level.* One of the most attractive features of a restructuring process based on the use of IEPs is that no one need lose his job. In most states, approximately half of the people employed by the school system are in non-teaching positions.[16] Many of these individuals are administrators who have no contact with children whatsoever. Currently, their jobs consist of making rules, implementing complicated policies, and devising training programs.

The many talented individuals who currently occupy themselves with the manufacture of paper in the offices of state, intermediate, and district bureaucracies are precisely the "hidden, scattered, and badly utilized" resources which need to be mobilized to save public education. Supervising the formulation and implementation of IEPs will require all of their expertise. To insure that no jobs would be lost, individuals currently employed in the bureaucracy would be offered the opportunity to be retrained as IEP coordinators. If they rejected the offer, they would be free to find employment elsewhere. If they accepted, they would find themselves in tremendously challenging new positions.

Under the proposed reforms, each IEP coordinator would be given responsibility for a particular school or schools, depending on the number of pupils in attendance. They would represent the state on the IEP committees, and they would be charged with enforcing the guidelines and ensuring that schools and families maintain their ends of the bargain. They would keep records and oversee the evaluation process. More importantly, they would serve as facilitators — helping schools to locate the resources and expertise needed to make the IEPs work. As their former responsibilities shifted to the local authorities or disappeared entirely, they would increasingly be empowered to put their expertise at the service of the local schools and the families whose children attend them. And while the new positions might not be as comfortable as the old ones, they would certainly be more challenging and exciting.

— *Guaranteeing equality of opportunity.* The redistribution of expertise should be accompanied by a redistribution of funding. It is unfair to hold a rural or urban school system to the same standards as a suburban system which spends twice as much per pupil. Simply stated, the disparities between the nation's wealthiest schools and its poorest schools are a disgrace. Following California's model, funds should be distributed on the basis of the number of students attending school per day. Application of this formula would provide added incentive for schools to work harder to meet the needs of their students. If a school does a good job, attendance will rise and more funding will accrue.

If affirmative action is to become an upfront investment instead of an afterthought, the federal government and state governments must expand support programs which have proven effective in meeting the substantive academic needs of disadvantaged children. State and federal governments might also be expected to provide incentives (higher wages, tax breaks, and housing subsidies) to attract top-notch teachers to inner-cities and depressed rural areas, as has long been the practice in Australia. While government cannot guarantee equality of outcome, they must guarantee equality of opportunity.

School and Community

The fundamental premise of the decentralization movement is that local schools should be allowed to make most of the decisions regarding instructional strategies, materials, and other means used in attaining the educational goals set forth by the state. Presumably, as schools are given more authority, they will become more flexible and responsive to the needs of their communities. Gradually, the increased permeability of schools will foster new relationships between schools and communities, blurring the distinction between one and the other and creating institutions of an entirely new sort.

The findings regarding school organization and administration which appear in the case studies are generally consistent with the basic principles which have emerged from the last several decades of "effective schools" research. Schools are effective when they have clear goals, rigorous academic standards, order and discipline, homework, strong leadership by the principal, teacher participation in decision-making, minimal interruptions of academic instruction for special programs, high expectations for student performance, and parental support and cooperation: in sum when there is a positive school climate.[17] Most of these characteristics were in evidence at the Hawthorne School in Yonkers, at schools using the Model Mathematics Project in Appalachia Unit O8, and at the best schools in West Virginia.

Assuming a competent and dedicated staff, the ability of a school to serve its community will depend on two factors: freedom from constraints imposed by the bureaucracy and legitimacy in the eyes of the community. In a decentralized system where students are provided with IEPs, the first issue will take care of itself. Gaining the respect of the community will largely depend on efforts made by the principal and teachers to break down artificial barriers between school and community and make all members of the community who have a legitimate interest in the school feel that they have access to the process. One thinks, for example, of Dr. Yazurlo's meetings with the minority parents' group at Hawthorne Junior High School or of the math classes that Linda Dell conducts for the parents of her students. While such informal forums must be continually explored and expanded, if the authority of the school is to be genuinely legitimized, formal mechanisms for community participation must be created. This might be accomplished by providing each school with a supervisory council, consisting of an elected body of teachers, parents, and other interested community members. The primary mission of this council would be to assist the principal in creating a positive school climate: to define the school's goals, to set academic and disciplinary standards, and to make major curricular and policy decisions.

Ideally, the council would also be responsible for hiring the school's principal. The council should seek an individual whose vision is consistent with their own and then vest her not only with the power to make day-to-day decisions but also to guide the school. Whenever possible, the council's goal should be to delegate authority, allowing the principal to lead and the teachers to teach. Although still controversial, councils of this sort implemented in Chicago are showing a great deal of promise.[18]

If the move towards decentralization of the nation's schools continues, tremendous opportunities will be afforded for schools and their communities to assume greater responsibility for the means by which students are educated. This will particularly hold true if students are provided with IEPs. Under ideal circumstances, the manner in which the goals outlined in each child's IEP are to be attained — the "how" of education — will be left entirely to the schools. Beyond broad decisions affecting general policy which will be made at the state level, decisions regarding hiring and firing, teacher training, use of staff time, scheduling, credit and placement, and the content and structure of the curriculum will be made by principals and teachers with advisory input from the school council.

While creating a positive school climate is extremely important, it is merely the foundation upon which a truly exceptional school may be built. Once the basics are in place, there is no simple formula for organizing a school. The success of a school depends on the ability of its leaders to respond to its community and shape its program to meet the needs of its student body. Increasingly, schools must organize themselves as flexible, dynamic, problem-solving organizations, constantly re-inventing themselves in response to the environment.

Promoting academic excellence must be considered the most significant challenge facing the nation's schools today. If a school is to be structured to encourage exceptional achievement, its administrators and teachers will do well to consider the types of issues which have been raised in the case studies presented in this volume. In particular, schools must make a commitment to flexible pacing, opportunities for early specialization, out-of-school learning, mentoring, and the creation of positive peer groups. What follows is a discussion of various approaches to implementing each of these strategies.

Flexible Pacing and Ability Grouping

We have come to think of the age/grade lock-step as a natural phenomenon and not as a human invention. There is nothing sacred or even particularly rational about the way our schools segregate people by age. In every respect, basing a student's educational placement on her abilities and accomplishments is simply more sensible. Ideally, schools would do away with the notion of grade-placement all together and automatically place each student in the course where the material was being presented at the appropriate pace and level of complexity. Since this is unlikely to happen any time soon, schools will have to continue relying on the various flexible pacing strategies which were explored in the case studies and discussed in chapter eight. These include: compacting, advanced level courses, grade skipping, early entrance, concurrent or dual enrollment, and credit/placement by examination.

While some of these flexible pacing and acceleration options do not require ability or achievement grouping, most do. If a subject is to be taught in a fast-paced, compacted course, the students in the class must all be capable of doing the work. The same holds true for an advanced placement course. There is no point in enrolling a student who hasn't learned Algebra in a Calculus course; nor is there any reason to introduce the pluperfect subjunctive tense to students who are having trouble distinguishing the present from the past tense. While rigid tracking systems are obviously undesirable, there is overwhelming evidence that high ability students make tremendous gains when they are grouped with students of like ability/achievement level and course content, instructional methods, and pacing are adjusted to provide appropriate challenges.

Some exceptional teachers take pride in their ability to teach classes in which students are performing on widely varied levels. By individualizing and placing students in small groups within the class for direct instruction and cooperative work, teachers like Linda Dell and Richard Wilkes are able to achieve tremendous results while teaching more than one subject in a single class.[19] Observing their classes one cannot help but conclude that learning is not a result of grouping so much as it is a result of instruction. Speaking with students who have participated in high level classes and low level classes, the same impression is reinforced. As Morgan Dagleish observed, "in level one courses, if you don't do your homework, you just want to dig a hole and put your head in it. In level two, ... it just doesn't make any difference at all."

Generally speaking, if there are any standards for students in lower level classes, they are geared to minimum competency and do not begin to provide the vast majority of students with optimal experiences. In a school system designed to encourage optimal performance from all students, expectations would be high in all courses because ultimately every child would need to meet the standards for promotion and graduation. Whereas all students would not be expected to attain the same levels of proficiency in all subjects at the same time, there would not be any classes in which teachers would not demand the best performance from their students.

Adopting clear standards for promotion and graduation and using IEPs to place students in appropriate classes would undoubtedly result in greater flexibility and quicker advancement of students to higher level courses. With or without IEPs, the goal should be to provide more students with opportunities to move through the basic curriculum more quickly than is currently the norm and to increase the options available at advanced levels. This will not only help to make school more appealing for academically talented students, it may also encourage students who are tired of school to concentrate on finishing early instead of dropping out.

Opportunities for Early Specialization and the Creation of a Positive Peer Environment

Joseph Renzulli, one of the most respected advocates of gifted education, has long advocated providing students with opportunities to delve into engaging projects in specific fields of endeavor. In fact, his Enrichment Triad Model was designed specifically to help students identify fields which might engage their interests and abilities and then to become absorbed by intensive projects: science experiments, oral histories, research, film-making, model-building, and so on. In general, school provides very few opportunities of this sort; in the case studies, students reported that their most absorbing and challenging intellectual activities frequently occurred in out-of-school situations. Caitlin Rawls received most of her writing instruction from professional writers not affiliated with her school and spent hours at home working on stories and poems; Michael Pastore pursued his interest in history through family travels and college coursework; Stig Nielsen explored science by participating in competitions and fairs.

While the enrichment triad model is preferable to the dabbling that goes on in most gifted pull-out programs and high school elective courses, some students are never given the opportunity to benefit from the program. Renzulli has come to recognize this short-coming, and has urged educators of the gifted to "... make every attempt to share with other educators the technology ... gained in teaching students process skills, modifying the regular curriculum, and helping students become producers of knowledge."[20]

As educating the brightest students increasingly becomes the responsibility of the whole school and not just of a few teachers, a primary job for educators of the gifted will be to ensure that the best practices from their field are integrated into the mainstream. This is already happening insofar as authentic problems are increasingly being included in the curriculum; instead of merely learning facts and skills, students are being asked to apply them from the start. An increase in the use of flexible pacing strategies will also prove advantageous. However, if one of the goals of reform is to give students genuine opportunities to specialize while at school, some restructuring will be in order.

In Yonkers, the use of magnet programs provides a fine example of a structural reform which encourages students to pursue in-depth specialties. In addition to the regular academic program, which is the same all across the city, each high school provides in-depth courses in a specific field of interest. There is a fine arts magnet, a video-production magnet, a technology magnet, and a law and medical magnet. Similarly, the Pasadena Unified School District has begun a pilot project in which specialized academies have been created within a high school. Academies focus on computer science, finance, graphic arts, space, health, environmental studies, and teaching, to name a few fields. Each academy has a partner in the community — a local business which helps to formulate that academy's program, provides extra funding, and helps to set up mentorships and on-the-job training experiences for academy students. Instruction is conducted by a team of teachers collaborating with a specialist. In addition to serving as a mentor in the field of specialization, the specialist helps the core subject teachers to devise materials and instructional approaches which reflect the concerns of the specialty.

According to a senior administrator for the Pasadena Unified School District, one unanticipated benefit of the program has been the creation of positive peer groups. Students in the Health Careers Academy, for example, are not all college bound doctors-in-the-making. Some aspire to careers as nurses, and many are interested in working in the rapidly expanding health technology professions. However, by studying together in the Health Careers Academy, students who might never interact in the more conventional high school context form deep and lasting friendships. More than any artificial attempts to structure classes for social interaction, providing diverse students with opportunities to work together in field a which inspires them may help to increase tolerance and understanding.

The academies have another structural advantage over the conventional high school; there are no electives. Students who choose to participate in the academies receive instruction in the core subjects in the morning, then participate in specialized programs in the afternoon. In this manner, emphasis is placed on delving into the specialty fields and the diverse needs of students are addressed. While an advanced student may spend her afternoons taking upper-level science courses at Occidental University or the University of California, another student might receive on-the-job training in specific technologies at Huntington Memorial Hospital. This arrangement addresses issues of equity and excellence in a simple and elegant manner. The most talented and ambitious students have opportunities for acceleration, and students with vocational aspirations benefit from state-of-the-art opportunities. At the end of the program, all students receive high school diplomas and at least one year of college credit from a California State University. Students who may have originally viewed their interests as vocational still leave all their options open.

In Brooklyn, New York, John Comer, Superintendent of Community School District 22 has proposed taking a similar tact in redesigning the district's elementary and middle schools. His suggestion is to extend the length of the day until 6 p.m. As in Pasadena, core instruction would be offered in the morning. Except in dire circumstances, this time would be inviolable: no pull-out programs, no counseling, no field trips, no assemblies. All of these services would be offered in the afternoons in programs known as clubs. In the clubs, students would be given the opportunity to delve into specific pursuits that interest them; special tutoring services would also be available during this time.

In Asia and Eastern Europe, specialized afternoon programs and magnet schools focusing on specific subjects have achieved tremendous results.[21] If we are to remodel our schools along these lines, it will be important not to recapitulate the mistakes of traditional gifted pull-out programs and high school electives. While participation might be required of elementary and middle school students, on the high school level it should be entirely voluntary, and a variety of choices should always be available. Although students should be provided with opportunities to change their minds, dabbling should be discouraged. Programs should be run by individuals with expertise in the area of instruction so that genuine mentor relationships can develop. When experts cannot be brought into the school, students should be provided with opportunities to work with individuals in the community. The IEP process could be used to place students in particular programs on the basis of ability and interest and to provide advanced placement and credit for work completed through such programs.

Breaking down the Barriers between School and Community

One way to gage whether the school reform movement is having a genuine impact on the quality of American education will be to examine the extent to which the artificial boundaries between schools and communities are eroded. Children in the United States, especially adolescents, are often systematically insulated from the realities of the adult world. Expectations are minimal and responsibility is continually deferred. At school, students interact with adults in extremely predictable and limited ways. Exchanges with younger children or seniors are virtually nonexistent. Even social events and extracurricular activities tend to preserve this distortion. In concert with the pandering of the popular media, age segregation has created an adolescent culture which is at once narcissistic and dangerously naive.

Individuals who oppose flexible grade placement invariably argue that children placed in classes with older students will suffer because they will become isolated from their classmates. Although we have come to accept the notion of age/grade peer groups as a natural phenomenon, it is almost entirely an artifact of our school system. Imperfect as they might have been, one room schools had the virtue that they allowed students to work on the appropriate level regardless of their age. At times, adults and young children sat side-by-side working on the same material with tremendously positive results.

One way of breaking down the separation between community and school will be to create as many opportunities as possible for adults to participate not only in the governance of schools but also in their day-to-day activities. College students and senior citizens make tremendous tutors and teachers' aids when their work is coordinated with a school's overall mission. Cross-grade tutoring has also proven extremely effective; Tyrell Green received a boost, for example, when he was allowed to tutor an older student in mathematics. This is an area where the federal government might take a leading role, providing stipends for senior citizens, college students, and even advanced high school students who are willing to work with students who have special needs. If classes cannot be made smaller, at least the ratio of adults to children should be raised.[22]

Collaboration between schools and other institutions such as universities, colleges, museums, banks, hospitals, voluntary organizations and businesses provide tremendous opportunities for students to learn new skills while interacting with adults in more realistic circumstances. The Pasadena Unified School District's "Partnership Pipeline to Success," which includes a Skills Reinforcement Project and the academy program outlined above, involves collaboration with 30 community organizations, including six universities and colleges, a hospital, two insurance companies, three banks, the National Science Foundation, and a variety of corporations and enterprises.

A more radical approach to mixing students of different ages would involve allowing adults who wish to complete their schooling or to brush up on particular subjects to enroll in high school classes. Linda Dell's mathematics classes for parents and Connie Strickland's classes on gifted education for other teachers are a step in this direction. In Yonkers, Assistant Superintendent of Schools Gladys Pack is attempting to implement a program which would similarly transform Yonkers city schools into institutions where adults are not only teachers but also students. She has invited experts from various institutions to set up shop at a number of schools where they are collaborating with teachers in the design of courses and curricula, holding seminars for teachers in their areas of expertise, and cooperating with teachers on research projects. Ultimately, this blurring of the lines between teachers and students, adults and children has tremendous implications.

Bringing adults into the schools is one way of breaking down the barriers between communities and schools; another is to situate more of the students' education in other community contexts. While some families currently take advantage of the learning opportunities available in their communities, schools generally do not explore community resources in any systematic fashion. Equipping schools with computer networks similar to the Baltimore Learning Network described in chapter eight would be a good first step in this direction. A computer network linking a community's resources would not only provide students with access to myriad sources of information, it would also serve as a springboard for collaborative projects and mentorships.

It should be obvious by now that many of America's best educational opportunities are not located in the schools. Most of the students whose experiences were discussed in this volume had opportunities to work with mentors in out-of-school situations. This allowed them to develop skills in the types of authentic situations that schools will never be able to emulate. Bob's work in his teacher's photography business, for example, paved the way for his future employment as a photographer. Every year, the Westinghouse Talent Search opens doors on careers in science for dozens of students. Similarly, programs like CTY have a profound impact, especially when students are provided with credit and placement for the work they accomplish.

Tapping into community resources is particularly important in fields where schools have traditionally been weakest. A student with musical talent will benefit more by taking master classes, playing in an orchestra, and having time to practice his instrument or compose music than he will from taking a smattering of music electives designed for the average student. Similarly, there is not a vocational school in the world that can provide students with access to the same technology that a business using state-of-the-art equipment can provide.

* * * *

The need for flexible pacing, mentors and opportunities for specialization are by no means limited to the academic subjects. If the nation's schools are to be effectively restructured, all of these issues will need to be taken into account. Decentralization and individualization must be implemented with the express purpose of providing students with opportunities that are both relevant and challenging. The barriers between teacher and student, adult and child, school and community must become more permeable, so that the individual student's desire to know may be nourished by the resources of the larger community.

Teachers as Mentors and Problem-Solvers

One of the ironies of the educational reform movement is that at the same time that teachers are increasingly being asked to teach students how to solve problems, they are neither being provided the opportunity to solve problems themselves nor being equipped to do so by the institutions that train them. Their position within most school systems is distinctly subordinate; they have little control over the aim and nature of the curriculum, little choice of materials, limited contact with colleagues, and minimal opportunities to take personal initiative. At the same time, the institutions charged with preparing teachers are so deeply mired in obscure theoretical debates and turf battles that it's a miracle anyone can teach at all. As experienced teachers will tell anyone who is willing to listen, teachers have very little say in setting standards for their profession. The result is a profession adrift, like Odysseus' ships, riding whatever wind prevails into the grasp of Cyclops, between Scylla and Charybdis, farther and farther away from Ithaca.

The fact that many teachers are not the masters of their own situation is not lost on students. They see their teachers battling with paper work, preparing meaningless lesson plans for central office files, and presenting material they've had no say in designing. They recognize their teachers' aggravation with over-sized classes, administrative indifference, constant interruptions for assemblies, club meetings, ball games, field trips. Because students know their teachers to be every bit as constrained by the school's structure as they are themselves, students have a tendency to question their teachers' authority. While this may not be a problem in itself — a flexible and self-assured teacher might turn the situation to her advantage by making allies of her students — it is a problem when the teacher reacts defensively, emphasizing order at the expense of dialogue, ideas, and learning.

According to the most widely accepted analysis, it is the teachers, their unions, and the tenure system that are to blame. If one could only make teachers accountable, the system would right itself. Just as there is always a glimmer of truth in the fog of accepted ideas, greater accountability would be a step in the right direction. But there is also a degree to which this sort of analysis is merely another instance of blaming the victim. Teacher accountability is meaningless if it is not linked to broader reforms in the administrative structure and the teacher education process. Teachers are short-changed by school systems. They are cheated by the institutions that claim to train them. And ultimately they are victimized by their own acceptance of subordinate, uninspired roles in the system.

On the structural level, teachers are cheated insofar as teaching is generally construed as a form of labor, the content of which is as rigidly delineated as that of any secretary or construction worker. When teachers attempt to take initiative, they are frequently squelched or pressured to conform. They are at the bottom of every school system's hierarchy — at the receiving end of orders, deprived of a voice in the operation of their schools. More and more frequently, they are provided with pre-fabricated, "teacher-proof" curricula. Their expertise is regarded with contempt, if it is regarded at all. Small wonder that their labor unions have traditionally focused on issues like pay, benefits, seniority, and hours.

Solutions to systemic problems will not come easily in that they are linked to the educational power structure. Officials in the school bureaucracies have a tremendous stake in maintaining the status quo. Decentralization, if it is implemented with an eye to providing students with an optimal match and families with voice and ownership, will necessarily improve the position of teachers in the system. Since officials and experts will be forced to interact with teachers on IEP committees, they will no longer be able to side-step the concerns of teachers when formulating policy. Similarly, in a decentralized system, decisions about the curriculum, scheduling, and employment would be made by principals and teachers, with the assistance of school-based councils. This sort of arrangement would provide teachers a greater sense of ownership of the events taking place in their schools and help them to feel better about their work.

Certain changes will need to be made in the structure of the school day if teachers are to take on effective new roles in a decentralized system. First of all, time will have to be set aside for teachers to interact with each other — to compare notes on students, to share ideas about effective teaching strategies, to design new lessons. Under current arrangements, preparation, assessment, and similar administrative tasks are performed whenever a teacher can grab a spare moment. Collegial interaction is equally haphazard and unstructured, giving most teachers the feeling that they are working in isolation. In this regard, we would do well to adopt the approach which prevails in schools in Japan, Taiwan, and China where teachers spend less time teaching and more time interacting with their colleagues, refining and polishing lessons, and tutoring students with special needs.[23]

One goal of decentralization should be to remove the obstacles which currently allow teachers and principals to blame the system for the problems in their schools. Once this has been accomplished, accountability will begin to take on a whole new meaning. While unions might be retained to negotiate contracts and to provide teachers a voice in the national debate, locally controlled schools would have every right to expect that arcane structures like seniority-based tenure would be replaced with mechanisms which could ensure greater accountability.

One particularly fertile idea is the rolling four-year contract.[24] Under this system, a teacher is hired for four years at a time. At any time during this four year period, the teacher may be rehired for another four years, subject to the same procedure. The four year time period gives a teacher who may be having problems time to improve but also provides the means for removing individuals who are chronic problems. To keep talented teachers in inner-cities and troubled rural areas, the federal government might link incentives — such as tax breaks and free homes for successful teachers — to the adoption of four-year rolling contracts and job ladders. If tenure is to be retained, it must become a mark of accomplishment (as is the case in most European nations) — a privilege earned by a teacher, not merely by putting in the requisite years of service, but rather through a record of prolonged and distinctive achievement.

While such arrangements may improve the performance of individuals already in the profession, they will not solve the problem of supply: how to attract and train talented individuals for the profession. While better salaries certainly would not hurt the profession, money is not a panacea. Reform of teacher education in the 1980's generally took the same shape as reform of pre-collegiate education: more requirements. In the name of raising standards, state departments added new exams and issued new lists of required courses. While there is no clear evidence that this sort of reform improved the quality of education, there can be no doubt that the addition of new requirements made a teaching career seem even less appealing to the thoughtful and independent people who make the best teachers.

Fortunately, recent years have witnessed a number of encouraging trends. Starting in the mid-eighties, several important studies, including the Holmes Group and the Carnegie Task Force on Teaching as a Profession, concluded that teacher education should be situated in "professional development schools" or "lead schools" where theory and practice are combined in apprenticeship programs.[25] Alternate certification programs have revitalized the profession to a degree by opening doors to more minorities, students from the nation's top universities and liberal arts colleges, and mature individuals with strong academic credentials and varied life and work experiences. Another fortunate outcome of the current debate about the manner in which teachers ought to be trained is that colleges and university education departments, fearing that they will be left out of the training game all together, have begun strengthening their ties with schools and placing greater emphasis on situating the education of teachers in the schools.[26]

Ultimately, the impetus for transformation of the teaching profession must come from teachers. Attempts to impose changes from above, no matter how well-intentioned, will inevitably meet with intense resistance, even sabotage. At any rate, school bureaucracies and education school faculties have too much invested in the status quo to provide genuine impetus for change. Teachers must begin challenging their subordinate roles in the system, taking responsibility for controversial decisions and focusing their energies on substantive educational issues. If a genuine transformation is to occur in American education, teachers must seize control of the profession's rudder and harness the winds of reform to their intentions.

In the case studies, the working methods of a number of particularly effective teachers were described in detail. If any generalization can be made, it is that their approaches cannot be reduced to a recipe or a list of steps which may be followed by anyone who would aspire to a career in teaching. The best teachers are distinguished by their dedication to the subjects they teach, their sensitivity to their students' individual needs, and their ability to inspire their students to become engaged in the pursuit of knowledge. Like the Kuba weavers from Zaire who adapt the decorative patterns of their textiles to the holes which naturally occur in the manufacturing process, the best teachers are masters of improvisation and adjustment. This is not to say that their work is without method; they have dozens of techniques and strategies at their disposal, derived from experience and the rich traditions of their disciplines. In the early grades, flexibility is the crucial factor. Teachers like Linda Dell and Susan Day are successful because their instruction is prescriptive; they teach students only those things which they don't know, keeping review to a minimum. At the same time, they strive to provide their students with opportunities to become actively engaged in learning, avoiding whole class instruction and lengthy lectures or drills. Conversely, they do not eschew lectures all together, recognizing that there are times when the whole class will need a broad overview of a new body of knowledge. The best teachers are expert guides and facilitators in discussion. They know when to group students for cooperative learning experiences and when to allow them to work independently. When they are not prodding, puzzling, or provoking their students with unexpected questions, they are modeling the processes of their discipline. They are masters of their own disciplines but they are not intimidated by other disciplines, and when necessary will cross the boundaries between disciplines with ease and self-assurance. For the best teachers, the goal is to assist students to learn. Any technique that works is a good technique.

The academically talented are distinguished from their classmates by the fact that they are able to process material more quickly and develop more sophisticated skills at a younger age. As a result, the need to work with a mentor — an individual thoroughly versed in the student's field of specialty — often arises much earlier. While it is not necessary for all teachers to be well enough versed in a subject to serve as a mentor to a tremendously talented youngster, it is important to find ways of providing the students who have the greatest need the opportunities to work with individuals who can guide and challenge them. If one cannot staff an elementary or middle school entirely with individuals who are experts in the subject that they teach and adept at teaching prescriptively, one would do well to provide the most talented students with opportunities to place into higher level classes. One of the signs of a truly great teacher is the ability to recognize the moment at which a student is ready to work with an even greater teacher.

* * * *

The Chinese poet Tai Hsu-lun once observed that a work of art is like the smoke which issues from a piece of jade: when you get too close to it, you lose the ability to perceive it. His point is similar to the one made at the beginning of this chapter regarding the position of the child in the educational system. The closer one gets, the more one becomes entangled in the system's workings, the more difficult it becomes to see a pattern or purpose. In chapter eight, certain features of an appropriate education were set forth and discussed, and in this chapter, a number of suggestions for restructuring the nation's educational system were suggested. Yet the question remains: for what purpose?

Even if we are able to focus our attentions on the individual child, to provide the best parenting, flexible schools, opportunities for specialization, and individualized instruction with caring and knowledgeable mentors; even if we are able to mobilize resources that are currently scattered or poorly utilized, to provide parents with a voice in the educational process, to recover the art of teaching; even if we can manage the tremendous investment of time and money that will be required to make excellence accessible to every child in every school; what will have accomplished if we do not have a purpose?

When it comes to education, Americans, who are otherwise a pragmatic people, have always believed in alchemy: it is an article of faith, a feature of the landscape as familiar and ineluctable as the Grand Canyon, that education transforms. That was the vision of Thomas Jefferson, the vision of W.E.B. Du Bois, the vision of every reformer in every reform movement including the present one. But before we can transform ourselves, we must know who we are and what it is that we want.

For as long as the school reform movement has been afoot, a rigorous debate has been raging in the media, in journals, in the academy (or rather the various academies), among scholars, politicians, and pundits on precisely this sort of issue. What does it mean to be an American? What should we teach our children? What unites us and what disunites us? Pluralism versus unity, tradition versus change, equity versus excellence, local wisdom versus professional expertise, the good of the individual versus the good of society. Again and again, the tremendous contradictions which are the fabric of our society have been laid bare in stark, millennial terms, so that one cannot help but suspect that something is going to happen, that we are on the verge of tremendous changes, and that transformations will occur whether we direct them or not.

However vitriolic it may become, the debate about our national identity and purpose is not nearly as disturbing as the specter of a generation (or large segments of a generation) cut off from that debate, engaged only by the pandering materialism of the commercial media and the narcissistic, unattainable promise of more "fun." Whether they want to or not, even those who argue that our intellectual tradition is bankrupt, that it has led us to a dead-end, are contributing to the tradition's renewal, for the genius of America has always been, as F. Scott Fitzgerald put it, "the ability to hold two contradictory opinions at once."

Why reform education? To add fuel to the debate, to exacerbate the contradictions to the extent that no amount of genius will be able to contain them, to destroy the tradition and to save it at the same time, to provoke further discussion, negotiation, and compromise, to demonstrate that America is no more possible without Spike Lee, Zora Neale Hurston, Oscar Hijuelos, and Amy Tan than it is without Allan Bloom, Edgar Allan Poe, and Herman Melville (or Tai Hsu-Lun for that matter), to make room for the hard work which is the basis of all creative production, to advance science, to improve our competitive position, to foster cooperation with other nations, to nourish children with hope, a sense of purpose, and the opportunity to become engaged.

Why reform education? There is also a bottom-line argument — one that has to do with the survival of the nation. The heavy industries which sustained the economy at the beginning of the century have long been stagnant, and growth in the service industries which characterized the last several decades has also slowed. Existing businesses are stymied by the difficulty of finding workers with adequate educations; every year, American industry spends 30 billion dollars retraining employees.[27] Gradually, employers are finding it easier to set up shop in other countries where labor is not only less expensive, but often better trained.

This situation is particularly ironic given the fact that currently 400,000 international students are spending 5 billion dollars a year to receive their higher education in the United States.[28] These are the most talented people from Africa, Asia, Europe, South America. They choose American universities because of quality. In crude economic terms, they return to their home with tremendous value added. This has caused some observers to worry that the universities are damaging the nation's competitive position. But they have missed the point: in America, we are capable of providing an optimal education. We have simply not mobilized the resources needed to provide every child with optimal conditions.

Those who ask if we can afford to mobilize these resources are guilty of mock-turtle logic. What we cannot afford is to allow them to remain scattered, unused, and neglected. Excellence is a resource unlike any other, for it is a resource which is capable of reproducing itself. The future growth of this nation lies in opening the best opportunities up to the broadest possible segment of the population. Our goal should be to allow each individual to become engaged in the learning process and to be limited only by his abilities and desire. We will only remain leaders in the world economy if we are able to position ourselves to add intellectual value to our most precious resources.

The flight of certain forms of labor intensive industry is inevitable; clinging to modes of production better suited to developing economies is not only nostalgic, it is foolish. In the future, sustainable growth will occur in stream-lined, small businesses in high technology fields such as communications, informational systems, transportation, education and biotechnology. Small businesses already account for 66% of growth. In so far as large businesses will have role to play, they will be highly diversified enterprises, with decentralized management structures, resembling loosely linked conglomerations of smaller firms. Massive bureaucracies and inflexible hierarchies will be no more appropriate in tomorrow's enterprises than they will be in the next generation of schools. Workers will need to enter the work force with highly polished basic skills and with the ability to analyze and interpret complex material. Basic research and development will become more important as we recognize that minds are our most important natural resources. Increasingly, machines will take the place of people in performing simple operations or work will be farmed out to developing economies.

The tremendous potential for transformation which lives in the minds and hearts of children is being lost in the mysterious machinery of a system which continues to serve its own purposes rather than those it was designed to serve. The case studies have demonstrated that there are many different approaches that families, teachers, and concerned administrators can take in attempting to recover our children from the process. More than any other endeavor, education must link the needs of the individual to the needs of society; in the classroom, one cannot serve one well without serving the other.

All across the nation, in the valleys and on the hillsides, in small towns and in the ghettos, in the fields and in the classrooms, there are children looking for challenges to master, ideas to engage their intellects and hearts, searching for markings which will help to direct them. As long as they are lost, so are we. And while we may not be able to provide them with any simple directions, we can at least share our maps and our knowledge of maps; we can show them how to stand back, and how to look at the landscape from a distance. Where they will go and how they will get there must be their own decision.

Notes

1. Advancement of Talent Among Precollegiate Migrant Children and Youth, CTY, p. 18.
2. Poe, E.A., "The Purloined Letter," p. 131.
3. See Maeroff, Gene I. "Assessing Alternative Assessment," in *Phi Delta Kappan*, December 1991, pp. 273–281.
4. For evidence that most students are capable of working at much higher levels than current expectations would indicate see Flanders, "How Much of the Content in Mathematics Textbooks is New?"; Renzulli, "The Reform Movement and the Quiet Crisis in Gifted Education;" Taylor and Frye (1988) "Pretesting: Minimize time spent on skill work for intermediate readers."

5. Over the years, schemes for flexible promotion have been suggested by a variety of individuals including William Wirt, Leta Hollingworth, James B. Conant, Theodore Sizer, and Chester Finn. For a discussion of Wirt's "Gary Plan," see Cremin, *The Transformation of the School*, pp. 154–57.

6. Purkey, Stewart and Smith, Marshall, "Effective Schools: A Review," Finn, Chester, "Toward Strategic Independence: Nine Commandments for Enhancing School Effectiveness."

7. Tyack, *The One Best System*, p. 13.

8. Chubb and Moe, p. 23.

9. See the *New York Times*, July 10 and August 8, 1990 and February 28, 1989, on private vocational schools which are more interested in "harvesting financial aid dollars than helping students." Under the guise of schools (cosmetology academies, computer training institutes, etc.) private vocational institutions have received millions of dollars in federal monies while providing students with worthless educations. See also Katz, *Class, Bureaucracy and Schools*, p. 10 on the organization of schools of New York City in the 1800's.

10. Hirschman, Albert O., *Exit, Voice, and Loyalty*, p. 13.

11. Brown vs. Board of Education 347 U.S. 483 (1954); San Antonio Independent School District vs. Rodriguez, 411 U.S. 1 (1973).

12. Demsetz, Harold, "When Does the Rule of Liability Matter?," p. 26.; Coase, R.H. "The Problem of Social Cost," p. 17.

13. Coase, p. 38.

14. See Chapter 11 for an extensive discussion of the Carnegie Unit.

15. Darling-Hammond, Linda, "Mad-Hatter Tests of Good Teaching."

16. *Digest of Educational Statistics* (1991) National Center for Educational Statistics, Washington, Table 80.

17. See Chubb and Moe; Finn, "Toward Strategic Independence," "Unsolved Problems," "We Can Shape Our Destiny;" Goodlad, *A Place Called School;* Purkey and Smith; and Sizer, *Horace's Compromise*.

18. Fitch, Clarence E., "Chicago School Reform: Who's the Boss?"

19. Instructions for grouping students for differentiated coursework in mathematics are provided in the Center for Talented Youth's Young Students Program's *Mathematics Sequence: Instructor's Guide* (1992).

20. Renzulli, Joseph S. and Reis, Sally M., "The Reform Movement and the Quiet Crisis in Gifted Education," pp. 32–33.

21. Unger, Roberta M., "Programs for Gifted and Talented Students in the USSR and Hungary ... " and Stigler and Stevenson, *The Learning Gap*.

22. For solid evidence supporting the common-sense notion that class-size *does* make a difference see Finn, J.D. & Achilles, C.M., "Answers and Questions about Class Size."

23. Stigler, J.W. and Stevenson, H.W., *The Learning Gap*.

24. Personal communication Rui Sousa.

25. Meade, Edward J., "Reshaping the Clinical Phase of Teacher Preparation," *Phi Delta Kappan*, May 1991, p. 667.
26. Meade, Edward J., "Reshaping the Clinical Phase of Teacher Preparation," *Phi Delta Kappan*, May 1991, p. 667.
27. Perry, Nancy J. "The Workers of the Future," *Fortune* (123) Summer/Spring 1991, pp. 68–72.
28. National Public Radio, "Market Place," May 15, 1992.

Bibliography

Adler M. The Paideia proposal. In: Gross B, Gross R. (Eds). *The Great School Debate*. New York: Simon & Schuster 1985.

Alley G, Deshler D. *Teaching the Learning Disabled Adolescent: Strategies and Methods*. Denver: Love Publishing Company 1979.

American Psychiatric Association. *Diagnostic and Statistical Manual of Mental Disorders*. Washington, DC: Author 1987.

Barnett LB, Favazza AE, Durden WG. Finding the gifted: A system that searches out and nurtures talented students. *American Education* 1983; 19(3): 40–43.

Barnett LB, Durden WG. CTY *advocacy and intervention in New Jersey: Documentation of early identification and out-of-school intervention with academically talented youth (Tech. Rep.)*. Baltimore: The Johns Hopkins University, Center for Talented Youth 1991.

Barnett LB, Corazza L. *Identification of mathematical talent and programmatic efforts to facilitate development of talent*. Paper presented at the William Stern Gesellschaft Symposium on Mathematical Talent, Hamburg, Germany 1992.

Bloom B (Ed). *Developing Talent in Young People*. New York: Ballantine Books 1985.

Bolton SK. *Famous Men of Science*. New York: Thomas Y. Crowell & Co. 1889.

Bordieu P. Cultural reproduction and social reproduction. In: Karabel J, Halsey AH (Eds). *Power and Ideology in Education*. New York: Oxford University Press 1977.

Brody LE, Benbow CP. Accelerative strategies: How effective are they for the gifted? *Gifted Child Quarterly* 1987; 3: 105–110.

Brody LE, Lupowski AE, Stanley JC. Early entrance to college: A study of academic and social adjustment during freshman year. *College and University* 1988; 63: 347–359.

Brody LE, Assouline SG, Stanley JC. Five years of early entrants: Predicting successful achievement in college. *Gifted Child Quarterly* 1990; 34: 138–142.

Brody LE, Stanley JC. Young college students: Assessing factors that contribute to success. In: Southern WT, Jones ED (Eds). *Academic Acceleration of Gifted Children*. New York: Teachers College Press 1991.

Bruner JS. *The Process of Education*. New York: Vintage Books 1963.

Chase RA. *The Baltimore Learning Network*. Baltimore MD: The Johns Hopkins University, Center for Talented Youth 1991.

Chubb JE, Moe TM. *Politics, Markets, and America's Schools*. Washington, DC: The Brookings Institute 1990.

Coase RH. The problem of social cost. *The Journal of Law and Economics* 1960; 3: 1–44.

Coles R. *Children of Crisis; A Study of Courage and Fear*. Boston: Little, Brown 1967.

Coles R. *Privileged Ones: The Well-Off and the Rich in America*. Boston: Little, Brown 1977.

Comer J. Educating poor minority children. *Scientific American* 1988; 259(5): 42–48.

Conant JB. *Thomas Jefferson and the Development of American Education*. New York: McGraw-Hill 1959.

Copeland ED, Love VL. *Attention, Please!*. Atlanta: SPI Press 1991.

Cox C. *The Early Mental Traits of Three Hundred Geniuses: Genetic Studies of Genius, vol 2*. Stanford: Stanford University Press 1926.

Cox J, Daniel N, Boston BO. *Educating Able Learners: Programs and Promising Practices*. Austin: University of Texas Press 1985.

Cremin L. *The Transformation of the School: Progressivism in American Education*. New York: Vintage Books 1964.

Cremin L. *American Education: The National Experience 1783–1876*. New York: Harper & Row 1980.

Cremin L. *American Education: The Metropolitan Experience 1876–1980*. New York: Harper & Row 1988.

Cronbach LJ, Suppes P (Eds). *Research for Tomorrow's Schools*. London: The Macmillan Company 1969.

Csikszentmihalyi M, Robinson RE. Culture, time, and the development of talent. In: Sternberg RJ, Davidson JE (Eds). *Conceptions of Giftedness*. Cambridge, England: Cambridge University Press 1985.

Csikszentmihalyi, M. *Flow: The Psychology of Optimal Experience*. New York: Harper & Row 1990.

Daniel N, Cox J. *Flexible Pacing for Able Learners*. Reston, VA: The Council for Exceptional Children 1988.

Darling-Hammond L. Mad-hatter tests of good teaching. In: Gross B, Gross R. (Eds). *The Great School Debate*. New York: Simon & Schuster 1985.

Dell L. *Developmental stages and the mathematically talented*. Unpublished manuscript 1992.

Demsetz H. When does the rule of liability matter? *The Journal of Legal Studies* 1972; I(13): 12–28.

Denkla MB. Executive function, the overlap zone between attention deficit hyperactivity disorder and learning disabilities. *International Pediatrics* 1989; 4(2): 155–160.

Dewey J. *Experience and Education*. New York: Collier Books 1977.

Du Bois WEB. *Writings*. New York: Literary Classics of the United States, Inc. 1986.

Durden WG. *The Johns Hopkins University Center for Talented Youth: Its place in American education*. Speech given at Duke University, Durham, NC 1985.

Durden WG. *The development of educational support systems for the academically talented: The Talent Search concept*. Paper presented at Developing Talent in Mathematics, Science, & Technology, Duke University Talent Identification Program, Durham, NC 1988.

Durden WG, et al. *Advancement of talent among precollegiate migrant children and youth: A report commissioned by the National Commission on Migrant Education*. Baltimore: The Johns Hopkins University, Center for Talented Youth 1991.

Einstein A. *The World as I See It*. New York: Covici, Friede 1934.

Eliot TS. What Dante means to me. In: Eliot TS. *To Criticize the Critic and Other Writings*. Lincoln, NE: Bison Book, University of Nebraska Press 1992.

Elliot RO. *Attention deficit disorder: Current understanding*. Unpublished manuscript 1988.

Feldhusen JF. Synthesis of research on gifted youth. *Educational Leadership* 1989; 46(3): 6–11.

Feldman DH. *Developmental Approaches to Giftedness and Creativity*. San Francisco: Jossey-Bass Inc. 1986.

Feldman DH. *Nature's Gambit*. New York: Basic Books 1986.

Feyereisen KV, Fiorino AJ, Nowak AT. *Supervision and Curriculum Renewal; A Systems Approach*. New York: Meredith Corporation 1970.

Finn CE. Toward strategic independence: Nine commandments for enhancing school effectiveness. *Phi Delta Kappan* 1984; 65(8): 518–524.

Finn CE. Teacher unions and school quality: Potential allies or inevitable foes? *Phi Delta Kappan* 1985; 66(5): 331–338.

Finn CE. Unsolved problems of the excellence movement. *The School Administrator* 1986; 43(2): 14–17.

Finn CE. We can shape our destiny. *Educational Leadership* 1986; 44(1): 4–6.

Finn CE. The biggest reform of all. *Phi Delta Kappan* 1990; 71(8): 585–592.

Finn JD, Achilles CM. Answers and questions about class size: A statewide experiment. *American Educational Research Journal* 1990; 27(3): 557–577.

Fitch CE. *Chicago school reform: Who's the boss?* Springfield, VA: ERIC Document Reproduction Service 1990.

Flanders JR. How much of the content in mathematics textbooks is new? *Arithmetic Teacher* 1987; 35(1): 18–23.

Flavell JH. *The Developmental Psychology of Jean Piaget.* Princeton, NJ: D. Van Nostrand Company, Inc. 1963.

Gallagher J. *Teaching the Gifted Child.* Boston: Allyn & Bacon 1985.

Gallagher J. The gifted: A term with surplus meaning. *Journal for the Education of Gifted* 1991; 14(4): 353–365.

Galton F. *Hereditary Genius.* London: Macmillan 1962.

Gamoran A. Organization, instruction, and the effects of ability grouping: Comment on Slavin's 'best evidence synthesis.' *Review of Educational Research* 1987; 57: 341–345.

Gardner H. *Frames of Mind: The Theory of Multiple Intelligences.* New York: Basic Books 1985.

Getzels JW, Csikszentmihalyi M. *Creative Vision: A Longitudinal Study of Problem Finding in Art.* New York: Wiley 1976.

Goldenberg C, Gallimore R. Local knowledge, research knowledge, and educational change. *Educational Researcher* 1991; 20(8): 2–14.

Goodlad J. *A Place Called School.* New York: McGraw-Hill 1983.

Gruber HE. On the hypothesized relationship between giftedness and creativity. In: Feldman DH (Ed). *Developmental Approaches to Giftedness.* San Francisco: Jossey-Bass 1982.

Guilford JP. *The Nature of Human Intelligence.* New York: McGraw-Hill 1967.

Gustin WG, Corazza L. Mathematical and verbal reasoning as predictors of scientific achievement. *Roeper Review* (in press).

Guterson D. When schools fail children. *Harper's Magazine* 1990; 281(1686): 58–64.

Hilliard A. Do we have the will to educate all children? *Educational Leadership* 1991; 49(1): 31–36.

Hirschman AO. *Exit, Voice, and Loyalty: Responses to Decline in Firms, Organizations, and States.* Cambridge, MA: Harvard University Press 1970.

Hofstadter R. *Anti-Intellectualism in America.* New York: Vintage Books 1963.

Hollingworth L. *Gifted Children: Their Nature and Nurture.* New York: Macmillan 1926.

Hornbeck DW, Salamon LM. *Human Capital and America's Future: An Economic Strategy for the Nineties.* Baltimore: The Johns Hopkins University Press 1991.

Howley C. *Intellectually Gifted Students: Issues and Policy Implications.* Charleston, WV: Appalachia Educational Laboratory 1986.

Jacobs K. *Legal issues and ADD.* Unpublished manuscript 1992.

Jackson B. *Fieldwork.* Urbana, IL: University of Illinois Press 1987.

The Johns Hopkins University, Center for Talented Youth. *Young students' achievement follow-up* (Tech. Rep. No. 8). Baltimore: Author 1992.

The Johns Hopkins University, Center for Talented Youth. *Young Student's Program Mathematics Sequence: Instructor's Guide*. Baltimore: Author 1992.

Kanawha County Department of Education. *Consultative/ collaborative model*. Charleston, WV: Author 1987.

Karnes FA, Marquardt RG. *Gifted Children and the Law: Mediation, Due Process, and Court Cases*. Dayton, OH: Ohio Psychology Press 1991.

Katz MB. *Class, Bureaucracy and Schools*. New York: Praeger Publishers 1971.

Keating DP. The study of mathematically precocious youth. In: Stanley JC, Keating DP, Fox L (Eds). *Mathematical Talent: Discovery, Description, and Development*. Baltimore: The Johns Hopkins University Press 1974.

Keating DP. A Piagetian approach to intellectual precocity. In: Keating DP (Ed). *Intellectual Talent: Research and Development*. Baltimore: The Johns Hopkins University Press 1976.

Kenner R. *Don't get de-geniused*. [Film in pre-production 1992].

Kozol J. *Savage Inequalities: Children in America's Schools*. New York: Crown Publishers 1991.

Krug D, Mills C. *The Skills Reinforcement Project: Math achievement of disadvantaged students*. Unpublished manuscript 1992.

Kuhn T. *The Structure of Scientific Revolutions*. Chicago: University of Chicago Press 1970.

Kulik JA, Kulik CLC. Effects of accelerated instruction on students. *Review of Educational Research* 1984; 54(3): 409–425.

Kulik JA, Kulik CLC. Effects of ability grouping on student achievement. *Equity & Excellence* 1987; 23(1–2): 22–30.

Kulik JA, Kulik CLC. Ability grouping and gifted students. In: Colangelo N, Davis GA (Eds). *Handbook of Gifted Education*. Boston: Allyn & Bacon 1990.

Learning Disabilities Association of America. *A guide to Section 504: How it applies to students with learning disabilities and ADHD*. Pittsburgh: Author 1992.

Lee GB. Moral education in the republic of China. *Moral Education Forum* 1990; 15(3): 2–14.

Lerner B. Good news about American education. *Commentary* 1991. 22–28.

Lupowski AE, Assouline SG, Stanley JC. Applying a mentor model for young mathematically talented students. *Gifted Child Today* 1990; 13(2): 15–19.

Lynch S, Mills C. The Skills Reinforcement Project (SRP): An academic program for high potential minority youth. *Journal for the Education of the Gifted* 1990; 13(4): 364–379.

Maeroff GI. *Don't Blame the Kids*. New York: McGraw-Hill 1981.

Maeroff GI. Assessing alternative assessment. *Phi Delta Kappan* 1991; 73(4): 273–281.

MacLeod J. *Ain't No Makin' It: Leveled Aspirations in a Low-Income Neighborhood.* Boulder, CO: Westview Press 1987.

Mansfield RS, Busse TV. *The Psychology of Creativity and Discovery: Scientists and Their Work.* Chicago: Nelson Hall 1981.

McDaniel ED, Soong W. *Comparisons of Self-Concept Scores of Children in America and in Taiwan.* Springfield, VA: ERIC Document Reproduction Service 1981.

Meade EJ. Reshaping the clinical phase of teacher preparation. *Phi Delta Kappan* 1991: 72(9): 666–669.

Merriam SB. *Case Study Research in Education.* San Francisco: Jossey-Bass Publishers 1991.

Miller RC. *The Model Mathematics Project: Appalachia intermediate unit 08.* Hollidaysburg, PA: Department for Exceptional Children 1986.

Miller RC. *Discovering mathematical talent.* Springfield, VA: ERIC Flyer: Clearinghouse on Handicapped and Gifted Children 1989.

Mills CJ. Sex roles, personality, and intellectual abilities in adolescents. *Journal of Youth and Adolescence* 1981; 10(2): 85–111.

Mills CJ. Academically talented children: The case for early identification and nurturance. *Pediatrics* 1992; 89(1): 156–157.

Mills CJ, Tangherlini A. Finding optimal match: Another look at ability grouping and cooperative learning. *Equity and Excellence* 1992; 25(2–4): 205–208.

Mills CJ, Durden WG. Cooperative learning and ability grouping: An issue of choice. *Gifted Child Quarterly* 1992; 36(1): 11–16.

Mills CJ, Stork EJ, Krug D, Sakamoto SO. Recognition and development of academic talent in educationally disadvantaged students. *Exceptionality* (in press).

Moore ND, Wood SS. Mathematics with a gifted difference. *Roeper Review* 1988; 10(4): 231–234.

Mordkowitz ER, Ginsburg HP. *Early academic socialization of successful Asian-American college students.* Springfield, VA: ERIC Document Reproduction Service 1986.

National Commission on Excellence in Education. *A nation at risk: The imperative for educational reform.* Washington, DC: Author 1983.

Nettles SM. Community involvement and disadvantaged students: A review. *Review of Educational Research* 1991; 61(3): 379–406.

O'Connor F. Writing short stories. In: Fitzgerald R, Fitzgerald S (Eds). *Mystery and Manners.* New York: Farrar, Straus & Giroux 1969.

Ochse R. *Before the Gates of Excellence: The Determinants of Creative Genius.* Cambridge, England: Cambridge University Press 1990.

Ogbu J. *Minority Education and Caste: The American System in a Cross Cultural Perspective.* New York: Academic Press 1978.

Oldenquist A. Social triage against black children. In: Gross B, Gross R (Eds). *The Great School Debate*. New York: Simon & Schuster 1985.

Paz O. The other voice. *New York Times Book Review* 1991.

Pendarvis ED, Howley AA, Howley CB. *The Abilities of Gifted Children*. Englewood Cliffs, NJ: Prentice-Hall 1990.

Perry NJ. The workers of the future. *Fortune* 1991; 123: 68–72.

Poe EA. The purloined letter. In: Poe EA. *Complete Stories and Poems of Edgar Allan Poe*. Garden City, NY: Doubleday & Co 1966.

Pressey S. Concerning the nature and nurture of genius. *Scientific Monthly* 1955; 81: 123–129.

Purkey SC, Smith MS. Effective schools: A review. *The Elementary School Journal* 1983; 83(4): 427–452.

Ravitch D. *The Troubled Crusade: American Education, 1945–1980*. New York: Basic Books 1983.

Renzulli JS. *The Enrichment Triad Model: A Guide for Developing Defensible Programs for the Gifted and Talented*. Mansfield Center, CT: Creative Learning Press 1977.

Renzulli JS, Reis SM. The reform movement and the quiet crisis in gifted education. *Gifted Child Quarterly* 1991; 35(1): 26–35.

Robinson NM, Robinson HB. *The Optimal Match: Devising the Best Compromise for the Highly Gifted Student*. San Francisco: Jossey-Bass 1982.

Roush RE. The Carnegie unit — how did we get it? *Educational Forum* 1970; 35(1): 71–74.

Schneider HW. *A History of American Philosophy*. New York: Columbia University Press 1963.

Shiang J. *'Heart' and self in old age: A Chinese model*. Springfield, VA: ERIC Document Reproduction Service 1984.

Silverman LK. *Mentorships*. Denver: University of Denver, Gifted Child Development Center 1991.

Simmons V. *The West Virginia model for academic instruction*. Charleston, WV: West Virginia Department of Education 1991.

Singal DJ. The other education crisis. *The Atlantic* 1991; 268(5): 59–74.

Sizer T. *Horace's Compromise: The Dilemma of the American High School*. Boston: Houghton Mifflin 1984.

Slavin RE. Ability grouping and student achievement in elementary schools: A best-evidence synthesis. *Review of Educational Research* 1987; 57: 293–336.

Southern WT, Jones ED (Eds). *The Academic Acceleration of Gifted Children*. New York: Teachers College Press 1991.

Stanley JC. Use of tests to discover talent. In: Keating DP (Ed). *Intellectual Talent: Research and Development*. Baltimore: The Johns Hopkins University Press 1976.

Stanley JC. How to use a fast-pacing math mentor. *Intellectually Talented Youth Bulletin* 1979; 5(6): 1–2.

Stanley JC. The case for extreme educational acceleration of intellectually brilliant youth. *Gifted Child Quarterly* 1976; 20: 66–75.

Stanley JC, Keating DP, Fox LH (Eds). *Mathematical Talent: Discovery, Description, and Development.* Baltimore, MD: The Johns Hopkins University Press 1974.

Stanley JC, Benbow CP. Youths who reason exceptionally well mathematically. In: Sternberg RJ, Davidson JE (Eds). *Conceptions of Giftedness.* Cambridge, England: Cambridge University Press 1985.

Steele S. *The Content of Our Character: A New Vision of Race in America.* New York: Harper Perennial 1990.

Stigler JW, Stevenson HW. *The Learning Gap.* New York: Summit 1992.

Tangherlini A. Of triggerfish and talented youth. *Harvard Magazine* 1990; Sep/Oct: 54–55.

Tangherlini A. The Skills Reinforcement Project: It's effect on students and their families. *Communicator: The Journal of the California Association for the Gifted* 1990; 20(5): 32–34.

Tangherlini A, Durden B. Verbal talent. In: *The International Handbook of Research on Giftedness and Talent.* Oxford, England: Pergamon Press (in press).

Taylor BM, Frye BJ. Pretesting: Minimize time spent on skill work for intermediate readers. *The Reading Teacher* 1988; 42(2): 100–103.

Terman L. *Mental and Physical Traits of a Thousand Gifted Children: Genetic Studies of Genius, vol 1.* Stanford, CA: Stanford University Press 1935.

Terman LM, Oden MH. *The Gifted Child Grows Up: Genetic Studies of Genius, vol 4.* Stanford, CA: Stanford University Press 1935.

Torrance EP. *Mentor Relationships: How They Aid Creative Achievement, Endure, Change, and Die.* Buffalo, NY: Bearly Limited 1984.

Tyack D. *The One Best System: A History of American Urban Education.* Cambridge, MA: Harvard University Press 1974.

Unger RM. *Programs for gifted and talented students in the USSR and Hungary: How does the West Virginia gifted program compare?* Paper presented at the 70th Annual Convention of the Council for Exceptional Children, Baltimore, MD 1992.

United States Department of Commerce. *1987 Census of Government, Finances of Public School Systems, Bureau of Census, vol 4.* Washington, DC: Author 1987.

United States Department of Education, National Center for Education Statistics. *The Condition of Education 1991, Elementary and Secondary Education, vol 1.* Washington, DC: Author 1991.

United States Department of Labor, Secretary's Commission on Achieving Necessary Skills. *What work requires of school.* Washington, DC: Author 1991.

Wallach MA. Care and feeding of the gifted. *Contemporary Psychology* 1978; 23: 616–617.

Webb JT, Meckstroth EA, Tolan SS. *Guiding the Gifted Child*. Columbus, OH: Ohio Psychology Publishing 1982.

Whitehead AN. *The Aims of Education*. New York: The Free Press 1929.

Wilson GM. *What Arithmetic Shall We Teach?* Cambridge, MA: The Riverside Press 1926.

Wolcott HF. A case study using an ethnographic approach. In: Jaeger RM (Ed). *Complementary Methods for Research in Education*. Washington, DC: American Educational Research Association 1988.

Yin RK. *Case Study Research: Design and Methods*. Newbury Park, CA: Sage Publications 1989.

Zimmerman E. Rembrandt to Rembrandt: A case study of a memorable painting teacher. *Roeper Review* 1991; 13(2): 76–81.

Zweigenhaft RL, Domhoff GW. *Blacks in the White Establishment?: A Study of Race and Class in America*. New Haven, CT: Yale University Press 1991.

Appendix I

The following seven suggestions are for parents who suspect that their children have academic talents requiring specific educational interventions. These suggestions were prepared in collaboration with Dr. Carol Mills, the Director of Research of the Center for Talented Youth (CTY) and a clinical psychologist with (twenty) years of experience evaluating the needs of students with academic talents and learning disabilities.*

1. TRUST YOUR INSTINCTS. If you have reason to believe your child has special talents or abilities, you are probably right. Of course, we all believe our children are bright and wonderful and special, but seldom do parents claim that their child is "gifted" or "academically talented" without some reasonable evidence.

2. SEEK THE ADVICE AND JUDGMENT OF A PROFESSIONAL. An independent assessment from a professional who specializes in assessment and child development can confirm your suspicions. A carefully chosen professional can provide information on your child's particular strengths, weaknesses, and learning style. In addition, she can give you advice on what to expect and what you can do to help develop your child's abilities.

---

* For more information on academically talented children and a list of organizations serving gifted and talented students, write to Publications and Resources, CTY–Johns Hopkins, 3400 N. Charles St., Baltimore, MD 21218.

3. BE AN INFORMED CONSUMER WHEN CHOOSING SOMEONE TO TEST YOUR CHILD. Take your time and choose the person to test your child wisely. You should seek someone with experience and training in psychological and educational testing; someone who has experience working with children, especially academically talented children; and someone who comes recommended by someone you trust (if possible).

Usually the person you choose will be a clinical or educational psychologist. Ask about the person's training (they should have a Ph. D. or M. D. degree from a reputable institution), specialty (it should be in one or more of the following: child development, testing, children with special needs), and experience (look for someone who has specialized in working with children and assessment for at least three or four years).

Ask them what tests they administer and whether they will give you specific recommendations and counsel concerning educational issues. They should be administering a reputable, individually administered test of intelligence at the very least. In addition, if your child is of school age or is capable of doing school-type work, the person should be administering a test of specific ability and academic knowledge. If the person will only give you a test score without specific recommendations and a consultation, find someone else. A test score or diagnosis of "gifted" is almost useless (you already knew this).

4. DON'T RUSH TO ENROLL YOUR PRESCHOOL CHILD IN SPECIAL PROGRAMS OR WORRY ABOUT STRUCTURING EVERY HOUR TO MAXIMIZE LEARNING. If you simply provide a rich, stimulating, and varied set of experiences for your child, her/his abilities will naturally unfold. Rather than setting up a structured learning environment for your child during the preschool years, strive to be responsive to your child's particular interests. An environment that provides exposure, stimulation, and that is responsive will ensure that your child's natural abilities and interest in learning will blossom.

5. IF IT'S NOT BROKEN, DON'T FIX IT. If your child is in school, is happy and well-adjusted, and appears to be rea-

sonably challenged intellectually, don't worry about changing anything drastically in his educational program just because he/she was identified as academically talented. On the other hand, if your child is unhappy at child, is obviously beyond the level of instruction in his class, or is exhibiting other behavioral problems (inattention, aggressiveness, anxiety), some adjustments in the school program may be necessary. The person who tests your child should be able to make recommendations in this regard.

6. SEEK A SUPPORT GROUP OF OTHER PARENTS AND LEARN AS MUCH AS YOU CAN ABOUT RESOURCES AVAILABLE IN YOUR COMMUNITY, STATE, AND NATIONALLY. Information on local laws and regulations can be obtained by writing to the director of programs for the gifted in your state.

7. BE PERSISTENT. As Mrs. Dagleish observed, "they will try to wear you down." Recruit allies within the school system. Often a sympathetic teacher, administrator, or counselor can open doors which would otherwise remain closed. Be firm and resourceful in your dealings with school officials, and make sure you document every meeting.

Appendix II

The following are seven suggestions for secondary schools working with talented ADD students that arose from the discussion and a careful examination of the research on the subject:

1. ADD students should have a homework assignment book in which the teacher initials the assignment at the end of class. This insures that the student has a proper record of what needs to be done and that individuals helping the student can do so effectively.

2. It would be immensely helpful to have a homeroom teacher, a tutor, or a resource room teacher assist the student with collecting all the materials that he/she will need in order to do nightly homework assignments. At home, parents should be willing to play a similar role — insuring that students complete assigned work and bring to school all completed assignments, pencils, pens, notebooks, and books.

3. Classroom teachers should be flexible enough to allow for modifications such as: word processed papers; oral examinations; front-of-the-class seating; time for individual "coaching".

4. In general, students with learning disabilities need to participate in activities and programs which give them opportunities to shine in their areas of strength and to develop their areas of weakness in non-threatening situations.

5. Placement policies should be kept flexible — placing students with teachers whose instructional styles are compatible with

their learning style and allowing for movement between ability groups.

6. All students (especially ADD students) would benefit from a move away from the traditional lecture-centered instructional model to a model which encourages students to participate actively in the learning process and in the development of mastery.

7. Communication channels should be kept open between students, parents, teachers, guidance staff, and administrators so that problems can be addressed in a timely fashion through collaborative efforts. The individual needs of each child should always be the focus of every intervention.

This list of suggestions is by no means exhaustive. For further information, contact C. H. A. D. D. Children with Attention Deficit Disorders; 499 N. W. 70th Avenue, Suite 308; Plantation, FL 33317.

Index